SHAPING THE FUTURE OF JAPANESE MANAGEMENT:

NEW LEADERSHIP TO OVERCOME THE IMPENDING CRISIS

LTCB International Library Selection No. 5

SHAPING THE FUTURE OF JAPANESE MANAGEMENT:
NEW LEADERSHIP TO OVERCOME THE IMPENDING CRISIS

TSUCHIYA MORIAKI

Professor Emeritus
The University of Tokyo

KONOMI YOSHINOBU

Management Consultant

LTCB International Library Foundation

Transcription of names

The Hepburn system of romanization is used for Japanese terms, including the names of persons and places. Long vowels are not indicated. Chinese terms are romanized using the pinyin system. The Wade-Giles system is used, however, for certain place-names outside mainland China. As for the romanization of Korean terms, the McCune-Reischauer system is used.

With regard to Japanese, Chinese, and Korean personal names, we have followed the local custom of placing the family name first.

This book was originally published in 1995 by
Japan Broadcast Publishing Co., Ltd. under the title
Korekara no Nihon-teki Keiei
© 1995 by Tsuchiya Morioki and Konomi Yoshinobu

English translation rights arranged with Japan Broadcast Publishing Co., Ltd.
© 1996 by LTCB International Library Foundation

First English edition published March 1997
by LTCB International Library Foundation
1-8, Uchisaiwaicho 2-chome, Chiyoda-ku, Tokyo 100, Japan
Tel: 03-5223-7204   Fax: 03-5511-8123

Translation and production by Simul International, Inc., Tokyo

Printed in Japan
ISBN 4-924971-04-9 C1334 ¥3000E

CONTENTS

PART II   What Is Happening inside Japanese Corporations Today?

PART III   What Changes Are Needed?

PART IV   Japanese Corporations Shedding Old Skin

Preface to the English-Language Edition

When informed that our work would be translated into English, we felt extremely honored. At the same time, however, we were somewhat concerned. This book was written to sound an alarm for the businesspeople of Japan. The discussions pertaining to the matters dealt with herein took place in 1993 and 1994. At the time, the Japanese yen was soaring and there seemed to be no end in sight. Japanese businesses were being encouraged to redouble their efforts to reduce costs to overcome the effects of the ascendant currency. We believed then that the fundamental problem of Japanese management lay in the fact that the nation's fundamental corporate philosophy and structure—which had been developed in the 1950s for the purpose of achieving economic growth—were no longer effective given the changed economic environment.

The yen peaked in 1995 and has since declined. Companies in export-oriented industries are now enjoying increased profits. If we were to conclude from this that the problems had been solved, this book would obviously be out of date. But there are still many problems that continue to plague Japanese management. In fact, the structure and approach of management continue to aggravate the problems faced by today's businesses in many areas of their operations. Japanese corporations are now engaged in intense competition with foreign companies, both in and outside of Japan. They are under pressure to transform their concepts and structures so that they might better survive this competition. Above all, the new concepts and structures must be recognizable to other countries, although uniquely Japanese attributes may have been added.

Japanese businesspeople today are aware of the problems pointed out in this book. They know that if they continue with the traditional ways, they are only courting disaster. But as many have not yet been directly burned, they continue to plod along, patching things up and putting off the painful yet necessary reforms.

It is our fervent hope that this book will encourage people to act, and that it will provide them with clues to creating new ideas for managing Japanese companies.

Finally, we are grateful to Messrs. Uehara Takashi and Shinkai Hisayuki of the LTCB International Library Foundation for initiating this project. We are also grateful to the staff of Simul International for their careful and efficient work throughout the entire process of translation and production.

TSUCHIYA MORIAKI
KONOMI YOSHINOBU

March 1997

Preface

With only a few years remaining in the twentieth century, Japanese society is about to change dramatically in many respects. As a matter of fact, it is being pressured to change. The world situation surrounding Japan has undergone considerable transformation, such as the cessation of Cold War hostilities. Japan has become an economic power, with its gross domestic product approaching that of the United States, and Japan's position in the international community has altered significantly as a result.

During the last half-century or so, as the Cold War raged around us, Japan pursued the task of catching up with the advanced countries as a national objective, and the nation built its political, governmental, and economic systems to achieve that objective. At the time the objective was established it was perceived as quite ambitious, and the concept and systems put in place to achieve the goal have taken root deep in the hearts of many Japanese. It is not easy to just throw away such a concept and systems merely because times have changed. For instance, it was once a matter of life and death for the Japanese to "dedicate themselves to exporting to earn foreign currencies." It goes without saying that adherence to such a practice today would lead to economic friction with other countries and could jeopardize the continuation of free international trade. Already more than a dozen years have passed since we first realized that change is required. Nevertheless, many people can still not completely rid themselves of the old concept. It would be wrong to deny that somewhere in the back of our minds we still entertain the possibility of a third oil crisis and the necessity of building reserves of foreign exchange for that eventuality.

To persist with an outmoded concept and systems would be neither accepted by the international community nor of benefit to

Japan's economy or society. Today, the appreciation of the yen has progressed beyond expectations, causing the hollowing out of Japanese industry in installments. Indeed, if this trend should continue unabated Japan in the future may very well not be producing much of anything. Such an eventuality could adversely affect not only the Japanese economy but also the psyche of the Japanese people. It could produce flabby and arrogant Japanese. That is why we must have the courage now to reform our antiquated concept and systems and explore new visions and strategies to implement those visions.

We can make this statement with respect to many aspects of Japanese society. It is true that since the days of the Meiji era—when the national strategy was to build a wealthy nation with a strong military—the Japanese have manifested a strong desire to catch up with the advanced countries. And although military means have long been abandoned and replaced by economic ones, this desire still guides the Japanese as they build their social institutions. In this sense, our educational system has not changed since before the war. Politics has been guided by this mentality as well. In public administration, it was a matter of pride for empowered government officials to be aware of this concept and to have their actions guided by it. But the time for change has arrived. And change will not be as simple as merely changing our means from economics to culture—much as we once changed our means from the military to economics—while at the same time maintaining our desire to catch up with the advanced nations. Perhaps our persistence in this desire may be what is obstructing independent, rational judgment on our part. Education, politics, and government—each must now cultivate a new vision and strategies.

This book addresses Japanese corporate management from the foregoing perspectives. Although individual corporations are managed to make profit, Japanese corporations have literally embodied the national objective described above. The pre-war slogan "Sangyo Hokoku" (Promote Industry to Serve the Country) was maintained after the war and is still alive and well in the back of the minds of many Japanese in the economic community. But perhaps one should not belabor the point. The important question now is what can be done to serve the country in the future. It must be understood that the traditional concept and systems no longer serve the best interests of the nation. On the contrary, they can now have adverse effects.

Corporate management is affected by changes to its environment more directly than education or politics or public administration. Individual corporations are by no means built on solid ground, and to survive they must adapt to changing circumstances and transform themselves. As a matter of fact, changes have already started as far as corporate management is concerned. We must examine and identify those changes.

It is true that some corporations still insist on maintaining the old systems, either because they are not sensitive enough to recognize the changes in their environment or because they are confused about objectives and means. It certainly requires courage to change one's concepts and systems to conform with changes going on around oneself. Above all, it requires the creativity necessary to trailblaze in untraversed territory. Many conflicting interests get intertwined, and pain can result. However, if you ignore the requirements of change you dig your own grave without even being aware of it.

We cannot begrudge Japanese corporate management its brilliant success in attaining the objective of "catching up with and surpassing advanced nations." But given the fact that the environment and conditions related to Japanese management have undergone great change, it would be lacking in resourcefulness to simply repeat the methods that proved successful in the past. You put the cart before the horse when you stubbornly hold on to old concepts and systems.

At times of reformation you often hear the word "self-denial." In the days when student protests were rife on university campuses, this word was thrust onto the teachers. Whatever its effect may have been in the past, it may well be necessary to willingly accept a regimen of self-denial in order to survive the ongoing changes in the business world. Half a century is too long a period for a given concept and systems to go unaltered. There is, after all, such a thing as system fatigue. It's about time we changed. What is happening to Japanese business management now, and how it is likely to change in the future—those are the subjects we will discuss in this book.

I must now touch upon how this book came to be written. The two authors share little in common in terms of age and background. I am a tenured professor at Tokyo Keizai University's economics department, with a focus on business administration, while Mr. Konomi has a technical background and has been a consultant with many corporations. Our collaboration began when I read the impressive series of articles Mr. Konomi wrote for *The Economist* magazine about 10 years ago that dealt with management strategies related to technological trends. Later, thanks to the efforts of Kitaya Yukio—who is now with Tama University but was then with the General Research Institute of the Long-Term Credit Bank of Japan—both of us became members of a research group, and during the ensuing three years or so we learned a great deal from one another. In many ways, Mr. Konomi has been like a tutor to me, explaining much of the real workings of business management.

In the course of our discussions we began to see that we shared a similar philosophy and critical approach with respect to the way things actually work. At that very time, as luck would have it, Ogawa Mario of NHK Press extended the helping hand that allowed us to summarize our discussions in book form.

Actually, three years passed from the time that tripartite collaboration began until the book was published. During those years the management environment surrounding Japanese businesses underwent many remarkable changes. The fact that we ended up taking three years to edit the text turned out, in the end, to be fortuitous because it meant that our discussions were not focused on temporal subjects but ranged over a longer span of time. Such is the serendipity that sometimes rules life. I willingly admit here, however, that I was the cause of the procrastination. My collaborators are blameless in this regard.

TSUCHIYA MORIAKI
July 1995

PART I

What Are the Structural Problems of Japanese Management?

Chapter 1 | Can We Foster the Entrepreneurial Spirit in Japan?

THE COLLAPSED REPUTATION OF JAPANESE BUSINESS

The international reputation of Japanese companies is collapsing. Not only Japan's corporations but also its politics and public administration are losing their once respected name. Tokyo had been considered—by Japanese and foreigners alike—to be the safest big city in the world until the sarin attack on its subway undermined that reputation so much so that foreigners are no longer as happy as they once were to come to Tokyo. Of course, in a book of this nature we shall limit our discussions to the matter of business management.

The international accolades given to Japanese corporate management reached their zenith during the 1980s. Japanese firms overcame with flying colors the oil crises that were visited upon them during the 1970s. Then, in the 1980s, they exported to the world such hi-tech products as video recorders and facsimile machines, which only the Japanese were able to manufacture successfully. And all the while Japan continued to chalk up huge trade surpluses. Japanese companies began to carry increasing weight in the world economy, and proud Japanese businessmen strutted down the streets of the world. Other countries were increasingly interested to know what was going on in Japanese companies, and a number of books came out in praise of Japanese management practices. Japanese words, such as *kaizen*, and English phrases coined in Japan, such as "just in time" (JIT) and "total quality control" (TQC), entered the world's lexicon. In fact, the methods and approaches for improving efficiency invent-

1

ed on the shop floor of Japanese manufacturers involved fresh thinking that overturned the traditional wisdom of European and American business. We were indeed very proud of ourselves for simply being Japanese. Japanese management as symbolized by lifetime employment and the seniority system was thought to be the new guiding light in the business world, and a number of scholars were trying to fathom the logic of it.

Today, there are very few who seem to be looking up to Japanese corporations. Even Prime Minister Mahathir of Malaysia—who once counseled people to "look east" and wanted to bring about the economic development of his country using Japan as a model—appears to have given up on Japan.

Why is it that their views on Japanese business changed so suddenly? And further, why is it that the international competitiveness of Japanese firms has declined so precipitously?

If Japanese firms have in fact lost their competitiveness, the first probable cause would be the appreciation of the yen. The sudden onslaught of the strong yen could well have wiped out the results built up through many years of hard labor.

The second cause would be the bubble economy and the impact of its collapse. On reflection, it seems incredible that during the bubble period almost everyone seemed to be flying high, having left their faculty for sober judgment on the ground. At the time, everybody referred to the bubble, but it didn't seem to occur to anyone that it might burst. All were racing ahead blindly, making one inflated judgment after another. The result has been a mountain of bad debt at banks and financial wounds that still haven't healed after 10 years. And all of that is casting a dark shadow over Japanese companies.

The strong yen and the bubble economy, then, have had a severe impact on Japanese companies. But the jolt is more in the nature of a demand that companies learn to cope with the new environment.

In addition to those two causes, we suspect there may have been a third cause—the emergence of problems inside Japanese companies—that worked to diminish firms' competitive power. Uncovering those problems is the principal focus of this book.

It can be generally stated with equal applicability to a human being, a corporation, or any organic entity that it adopts certain behavior patterns that conform to the particular environment in which it finds itself and then evolves and grows in that direction. As a result of this growth, the size of the entity increases and causes its internal mechanisms to change in line with the enlarged dimensions. Its influence over its external environment may also increase to the extent that it can alter the conditions of that environment. Precisely because it has adapted nicely to changed circumstances, it can in some cases end up creating conditions that preclude it from adapting any further to the environment.

If Japanese companies have inadvertently created such conditions of incompatibility to environment, they would be well advised to realize it quickly. In the course of our dialogue, we, the authors, have come to realize that we share a sense of crisis in this regard— a belief that the writing is already on the wall. Because of this shared foreboding, we have decided to delve into the matter together.

MARATHON RUNNERS WHO TOOK A WRONG TURN

We will closely examine the question of incompatibility to environment in chapter 2 and succeeding chapters of this book. We will also touch on questions pertaining to the bubble and its aftermath in and after chapter 2. We will not discuss the matter from a financial policy standpoint. Rather, we will address it by looking at the conditions the new realities are likely to impose on the future activities of Japanese companies. Today, the very fact that the consequences of the bubble's burst remain unresolved may be what is hindering effective, vigorous corporate activity. One of the things we want to assert in this book is that the thwarting of the entrepreneurial spirit could prove to be a major source of ills for Japan's future economy.

To proceed with our discussion, let us begin with the impact of the strong yen. During the 1980s, when the dollar was maintained at a relatively high level on President Reagan's watch, Japan had a very strong competitive position in exports, both in terms of quality and price. Partly because of the stagnant domestic economy,

Japanese corporations depended on exports and expanded their facilities with a view to bolstering exports. As a result, many Japanese industries have built a structure in which equipment is idled when the possibility for exports is removed.

The rapid rise in the value of the yen began 10 years ago, in 1985, after the finance ministers and presidents of the central banks of five advanced nations signed the so-called Plaza Accord, designed to weaken the strong dollar. The rate at the time was ¥242 to US$1. The yen quickly ran past ¥200 and went progressively higher, to ¥180 and then to ¥150 to the dollar. Japanese companies in the export industries, forced at times to operate at a loss, worked assiduously to reduce costs in order to survive. No sooner had their diligence borne fruit and successfully overcome the effects of the strong yen, than they were buffeted by a further escalation, compelling them to redouble efforts to cut costs. This discouraging cycle was repeated again and again. In time, the strength of the yen no longer reflected economic reality. Whenever another wave of the soaring yen surged, a new group of Japanese companies reached the limit of their ability to adjust, and they went out and bought foreign firms or invested in real estate overseas. Life insurance companies invested in foreign bonds and kept incurring foreign exchange losses each time the yen climbed another notch.

Following the Plaza Accord, the Japanese government did its best to try to promote imports and encourage domestic demand by lowering the official discount rate and investing more in public works, which made use of the vitality of the private sector. Ironically, these efforts were too efficacious. They resulted in a rise in real estate and stock prices and, in time, brought about the bubble boom.

In the midst of this boom, the yen temporarily stabilized. But as soon as the domestic economy slowed, the yen soared yet again and a new threat to industry resulted. The yen's rise was particularly remarkable in 1993, when the rate went from ¥120 to the dollar to ¥110 in the spring, before going above ¥100 momentarily in the summer. At the time, many businesspeople shuddered at having had what some described as a "glimpse into hell." Nobody then imagined that we would ever experience the throes of agony that were felt when we actually arrived in hell—a yen in the range of ¥80 to ¥90 to the dollar, where it now resides.

In light of this upswing in the value of the yen, it would be pointless to discuss the export competitiveness of Japan's industrial products. It would be missing the mark, however, if we were to argue that Japanese business lost its international reputation because of the rise of the yen but that Japanese companies should not be held accountable for this because the appreciation of the yen was caused by speculators. To be sure, Japanese companies understood that they were engaged in a game with a certain handicap called exchange rates and that they were vying to win using their competitive strength under that handicap. In realty, the rules of the game were such that whenever Japanese players' hard work appeared to win them a victory they saw the handicap raised even higher, even while the match was still under way. Nonetheless, a review of the history of international trade friction indicates that the game already permitted a midcourse correction of the rules themselves.

When you see businesspeople screaming at the escalating yen, faulting the government for ineffective policies, blaming speculators for their unsavory activities, or otherwise taking it out on others, one wonders if they might not have misunderstand the rules of international trade under the floating exchange rate system. Have they been dedicating themselves to inappropriate endeavors while striving to follow rules they did not understand, much like marathon runners who keep running without realizing they have taken a wrong turn? If they had been certain of the rules, they would have been able to redirect their efforts. If so, the changes in the industrial structure being urged now might have been undertaken in earnest much sooner.

THE UNITED STATES THAT RECOVERED FROM DEINDUSTRIALIZATION

Whenever the yen soars suddenly, the press and the whole nation spooks and blames the government for its lack of an effective policy. But why have we been so scared of the yen's appreciation?

When you examine the history of the process, you see that our inordinate fear of the rising yen might arguably have had the effect of egging on the speculators, resulting only in a further ascendancy.

From the standpoint of companies engaged in exporting and importing, stable exchange rates are best. That makes it easier for them to set up numerical targets and plans. Change is anathema to them. In their situation, it is just as spooky to see the value of the yen drop precipitously as to see it shoot up. In particular, since our country must depend on imports to meet almost all of its needs in terms of fuel and natural resources we should be more fearful of a weaker yen and the inflation that would ensue as a result. One of the reasons we are frightened of the strong yen may be our concern about the effect of the reverse swing, which will no doubt come soon enough.

We fear the escalating yen because we believe it will make it more difficult for us to export goods and that our economy will suffer—with the result being increased bankruptcies and unemployment. It is because of this concern that the government has taken measures to stimulate the economy at each new instance of the yen's appreciation.

During the first half of the 1980s—when the yen was lower than ¥200 to the dollar—firms that exported their products, such as automobile companies, were claiming that an appreciation of even ¥1 would wipe out profits worth billions. Some years have passed since then, and the yen has moved dramatically, to the point where it almost seems impossible that these companies are still able to be profitable given the exchange rates prevailing today. They are able to do so because of the grueling efforts they have made at cost reduction and because of the other steps they have taken to offset the strong yen, such as the foreign purchase of materials and parts and the shifting of their production overseas.

Still, many local small and medium-size companies that have focused on exports can no longer export their products profitably because of the strong yen. They face the alternatives of switching production to products for domestic consumption, moving production overseas, or going out of business.

It is an effective response to the soaring yen for companies to move their production operations overseas or procure supplies and components from abroad. From the standpoint of Japan's overall economy, however, these measures are cause for some unease because they result in cutbacks in domestic production and employment. This is the so-called deindustrialization, or hollowing out, of industry.

The authors contend that industrial hollowing out cannot be helped. We must by all means avoid the kind of deindustrialization that may result from companies falling by the wayside because they can't go on producing in Japan. If, on the other hand, deindustrialization results from Japanese companies deciding on their own to go overseas, then it could well be a good thing. Some argue that when Japanese corporations begin production abroad, productivity will increase in those offshore locales, and that those local operations will turn to Japan for capital goods and other products that only Japan can supply, thereby helping maintain Japanese exports. We are not saying that the hollowing out of industry is something about which we should not be concerned. Indeed, it could very well mean Japan's trade surplus would continue as before, which could invite another onslaught of the strong yen at any time. What we argue is that the transformation of the industrial structure that is being sought now may make little progress unless we go through this hollowing out with the help of the strong yen.

A foreign example may help us understand the mechanism involved. From the 1970s through the 1980s, when the dollar was maintained at a high value, the United States carried out deindustrialization with a vengeance. Companies actively outsourced supplies overseas when they thought it advantageous to do so; they often closed their domestic plants and started production overseas. As a result some lost their competitive position completely, such as producers of television sets, and a number of entire industries disappeared. The phrase "hollowing out" began to circulate about this time. Strangely, few argued that it was the wrong thing to have happen. The results today show that the United States used this hollowing out as an effective means to replace the oligopoly of big business with a new industrial system centered around young, vigorous firms.

An industry that seems to have disappeared because of hollowing out may yet see a new emergence when the dollar weakens and its competitive position recovers vis-à-vis imports. In this sense, the most important thing to cultivate is the entrepreneurial mettle with which to take risks and seize opportunities and a system to help entrepreneurs do so. Just when the industrial system dominated by traditional big business was being shaken up, research parks sprang up in many parts of the United States, with local governments and universities together helping new companies get started.

As everyone knows, business schools in the United States are busy offering education in business administration. Just the reverse is true in Japan. In the 1980s, when the U.S. industrial system centered on large businesses was about to crumble, the reputation of Japanese management was rising sky-high. Observing this, we wondered about the significance of the education offered in the business schools. Today, we are embarrassed that we entertained such doubts. The American business schools were not turning out bureaucrats in big business; they were fostering entrepreneurs who were willing to bet on a business venture.

THE END OF THE "WORLD FACTORY"

Let us cite another, older example. Nineteenth century England was literally a world factory, exporting manufactured products all over the globe, including to its many colonies, and in doing so it maintained an overwhelming surplus in its trade balance. It eagerly exported capital as well and received huge interest income. During the latter half of the nineteeth century, England was reluctant to transfer overseas the technology of its domestic industry to maintain this system, as it sought—in concert with the trade unions—to avoid the hollowing out of its industry. When new industries emerged in the United States and Germany, England fell behind in transforming its industrial structure because it had clung for too long to its cherished industries. It has since become a nation with chronic deficits in trade.

The gold standard ruled international finance then. Since England had hoarded a lot of gold throughout the nineteenth century, it was able to sustain deficits of considerable size remarkably well. One could argue that precisely because it kept sustaining trade deficits during the first half of the twentieth century, it failed to foster new, competitive industries.

After the Second World War—when international finance changed to a fixed exchange rate system based on the U.S. dollar—the United Kingdom attempted to promote the competitive position of its domestic industry by devaluing the pound sterling a number of times. But its industrial structure was now a service-dominated one, with an increased concentration of employment in that sector. To be sure, the British health care system is well maintained, the City remains the center of world finance, and the hottest political and economic information finds its way into London. But because the number of people engaged in manufacturing is very small in Great Britain, whenever there is an upturn in economic activities foreign imports increase faster than domestic production. And it is in the service industry that we see employment rise at such times. Fewer people work in manufacturing, and the structural trade deficit remains unremedied. The living standard of Britons is steadily declining.

During the 1970s and 1980s, Japan prided itself on being a "world factory." With its chronic trade surplus, Japan has accumulated a huge amount of foreign currency year in and year out. But under the floating exchange rate system, Japan is constantly handicapped by the unceasing advance in the yen's value, making hollowing out inescapable. That is why the current extreme trade surplus will not last. In the near future, the strong yen could reverse its course and turn weaker should the trade balance turn to deficit, or a third oil crisis could send energy prices skyrocketing and the resultant panic could start the yen falling. In either case, we ought to be prepared for a possible reversal to a weaker yen.

In light of the foregoing discussion, there seems to be one important issue that might well determine if Japan is to share the fate of Great Britain, and that is whether or not the spark of the entrepreneurial spirit is to be fanned or doused in Japan. At the same time that it brings hardships, the rising yen offers an abundance of business opportunities, and more entrepreneurs ought to come to the fore and seize on those opportunities with alacrity. Today, we have regulations that frustrate entrepreneurs, and the consequences of the burst bubble still seem to hobble the building of a support system for them.

We must not procrastinate in implementing deregulation or in disposing of the negative aftereffects of the bubble. If the entrepreneurial spirit does not emerge in full force at the time of the weaker yen, it would indeed be a tragedy. It could perpetuate the deficit structure that was created by the hollowing out of industry. And if the enterprising spirit is killed, it may not be possible to find our way to recovery from the deficit structure. As we proceed with deindustrialization, some industries may disappear. But that shouldn't worry us too much. As long as entrepreneurship is alive and well, it will be able to resuscitate such industries the next time the yen weakens and new business opportunities present themselves.

Entrepreneurism may be a product not only of economic conditions but of social and cultural ones as well. In a culture that values conformity with the prevailing tides and keeping up with the Joneses, it may be difficult to nurture the self-assured, risk-taking, enterprising mind, although such a culture may be conducive to fostering the erstwhile virtues of Japanese management. We are not suggesting that Japan's cultural environment necessarily makes it harder to foster the enterprising spirit. Should that prove to be true, however, it behooves us to change that cultural climate. Otherwise, Japan's economic society may have nothing to look forward to in the twenty-first century.

Chapter 2 | # The Crisis We Face

The Japanese management approach has attracted the attention of many of the world's business administration researchers over the past 10 years or so because of the competitive strength of Japan's exports. Not so long ago, many European and American scholars were focusing their attention on a number of Japan's strengths, ranging from the Japanese-style production system and the structure of Japanese corporations to the nation's personnel system and even its cultural environment. Today, however, we find ourselves being forced to take another look at the very same management approach that was praised to the skies only a few short years ago. It is clear that we face a crisis. Japanese executives who in the past had complete confidence in the Japanese system of management now seem to be adrift, having been deprived of their moorings.

Why is it that the Japanese managerial approach doesn't seem to work any more? That question leads naturally to others. What is "Japanese management" all about? Would it be prudent to continue employing Japanese management practices? What should we do if we discover that such practices no longer contribute to effective business operations?

In seeking solutions to these questions, the first thing that must be remembered is we are not talking here of Japanese management having reached its limits, but rather of a situation where European and American businesses have schooled themselves in management know-how similar to the Japanese variety and thus have eliminated the gap between Japanese and foreign corporations. European and American companies have invigorated their management by introducing many of the advantages of Japanese management into their operations. There has been a lot of soul-searching in European and American companies over the fact that they did not pay as much attention as did Japanese firms to shop-floor operations and operations management. European and American managers seem to have been given quite a jolt when they heard that employees in Japanese companies were being urged to submit ideas for management improvement. Driven by a considerable sense of urgency, they were eager to learn from the Japanese system. As a result, Japanese management no longer possesses a great body of exclusive know-how.

The second issue of importance is the numerous ill-advised decisions taken by many Japanese companies during the era of the bubble economy. The Japanese system of business administration —once considered the very bedrock of Japanese business—has never been so shaken as it was during the latter half of the 1980s. How is it that managers who believed wholeheartedly in the excellence of Japanese management never seem to have pondered the risks inherent in excessive investment and self-centered judgments made without regard to the market? We will address that question, and try to discover the causes behind such misjudgment.

The third important issue is the politically motivated criticism leveled by the U.S. government at various structural features of Japanese management that were once considered meritorious. Lately, discussions on these structural features have for the most part taken place during government-to-government negotiations aimed at improving the balance of trade between the U.S. and Japan. Such discussions have had a macroeconomic focus and have centered around a political agenda and are not often convincing to those of us who study business administration.

Focusing on the three issues described above, we will review the current crisis faced by Japanese management.

JAPANESE MANAGEMENT STRUCTURE UNDER ATTACK

Japan's competitive strength in exports is seen by many as a successful outcome of Japanese management practices. Today, such functional aspects of Japanese management as making long-term investments or resolutely pushing ahead with investments that are worldwide in their perspective are being subjected to criticism from Europeans and Americans. It has been pointed out, for example, that a Japanese corporation can keep on investing on a long-term basis because of the existence of certain characteristics unique to Japan. One of them is the bank-centered financial structure, which leads to a strange system of business transactions; according to this criticism, the corporation is supplied with long-term capital thanks to unofficial, customary relationships with the banks. Excessively low-cost capital has been the subject of many studies by economists. In short, the criticism maintains that it is unfair that Japanese corporations should be able to procure funds at low cost through inequitable dealings with the banks. Japanese corporations have thus been able to carry out even foolhardy investments on a long-term basis and keep up with the expanding size of the world market.

Additionally, it is said that a high rate of savings is the backdrop that allows Japanese corporations to continue with long-term investments. This point has become politicized, principally from a macroeconomic perspective. A high rate of savings means less money is consumed. Corporations thus make investments on the basis of money they have saved. This flow of funds supports Japan's export-oriented economic system. Unless Japan's investment-oriented economy is transformed into a more consumption- oriented one, Japan's international competitive position will never wane, and its trade surplus will persist. Thus runs the argument, which has been repeated time and time again.

Critics also charge that investors don't ask for any increase in the meager dividends that Japanese corporations pay to their stockholders. We also often hear disapproving comments about the Japanese corporate practice of cross-ownership of shares among firms, which helps form an investment-oriented system, and that Japanese corporations, instead of focusing on making profits, are aimed at mere expansionism.

The essence of these complaints is that Japanese government and corporations have let loose an export-led economic structure and that it's wrong to have a system that aims at world domination.

Unfortunately, no convincing counterarguments have been put forth from the Japanese side. Instead of countering the criticisms, we often hear assertions that Japan's economy should transform itself into a consumption-type economy in affirmation of the American view. The arguments that are made rarely go much beyond pointing out that the problem lies with the American savings rate, which is much lower than that of Japan.

It was during the Structural Impediments Initiative (SII) talks held when Ronald Reagan was the U.S. president that such issues were debated in a public forum. On the one hand, many U.S. corporations depend on Japanese products to such a degree that they cannot restrict their imports, while on the other hand they find it extremely difficult to increase their exports to Japan, no matter how hard they try. In short, they can neither curtail Japanese imports nor increase their exports to Japan. When all steps had been exhausted in the effort to attain equilibrium in the trade balance, there emerged a series of criticisms against the uniqueness of Japan's economy, condemning Japan's business practices as unfair. During these SII talks, the participants discussed the different corporate environments that prevail in Japan and the United States, trying to determine why things seem to work out well in Japan and not so well in the U.S.

The SII negotiations not only brought the uniqueness of Japan's economy into sharp relief, they also made clear certain major problems that had not been sufficiently aired previously. These problems all relate to the management environment as seen from the perspective of business executives and can be divided into four areas: (1) the relationship between shareholders and management; (2) the relationship between workers and the corporations that employ them; (3) the relationship between capital procurement and corporations; and (4) the relationship between parts makers and assemblers.

The involvement of Japanese corporations in each of these relationships can be thought of as the soil that supports Japanese management. The kind of management environment in which corporations find themselves has a great impact on their performance. In the case of Japanese corporations, their environment allows them to continue Japanese-style employment practices. The environment supporting American corporations, conversely, allows them to operate on a short-term perspective and focus corporate judgment on profitability and returns to shareholders. Examining the differences in management environments also affords us an opportunity to look at how the management environments may change in the future and what transformations Japanese management—which has been supported by a particular environment—may have to undergo.

The Relationship between Shareholders and Corporate Managers—Shareholders Who Make No Demands

According to a story told by an American manufacturer of semiconductor equipment, a shareholder of the company demanded that it sell off an unprofitable department after recession had caused a deterioration in the company's performance. A Japanese semiconductor machinery maker, on the other hand, which suffered from similarly worsened earnings due to recession, pursued a strategy of technical development to prepare for the next stage of technological innovation. The widely divergent directions taken by the two companies is indeed instructive.

The shareholder of this American company was a so-called venture capitalist. American venture capital fosters entrepreneurs, but in the face of a crisis such as a business recession it can also demand that management take actions that might nip company growth in the bud rather than actions that further growth.

Japanese corporate managers have been relatively free from control by shareholders and have been able to run the company as they saw fit. American managers, on the other hand, can be deprived of their right to run the company if they do not take those actions demanded of them by the shareholders.

Generally speaking, investors want to recoup their capital and be paid dividends. Because of this, American managers tend to concentrate their efforts on turning a profit so they can pay out dividends. And while it would be inaccurate to say that Japanese investors do not demand dividends, they are more likely to leave corporate decisions to managers. As a result, Japanese managers

—being little restrained by shareholders—can make decisions and investments beneficial to their company and employees.

Another story has been told of a post-bubble committee meeting at the Ministry of Finance. There was a heated debate about placing more emphasis on dividends in order to raise stock prices. One committee member told another member, who represented an insurance company and was in favor of higher dividends, "If you want to support a proposal to increase payout ratios, you should raise the matter at the shareholders' meetings of the companies you invest in, rather than raising it at a government committee meeting." The man was nonplussed as he sat through the rest of the discussion. This story suggests the extent to which Japanese investors hesitate to express their views at shareholders' meetings. It should be the duty of a life insurance company to be resourceful in investing the pool of collected premiums for as high a return as possible. Instead, they remain largely idle and refrain from making just demands.

Banks and insurance companies are major shareholders in many large companies. Perhaps because they are familiar with the financial conditions of the companies through their communications with them in advance of general meetings, they rarely make demands at shareholders' meetings for things such as higher dividends, except in very special cases. Accordingly, Japanese managers make business decisions to benefit themselves, their companies, and their employees. One must conclude, therefore, that they operate according to judgment criteria that are different from those of American managers, who think principally in terms of the interests of the shareholders. Because Japanese banks want to continue to lend aggressively, it is perhaps inevitable that their approach to loans is different from that of American banks, which specialize in extending credit for short-term working capital. In Germany, banks and corporations are even more closely interrelated, to the point where the interests of capitalists and managers are almost merged.

Nowadays, however, some form of restraint is seen to be needed in Japan, much as in the United States, where the dominant power of investors exercises restraint on managerial actions. This need is evident from the fact that runaway capital spending during the bubble economy ended up creating a slew of profligate investments. That situation raises a fundamental question related to the essence of capitalism: What indeed is a company, and for whom does it exist? It should be understood here that the authors do not advocate simply reinforcing the authority of capitalists. We will make known our views on this matter from time to time as we move forward.

The Relationship between Workers and the Corporation—Great Store Is Set in Maintenance of Employment

Employment contracts in America are very different from those in Japan. Employees can be laid off at any time, even when a company is not suffering from poor earnings. Corporate managers can fire employees to maintain or boost dividends. Consequently, workers with an American company endeavor to improve their abilities: a lathe operator may want to run his or her machine more skillfully, and a salesperson may want to do a better job of selling. Otherwise, they may not be able to find a job with another company should that need arise. In other words, individual workers have a strong desire to enhance their profession skills, while what they do for the company is of secondary concern.

Some time ago, a man who looked to be somewhat learned was observed working as a cleaner at the Seattle airport. He said he had been laid off by Boeing Co. and was waiting his turn to be recalled. U.S. companies have a seniority system whereby laid-off workers are called back to work in accordance with the length of their service with the company, the longest-serving worker being the first to be recalled. U.S. unions value this system. In Japan, managers endeavor to keep employees on the payroll as long as possible by cutting their own salaries before resorting to dismissal. Few American companies replicate such efforts. This former Boeing employee wanted very much to stay in Seattle rather than move to another community to look for a job with another company. Consequently, he had no alternative but to await his recall.

Companies are actively bought and sold in America, and shareholders—looking for a higher return on their investment—

tend to agree readily to the proposed acquisition or sale of a company. Whenever it happens, incumbent managers may be fired or new managers installed at the behest of the new capitalists. It would be interesting to know how such acquisitions are viewed by employees in general.

Verbatim, a manufacturer of floppy disks now affiliated with Mitsubishi Chemicals, used to be one of the world's leading corporations. Quality claims against the company resulted in poor earnings, and it was bought out by Kodak, the famous maker of film. Concerned that in the future photographic film might be replaced by magnetic memory, Kodak wanted to have its fingers in the magnetic products pie, much as Fuji Photo Films has. Verbatim, on the other hand, thought that for the sake of long-term survival it was better that it become part of a large company involved in photographic film rather than going it alone with magnetic products only. Thus, Kodak's purchase of Verbatim made sense on both sides. Some executives and managerial staff stayed with the company under the new Kodak management, while others resigned. We were interested in gauging the feelings of middle managers of the acquired company. It so happened that we had the opportunity to speak with some of those middle managers. What did they think of the acquisition? What were their feelings toward the new shareholders? Their responses to these and other queries were quite interesting: "Our company's owners may have changed, but our jobs haven't. Our senior managers are on edge in dealing with our new shareholders. We are not interested in the shareholders. We don't think there will be any change in the company. Our technology is what supports the company."

We were happy to learn from the interviews that some middle-level managers in an American company do work for the company and for the business of the company.

Under employment arrangements in an American company, employees can, in general, be discharged from their jobs at the whim of their managers, without cause. Under such working conditions they aren't likely to feel they should work hard to improve their operations or otherwise dedicate themselves to their jobs for the sake of the company. Such feelings on the part of the workers are an inevitable result of the employment practices in the U.S. This American-style employment system cannot be condemned out of hand, because it does provide for mobility of labor, which is beneficial from the perspective of society as a whole. However, if you compare the American workers' sense of identification with their company and that of Japanese workers enjoying lifetime employment the difference is striking. Implementing Japanese employment practices, we are better able to construct a highly flexible production system on the shop floor, such as the development of multiskilled workers. There is no doubt that such differences in employment contracts affect the workers' motivation.

A different view can be offered with respect to white-collar jobs for which there is no clear-cut definition of specialty. In the U.S., the specialty of white-collar jobs has been at issue in recent years. Companies employ few unnecessary managers, and that is one of the reasons why American companies incur less fixed costs. In contrast, Japanese companies now have such a high percentage of managerial and white-collar employees that it is increasingly difficult to maintain the lifetime employment system. One can no longer argue that the Japanese employment system excels in every respect. Has this situation resulted from reckless hiring of a large number of white-collar workers or from the unraveling of the lifetime employment system itself? It is an issue that deserves very careful attention.

The Relationship between the Capital Market and the Procurement of Funds by Corporations—Dependence on Bank Loans for Long-Term Capital

Let us look again at the case of the American semiconductor machinery maker referred to earlier. What would have happened if this company had been a Japanese company and the stockholders asked the management to continue paying dividends during a recession? Japanese shareholders would likely be just as concerned with the future business of the company as would American shareholders, but Japanese managers would likely find other means of procuring funds, perhaps through negotiations with banks they customarily deal with. The shareholders and the banks—were they possessed of an adequate understanding of the company's technology and its future market—would probably support the continued operation of the company. It is highly unlikely that shareholders of a Japanese company who had little understanding of technology would press the company to downsize to equilibrium in order to insure a return on their investment. In this sense, when business operations run over a long period, over a number of annual earnings reports, support of the investors and banks is indispensable to their continuation.

The function of American banks and capital markets is different from those of Japan. In America, the only way to secure funds for long-term investment is to raise them in capital markets. In Japan, such funds are made available mostly through indirect financing or through banks. One can make an investment over a considerably lengthy period of time as long as the banks consent to it. In essence, the principal function of American banks is to provide short-term working capital, while long-term capital is obtained, in principle, directly from capital markets. Unless an investment is recouped in a short time and dividend payments to the capital markets continued, one cannot raise capital at low cost and under favorable terms. This is the reason American managers must focus on short-term profits in the stewardship of their companies.

During the bubble economy in Japan, the securities markets became vitalized, and it was no longer rare for companies to steer clear of the banks. However, with the bursting of the bubble the proportion of indirect financing through banks increased again. Today, bank loans remain the basic source of long-term capital. Because of BIS rules (regulatory capital ratios set by the Bank for International Settlements), Japanese banks have been limiting their loans recently to those with terms favorable to them and have become more profit oriented. On an international comparative basis, however, funds can still be obtained at low cost from Japanese banks, and profitability cannot be said to be high by international standards. There has been no change in the terms of loans characterized by long-term lending as well as low interest.

Parts Makers and Industrial Structure—Independent Parts Makers Promote Competition

The automobile and automobile parts industries, which have been in the forefront of trade friction between the U.S. and Japan, have been called leading industries, with their products accounting for a very large percentage of total Japanese exports. The structures of the American, European, and Japanese auto and auto parts industries differ from one another in many respects.

Japan's dealership networks have come under attack for being overly influenced by manufacturers, as they are vertically connected under *keiretsu* to specific auto companies. These days, automobile dealers are being encouraged to handle foreign cars without being constrained by their relationship with principal domestic manufacturers.

The relationship between Japan's automobile companies and their parts suppliers has also come under attack. Until quite recently, individual parts manufacturers had been integrated into the *keiretsu* organizations of the respective automobile manufacturers and identified as, for example, Toyota-group or Nissan-group suppliers. As a matter of fact, the U.S. auto companies are in no position to raise a hue and cry over their Japanese counterparts because General Motors, for instance, manufactures major components within its own organization. Ford Motor Co. has a steel subsidiary called Rouge Steel. It is so structured that it can make almost anything in-house. Their objective may have been to improve their competitive position by putting important parts to advantageous use for themselves without releasing them to other companies.

In Japan, there are many components makers, and auto companies buy their parts from them for assembly. This fact exerts great influence on the competitive environment. For example, if one wants to start an auto company one can purchase parts from parts vendors and make cars in a short time and with small investment. Without making efforts in the development of individual components one can concentrate on developing specifications and special features for the final products for sale to segmented markets. One could argue, therefore, that Japan's auto industry has a lower entry barrier than the U.S. auto industry. As a result, Japan ended up having as many as 10 automobile companies, constituting a unique competitive situation.

Assemblers have faced severe competition. This is a completely different environment from that of the three-company oligopoly of the U.S. As any economics textbook will tell you, an oligopoly lessens competition among companies, and American automakers have neglected to compete; have reduced investment in essential components, such as engines, which require large developmental cost; and have concentrated on enjoying profits. When they realized what was going on, Japanese auto companies had beaten them. And they grew desperate. That is the story of the international competition between American and Japanese automobile firms.

Although Japan's *keiretsu* structure has begun to crumble during the auto recession, there has been no change in the continued separate existence of auto parts makers and automobile makers as assemblers. In Europe—where, as in Japan, they have a number of small auto manufacturers—an oligopoly in the parts industry has progressed to the extent that it has created a gigantic auto parts maker, Bosch. Because of this, small-scale auto parts makers can operate successfully only if they can find a specialized market, such as that for sports cars.

A similar structure of excessive competition can be found in Japan's electric machinery industry. More than 15 companies constitute Japan's appliance industry. The widespread existence of electronics components manufacturers is one of the major factors that enables so many companies to survive in this industry. In fact, if the Akihabara district of Tokyo is scoured for parts an amateur might very well be able to put together a radio or a television set. When so many parts makers operate and sell their wares freely, they necessarily run into excessive competition. And that's how they have built an industrial system that can win in severe international competition.

THE FAILURE OF LONG-TERM MANAGEMENT PLANS

That Japanese management is on the verge of a crisis is evident in the failure of its long-range management planning. The formulation of management plans is a very important part of participatory Japanese management. In making long-term management plans, many companies first establish a general direction through what might be called a policy for the formulation of management plans. Each operating department presents its views regarding the general policy and sets forth its particular plan, which is then consolidated into overall corporate plans. The very act of putting together long-term plans is characteristic of Japanese management, and the process by which it is done is quintessentially Japanese.

There were three recent periods during which Japanese corporations zealously engaged in long-term planning. The first such boom was the period preceding the oil crises; the second covered the period from the end of the oil crises until the Plaza Accord of 1985; and the third involved the period from 1986-1987, until just before the collapse of the bubble. Each enjoyed a relatively stable management environment, and the economy grew consistently. During the times between these periods, on the other hand, there were valleys of drastic change.

Normally, it is during times of reformation that management is in need of long-range plans. But, setting aside that argument for now, let us here consider the types of plans that were formulated and their functions and results today.

The first boom occurred in the midst of the high-growth economy of the 1960s. The phrase "long-term management plans" was itself a novelty then, and the newly created corporate planning departments played a central role in creating a future vision in numerical terms. Then, after the oil crises, when Japan was faced with serious energy issues and a decline in the international competitive power of its industry, long-term planning was taken up seriously, by the materials industry in particular. Long-term planners for players in the nonferrous metals industry, such as aluminum and copper producers, wrestled with the question of how to survive as going concerns after they had moved their upstream smelting operations overseas. In their completed plans, chemical firms all announced a greater emphasis on engineering plastics, biochemistry, materials for the electronics industry, and fine chemicals, while steel companies announced their diversification into new hi-tech materials, electronics, and the service industry. We recall being somewhat puzzled about the uncanny similarity of the corporate plans among companies in the same industry. A number of companies were intent on becoming trillion yen companies and presented numerical targets in their plans.

All of these long-term plans went bust due to the yen's appreciation following the Plaza Accord. As oil prices declined and the yen's relative value went up, the companies failed to achieve the trillion yen sales goals they had set. Biotechnology is still in the developmental stage, and they have nothing much to show for their efforts. They did achieve some results in fine chemicals, but they apparently did not go much beyond supplying in bulk to pharmaceutical companies. In the electronics field there were so many new entries that few made any appreciable profit and a good number of them had to withdraw from the field.

Chemical manufacturers were not the only companies whose long-term plans went awry. Steel producers launched into the leisure industry, but their golf courses and theme parks modeled after Disneyland and built on vacant land don't seem to be profitable. Their entry into the electronics industry was a disaster, and most of them are working madly trying either to withdraw from or downsize their ventures. Long-term planning has thus been a failure in most companies.

But the fact that Japanese firms were carrying out a diversification of business within their own companies to maintain employment rather than changing to some other industry was for a time acclaimed overseas as the quintessential manifestation of Japanese management know-how. The Japanese way was totally different from the American way, in which long-term planning by top management is imposed on the rest of the organization or a handful of corporate planners concoct very abstract plans. After the burst of the bubble, however, we have seen some sorry spectacles, with Japanese companies doing away with diversified business departments under the slogan "Return to Your Main Business," introducing a system of early retirement for white-collar workers, and furtively picking out employees to be downsized by "tapping them on the shoulder."

Why did long-term planning end in such a debacle for most big companies? Was it due to a lack of precision in the plans? Was it due to poor execution? Or was it due to unforeseen changes in the corporate environment? It is imperative that Japanese managers determine the causes of the fiasco. Corporate planning is a very taxing operation, involving all staff members, but with a central role given to a company's controllers office or corporate planning office; it is a very important exercise, as it affects the future of all employees. And because that operation has failed in most cases, we cannot dismiss it simply by reciting the mantra that "this is the time for us to return to our principal business."

What was the central cause of the failure? That is the question we want to pursue in this book. At this stage, we can only say for certain that the process of participatory long-term planning—once touted as the embodiment of Japanese management—has come to naught.

We don't want to take refuge in the plausible conclusion that long-term management plans just don't work when circumstances undergo substantial change. Unfortunately, however, that seems to be exactly what has happened. The sum of that thinking is that long-term plans of strategic diversification formulated before the Plaza accord of 1985 could not be implemented and had to be amended after the accord because of the strengthened yen and weakened dollar. The reformulated long-term plans made during the bubble period looked forward to greater globalization and diversification, but they collapsed when the bubble collapsed, making it difficult for companies to raise money and causing the market to change considerably.

The situation of most companies that have abandoned corporate planning may be likened to a ship adrift on the ocean without a compass (management policy), not knowing which way to go. Where in the world did Japanese management go wrong?

THE TRUTH OF THE SUCCESS OF SUCCESSFUL COMPANIES

Among the ruins of collapsed long-term plans we can find a few successful exceptions. But before looking at some of those, let us first review the relationship between the management environment and corporate earnings, as these are very closely related. The left side of figure 2-1 on page 28 shows the changes in the ordinary profits of electrical machinery and automobile companies with annual sales of ¥500 billion or more from 1984 to 1986, during which time the yen moved to higher ground. The x-axis shows the percentage of products exported, while the y-axis shows the change in ordinary profits.

You will note that companies with higher export percentages experienced worsened results on account of the weaker dollar and that their ordinary profits declined considerably. Companies in the computer and telecommunications business, such as NEC Corp., Mitsubishi Electric, Hitachi, Toshiba, and Fujitsu were exceptions, and they did slightly worse than the average of other industries because of the compound effects of the recession in personal computers and semiconductors. These results show that the earnings of Japanese companies after the Plaza Accord were interrelated with the two factors of the stronger yen and the percentage of their products exported. There is not much differential in earnings among the companies, with earnings mainly influenced by business environment. In other words, the stewardship of a company had only a minor effect on its performance. One might say that the results were not so much the measure of management skills as the evidence of the influence of environment.

The right side of figure 2-1 on page 29 shows the changes in ordinary profits during the Heisei recession, when the yen appreciated to a value greater than ¥110 to the dollar. The chart reveals that, as in 1985, domestic-oriented industry was not much affected by the soaring yen. Companies exporting a large percentage of their products continued to do poorly. Among electrical appliance makers, JVC hovered above the break-even point, while Sharp, with a similar percentage of export products, managed to keep profits from falling more than 20 percent or so. That situation is different than the strong yen period of 1985 in that substantial differences in competitive power among companies in the same industry are evident.

In the automobile industry, Mazda and Nissan are having a difficult time, while Mitsubishi Motors has barely suffered a decline in profit. We are not sure if this is due to a difference in competitive power. Perhaps the divergent performances are ascribable to the way these companies deployed their investment strategies during the bubble period. Mitsubishi Motors did not undertake much capital spending; with disciplined management, it marketed good-quality products at low prices. It had a small market to begin with, and it escaped the adverse effects of being adventuresome. It made profit by exporting key components, such as engines, to South Korea and the United States. Mitsubishi recreation vehicles were a nice success story that added to the bargain. Mitsubishi management ran the company differently than did its counterparts at other auto companies. We can surmise that Mitsubishi Motors did not see its profits decline when others did because its management distinguished itself in terms of its investment strategy, business structure, and product strategy.

Computer makers and telecommunications companies chalked up some poor results during the Heisei recession. In recent years, the supply and demand balance has improved somewhat—prices have gone up, and business is recovering. Differences in competitive power among companies are evident. Oki Electric Industry—whose corporate culture is reputed to be similar to that of NTT—had, along with Hitachi and NEC, serious earnings problems, leaving a wide gap in comparison with other makers. But, thanks to the successful strengthening of its semiconductor business, earnings have improved dramatically.

Differences in earnings among different companies are now very obvious. While it may invite controversy to attempt to ascribe these results to differences in corporate management, certain structural differences of some companies have by this time been so clearly exhibited that it is no longer possible to evaluate the performance of all companies by alluding to the impact of

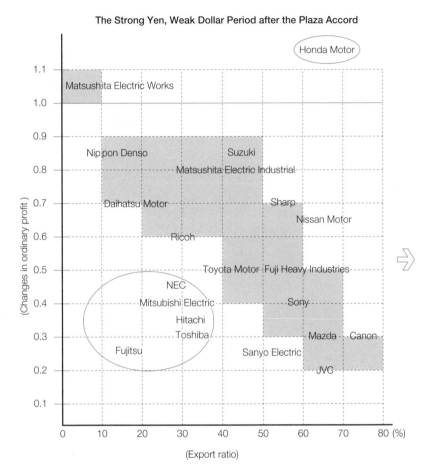

The Strong Yen, Weak Dollar Period after the Plaza Accord

Fig. 2-1. Foreign Exchange Fluctuations and Changes in Corporate Earnings

Notes: 1. Changes in ordinary profit from FY1984 to FY1986.
2. Electronics parts makers sustained greater impact than others because of the added factor of a semiconductor recession. Generally, the higher the producers, export ratio, the greater the rate of earnings decline.

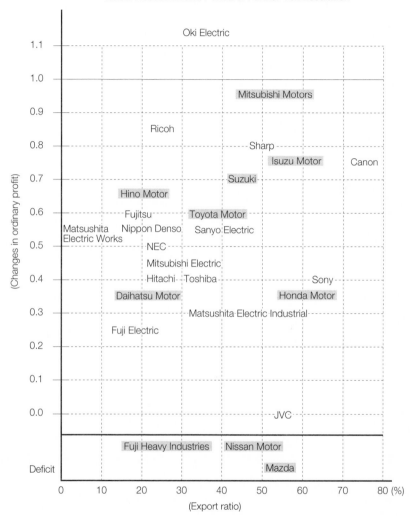

Heisei Recession and Period of Further Yen Escalation

Notes: 1. Changes in ordinary profit from FY1990 to FY1994 (based on earnings forecast).
2. The chart shows companies in the electrical machinery and automobile industries mostly with ¥500 billion or more in sales (based on FY1990).
3. Changes in earnings differ from one company to another in the same industry.

circumstances. Only a few years separate the period immediately following the Plaza Accord and the Heisei recession, but it is most revealing to examine how management changed during this brief interval.

In the office equipment industry, for example, Canon's solid performance is supported by such illustrious products as laser beam printers (LBPs), bubblejet printers, and copiers. How did these come to be developed? How was it possible for Canon, which in the past had specialized in cameras, to develop these new products? A review of the process of development makes clear the skill with which Canon managed technology.

Having been engaged in the manufacture and development of cameras, Canon possessed a wealth of optical technology. The company combined this with photographic development technology to produce copying machines. Similar diversification of products took place at Ricoh, Minolta, and Konica, so that Canon by no means monopolized such successful diversification. By digitalizing its optical technology, Canon came out with LBPs. The company is said to have managed technology very well and went on improving on some of its existing technology to diversify its products. Many other camera makers also had a similar lineup of products. It is hard to say with certainty, therefore, what were the critical points in technology management and precisely where Canon excelled.

Canon has distinguished itself from others by having developed small copying machines, often called minicopiers, and small LBPs. Who developed these? It is said that the inventor is not a career employee of Canon but someone who joined the company after having worked for Oriental Photo. An image development process called jumping development—for which Canon owns the patent—was added to the existing technology, and that led to the introduction of small copying machines and small LBPs. It is reported in some quarters that Canon bought this particular development technique from a defunct company called Kinoshita Research. Perhaps Canon was adept at using outside resources in running its operations.

We have also heard that in the course of making considerable investments aimed at diversification Canon had accumulated so large a deficit that it wanted to discontinue its venture into copier development. At that time, so the story goes, employees engaged in the developmental effort put the company on notice that they would resign if it discontinued the work. Managers were in a bind, but they decided to postpone termination of the project for awhile. In time, business recovered and the pressure to terminate lessened. We are not certain as to the veracity of this story, but one might say that the managers' decision to wait and the strength and enthusiasm of the company's employees together created today's Canon. Afterwards, Canon entered into agreements with Hewlett Packard of the U.S. and Olivetti of Europe in order to pursue its strategy of becoming a dominant presence in the world market. Smart business decisions—holding down the prices of its products and making drums and toners exchangeable—built its profit structure. It developed production technology that enabled it to make products at low cost. Canon's outstanding performance today is the result of its efforts to marshal its corporate resources in this manner.

In terms of the interaction of employee enthusiasm and corporate management, companies can tell all sorts of stories, some happy and others not so happy. Sony initially made its mark with videocassette recorders but failed in its beta format strategy and had to play second fiddle to the VHS camp. The only way that Sony could recover from that failure was to make a success of 8 mm video technology, and the company devoted itself to its development. Those efforts have borne considerable fruit, and today it has succeeded in the second generation 8 mm video.

In the story of the rejuvenation of NEC through "C&C" (computers and communications) there is little doubt that Kobayashi Koji and Sekimoto Tadahiro, who were then middle-level managers at NEC, worked furiously on the development of C&C, relying on their keen insight into the company's future to build the foundation for the success of today's NEC. Very often it is those employees working at the operations level who have the ability to look into the future and foresee unrealized markets and who continue with developmental efforts in the face of temporary failures, be it with electronic switches or computers. It is often the people in the field who can make proper judgments about the best strategy for the future. This is not to deny that some exceptional managers with liberal arts backgrounds have the ability see the future clearly. It would be safe to assume, however, that there is little guarantee that today's managers can make the proper business decision at every turn.

It would seem to us, then, that middle-level managers in charge of field operations must provide the principal driving force behind Japanese corporations. Of course every company will have its own intriguing history in this regard, its own share of episodes relevant to the question of whether it owes its growth to the competence of senior management or to middle managers' command of factory operations and their insightful outlook for the future.

In Japan's electric appliance companies—whose products have dominated the world market—most decisions on product design and specifications were made by engineers in the factories. One could argue that it was the unrestricted climate that allowed plant engineers to visualize desirable products for worldwide marketing and then build them that turned today's appliance makers into global manufacturers.

Methods of developing products in accordance with strategies taught in business administration textbooks should be seen as no more than one alternative. Unfortunately, the management planning we have been discussing may not be anything more than a method of this nature. Therein may lie the problem of today's management without substance.

THE TURNING POINT BROUGHT ABOUT BY THE BURSTED BUBBLE

What happened inside corporations when the bubble burst? The basic approach companies took was to implement large-scale rationalization programs to avoid red ink. Managers today are not in a position to rely solely on their instincts when they can no longer forecast the needs of the market or the trend of technology.

The seniority-based compensation system once considered one of the major pillars of Japanese personnel management has just about fallen apart; as for lifetime employment, people are almost equally divided between those who feel the system is no longer needed and those who believe it should be continued.

You cannot hope to achieve immediate results by holding seminars on innovation in management or reforms in business operations or by resorting to other forms of exhortation within the company. In fact, many employees feel pressured by the very word "restructuring." Bold new ideas for the future are necessarily hard to come by in such a gloomy atmosphere. Managers who are not familiar with technology will have to turn to someone else for help in deciding whether a new development proposal is good or bad. They ask other companies for their views and deftly arrange for people outside the company to offer advice. It is extremely disappointing to have managers come back and say, "We've got professionals agreeing with us. We should quit this project or venture. And you have to take responsibility for it." However, such an atmosphere is gradually spreading. One wonders if such managers are qualified to discuss the merits and demerits of Japanese management.

The most important function for any manager is to clearly grasp when a business turning point is at hand, orient the company in the direction of a new business structure, and then take the helm as the company moves in that new direction. In this sense, Japanese companies, particularly those whose senior management consists principally of bureaucratic managers who came up from the ranks of salaried men, find themselves at a major crossroads.

Until only a few years ago, many managers were concerned they had expanded their realm of operations so much in anticipation of successful business diversification that they lost sight of their main business. They very much wanted to retrace their steps and review the scope of their business. Many companies changed their logos and created new identities for themselves while actively carrying out so-called corporate identity programs. Many companies are now engaged in a soul-searching effort aimed at trying to understand the significance of such activities. Brainy, all-knowing consultants and image creators proliferated like wild-flowers in the boom days. Lots of people were busy seriously debating such questions as what should be the social mission of the company or what business structure should the company have. What was it all about? As soon as the bubble burst these discussions ceased.

Many companies that once proclaimed their environmental consciousness and touted their philanthropic activities appear to be soft-pedaling now. It is quite obvious they never seriously cared about the social environment. Would it be too much to say they have betrayed the shallowness of corporate Japan?

There is also the issue of employment. It is now clear that large companies in particular hired an excessive number of new employees during the bubble period. They are beginning to downsize middle managers and gray workers rather than the younger workers they hired to excess. Some employees are being "tapped on the shoulder" and laid off, while others are being seconded to subsidiaries. Moreover, employees in age groups that would have heretofore found jobs elsewhere are being compelled to live a pensioner's life—a crushing blow to their expectations. Instead of layoffs, some companies have moved quickly to put a lid on rising wages with wage cutbacks or by switching to the so-called fixed annual salary schedule. Some managers tell their charges that "if you don't work harder, you won't get any more raises." This is a far cry from the traditional concept of Japanese management.

Finance is also a very serious issue. In the same way that they hired far too many employees during the bubble, firms also raised a huge amount of unneeded money through equity financing and invested much of that in stocks and real estate. They are now being pressed for repayment on the equity-related bonds. Convertible debentures cannot be converted to stock; it has become impossible to exercise the warrants that were attached to bonds. Only management's duties to the stockholders have increased.

Once-peerless Japanese management has sunk so low it is now hard to believe it once enjoyed the world's acclaim. Observers are truly bemused. There is no question that Japanese management faces a gargantuan turning point.

We say this because, first, that's the feeling we get when we view Japanese management through the words of American scholars and students and assess arguments over political conflicts between the U.S. and Japan. Second, the proof is in the virtual breakdown of long-term planning. Third, there seems to be a narrowing in the domain of acceptable activities for middle managers—who, along with some senior managers, were once the prime movers behind management innovation. Fourth, the wave of restructuring that has taken place since the bubble burst has made it imperative that traditional Japanese management practices undergo tremendous change.

Chapter 3 | Japanese Management from a Historical Perspective

We will begin this chapter by taking a look at changes in the business environment from a historical perspective. We want to discover the ways in which the business environment has changed and how Japanese corporate management has changed in response to those changes. It is important to analyze the relationship between Japanese corporate management and the business environment in historical terms because the manner in which a company is managed depends in large measure on how skillfully its management responds to changing circumstances. It is also important to identify and examine the causes of the success Japanese corporations have enjoyed in the past, as this will help to determine whether that success derived from the approach taken by Japanese firms in response to changing circumstances— as distinguished from that taken by American and European firms—or whether it was due to the particular vitality of the corporate organizations involved.

LUCK AND ECONOMIC GROWTH

What were the changes in circumstances that have significantly altered the direction of corporate management from the end of World War II to the present?

Immediately after the Second World War, Japan found the level of its technology far below that of the U.S. and Europe, with a slew of dilapidated facilities that lacked the capacity to supply needed products. There is no question that the Japanese government's deft policy decisions at the time—which encouraged the introduction of foreign technology and guaranteed the funds to pay for that technology—went a long way to revitalizing the private sector. During that period, the preferential allocation of precious resources favored select industries and an all-out effort was made under the government's leadership to reconstruct the war-torn economy. It was not the time to be concerned about the independence of private business or the freedom of corporate managers; of necessity, government policy and the policy of private business were in agreement. The major objective of the government was to build a foundation for industrial reconstruction, and it limited the recipients of its priority investments to a handful of priority industries, such as energy and steel.

The proposed entry of firms other than Japan Iron & Steel Co. into the steel industry caused quite a stir because of concerns about excessive investment. The Japanese government did not believe the automobile industry could catch up with American or European auto manufacturers, and it provided little active support to this sector, although neither did it throw any impediments in its path. We must not lose sight of the fact that the assiduous efforts of Japanese industrialists during this period were instrumental in ensuring the subsequent advances made by industry.

At the same time, General Douglas MacArthur's occupation policies were also having a tremendous impact. Certain old business executives were driven out of their positions—forced to take their share of the responsibility for the war—while others were removed through the dissolution of the *zaibatsu*. Inevitably, the stewardship of many companies devolved onto the shoulders of amateurs, strangers to the tasks required to run a company. Yet they worked at it furiously, which may have given birth to the celebrated vitality of Japanese business. It should also be acknowledged that agricultural land reform and labor union activities had the salutary effect of accelerating the expansion of the consumer goods market. Undeniably, Japan followed a rather delicate path of transformation.

Something else that can only be termed fortuitous—as it was helping to rebuild Japan's industry—was the international situation that prevailed at the time. The Cold War between the U.S. and the U.S.S.R. caused the Allied powers to make a major shift in their basic occupation policies in favor of facilitating the reconstruction of Japan. More directly, the Korean War gave Japan a special procurements boom, which was a much needed shot in the arm for its moribund economy.

As the special procurements boom was giving Japan some breathing space, many Japanese corporations enthusiastically imported technology to try to catch up with the advanced nations of the West. The introduction of technology from U.S. and European companies into Japan's chemical industry—which was lagging considerably in this regard—is an excellent example of the way technology was imported. The technology imported by the chemical industry during the 1950s and early 1960s related to nylon, polyethylene, polyester, and polypropylene. Firms absorbed the technology, manufactured products, and sold them in the domestic market. As the technology was improved upon, chemical companies gradually began exporting their products overseas. Likewise, the automobile industry imported technology—from Renault and Hillman—and worked hard at absorbing it into the manufacturing process. In addition to such efforts, which certain industries undertook to narrow the technological gap in their own area of business, some industries—the chemical industry for example—imported whole sets of technology in order to create a new type of business within the framework of an existing business group of the old *zaibatsu*. There were a number of such cases. It is well known that Komatsu, a maker of construction machinery, imported a number of different technologies, such as those related to power shovels and tunnel-boring machines, mostly from its counterparts in the U.S.

It was during this period that the skill with which these technology transfers had been effected began to make a difference in the business results of Japanese corporations. And the introduction of technology was not limited to machinery. Ajinomoto actively brought in American technology. It set up a joint venture with a French firm to make layered cheese. These efforts built the foundation upon which the diversified general food manufacturer of today was erected. With these technology transfers functioning as a catalyst, the diversification of corporate activities made significant progress. The creation and publication at that time of a management theory that supported these developments had a great impact on corporate management. The protagonist was Peter F. Drucker. Such concepts and methods as "creating customers" and "decentralized organization," which Drucker proposed in his writing, went over very well with contemporary managers. This was a time when phrases like "market segmentation" and "differentiated marketing" and concepts such as chain-store organizations in the distribution industry sounded so refreshingly new that Japanese companies absorbed them with awe and fell all over themselves trying to embrace these new examples of Western management know-how.

As a result, Japanese manufacturers of bicycles, cameras, and watches became the first domestic companies able to compete with European firms, and they gradually made their appearance in the world market. The Japanese were praised for the skill with which these products were made. Also beginning to bear fruit was the strategy of priority investment in steel, shipbuilding, and other heavy industry, as well as the strategy of enlarging the scale of operations, which was successfully employed by the chemical industry to catch up with its competitors in the West. At that time, giant corporations in Europe and America were transforming themselves into multinational corporations; in the U.S., mergers and acquisitions were being undertaken at a brisk pace. However, conglomerates and mergers were still alien phenomena in Japan at this time.

Propelled by these investment and growth strategies, as well as by expanded consumption, the Japanese economy grew continually until it encountered the major obstacles that were the two oil crises—the first in 1973 and the second in 1979. These events made it painfully clear that Japan lacked international competitiveness in the area of energy, which is in fact the very infrastructure of industry. The Japanese economy recognized the need to explore ways of sustaining its growth without relying on energy. Fortunately, Japan chose to be competitive through knowledge-intensive, technology-driven industries rather than with energy-consuming industries. However, many materials-production industries that consume large quantities of energy—such as the aluminum smelting and pulp and paper industries, as well as the still-controversial soda and glass industries—were forced to follow a path of stagnation due to the oil crises.

The oil crises occasioned other significant changes in corporate management. One of them was the change in the location of the materials industries; their upstream processes had to be relocated offshore, accelerating the trend of multinationalization. This was the beginning of a major transplanting overseas of Japan's industry, something that had already taken place in the textiles industry. Another interesting development was the internationalization of pricing decisions. We begin to see at this time the globalization of price leadership, unfettered by any domestic market situations or marketing actions.

Although Japanese corporations weathered the oil crises relatively well, they soon had to grapple with the next major change in the business environment, which was precipitated by the Plaza Accord of 1985. This change was the rising value of the yen, which is still the principal problem facing Japanese management today. The escalating yen struck hard at many assembly operations, especially export-oriented industries, and many were compelled to shift their operations overseas.

But foreign exchange was not the only cause of this new environment; its appearance was accelerated by political friction with some of the advanced countries. Trade became highly politicized through quantitative restrictions on exports and antidumping litigation. One could argue that what is at issue today is, once again, the system of interactions between the Japanese government and Japanese industry since the war.

It is not clear to what extent the market share of foreign semiconductors agreed upon by governmental negotiations is relevant to the desire of customers to buy foreign products. The U.S. demands that Japan and other countries buy more American products, but it cannot prevent its own multinational corporations from investing abroad. When we asked U.S. government officials about this, a typical reply was "The U.S. government has no authority to control private business." When asked why then they make demands on Japan, their response was "The Japanese government does have influence over Japanese corporations. It ought to do whatever it can if it wants to see the U.S.-Japan trade balance move toward equilibrium." In effect, then, the source of today's friction lies in the relationship between the government and industry. What is being questioned is the stance of big corporations that proclaim import targets at the insistence of the government.

Another development is the emerging contradictions between the financial policies of the Ministry of Finance and the industrial policies of the Ministry of International Trade and Industry. In their desire to see amortized the unrealized loss from the burst bubble and to see securities firms revitalized, they have shown a readiness to intervene in the stock market and prevent stock prices from falling, and that is lessening the risk of investment by overseas investors in Japan. Why do foreigners continue to invest in Japan despite the fact that Japanese securities are, relative to the securities in other nations, the least attractive and yield the least income? Why is it that Japanese insurance companies cannot make up their minds and invest overseas? The answer to the second question is they are afraid that the government's policies will cause the yen to advance further and that they will see their unrealized losses increase. They are caught in a web of their own making. One consequence of all this is that the most competitive industries vie with one another in moving production operations overseas, causing the further hollowing out of industry.

Once you go overseas, it is no easy task to run a business there. Unlike in the materials industries, with their equipment-intensive structure of production, the most important aspect of management know-how in labor-intensive assembly operations is how best to utilize the local work force. It presents a daunting challenge to Japanese managers who have little experience in utilizing employees of different ethnic backgrounds. After coping with the oil crises and the surging yen, Japanese managers now find it necessary to acquire management know-how that is, literally and substantively, global in nature.

DIVERSIFICATION STRATEGIES THAT FAILED

Let us take a look at the trends connected with Japan's corporate strategies. Whereas Japan's materials industries began to globalize soon after the oil crises, it was not until after the Plaza Accord that many machinery firms, including assembly firms, were obliged to deploy their operations overseas in earnest. Until then, they had been hard at work trying to diversify. While Japanese companies were up to their ears in diversification strategies, multinationals were already in action in the West. In America, Ford, IBM, ITT, and others were poised to conquer the world with their technological prowess. Those companies had effective political clout over their host countries and had acquired know-how to deal with any conflicts with them.

These gigantic Western corporations, which had made great strides in the world market, set out to make changes in their business structure in the 1980s by means of mergers and acquisitions. Their managers must have decided that, having satisfied consumer demand for the time being, the most important task for management was to emphasize and focus on stable growth. Japan's appliance industry and automobile industry, which had no equals in the world, were late in reinforcing their overseas operations because they first had to overcome the confusion brought about by the oil crises.

A comparative examination of the major management strategies undertaken by Japanese firms and those undertaken by American and European firms shows that the Japanese were often a step behind the West.

Japanese companies were late in coming out with a diversification strategy, late in going global, and, most critically, late in effecting stable growth for themselves. During the Heisei boom, when the bubble economy was in full swing, many giants of Japanese industry paid no attention to the maturing market and concentrated their efforts on the expansion of their manufacturing capacity for existing merchandise. When the boom went bust, they found they had surplus personnel and excess investments. At the same time, the soaring yen prompted them to question their international competitive strength, something they had never doubted in the past. The bubble's burst thus found Japanese companies saddled with the dual burden of their belated response to the maturing market and superfluous investments.

Many companies did anticipate the changing market and intensified their diversification efforts. For example, Nippon Steel Corp. and other steel companies all followed one another into the electronics field. Toray Industries and other chemical companies entered the electronics and pharmaceuticals sectors. Many companies in the materials industries set their sights on floppy disks and optical disks, and even those who had never commercialized their ventures on a full-fledged basis did undertake a great deal of investment in research and development. Some companies even began making hard disks. Also, since specifications for copying machines changed from metal drums that use selenium and tellurium to organic semiconductors, many firms in this industry invested in developmental work.

We will refrain here from giving a detailed explanation of all the results brought about by these efforts. Kao and Mitsubishi Chemicals succeeded in entering the field of floppy disks; companies other than Mitsubishi Chemicals set up ties with hardware makers of organic semiconductors but had to suspend their joint development, many of them ending up withdrawing from the venture. Comments regarding the semiconductor field—where all-out efforts are still ongoing—would be premature at this point. It can be said, however, that at the present time only a few companies have succeeded.

The materials industries are not alone. The assembly industry also made investments to diversify into the leisure industry and the housing industry. Here again it is harder to find successful cases than failures. The crux of the issue comes down to this: Did they think they could bring it off if they spent enough money? Or were these merely cases of profligate investment?

Doing as the Joneses Do

Japanese companies have traditionally believed that emulating what other companies in the same industry are doing is proof of their competitive prowess. In contrast, American and European firms generally believe that the prime determinant of successful management is the achieving of differentiation from other companies, which will lead to an improved profit structure and enhance the firms' own identity. Thus, there are two vastly different concepts at work here.

Nowadays, everybody talks about how attractive the multimedia market will become in the future, and almost all companies in related fields in Japan want to enter it. The results are excess supply, necessarily stiffer price competition, and the inability of any of them to make profit. One could also argue, however, that it shows that Japanese companies are inclined to make investments in an active way and are equipped with the financial and technical resources to do so.

In the past, management's goal was to ensure there was no lagging when it came to entering growth markets, and this competitive spirit was the principal source of vitality for the economy. This same behavior is now being faulted. Many now criticize firms for going too far while trying to keep up with the Joneses.

Conspicuous examples of this type of copycat behavior are found in the diversification strategies undertaken by firms. Many chemical firms, for example, set their sights on diversifying into fine chemicals, biochemistry, engineered plastics, pharmaceuticals, and electronics. For a time, these companies were even drawing up similar diversification plans. Chemical companies were not alone in trying to emulate the Joneses: steel companies went into electronics, the service industry, and plant exports. The materials industries and the appliance industry wanted to try their hand at information technology. Of particular motivation for the appliance industry in this regard was the knowledge that it would soon be a mature industry. Many firms in the materials and appliance industries saw themselves growing into general electronics companies in the future. Sony's entry into the world of word processors and workstations and Matsushita's foray into the word processor and personal computer markets are just two examples of the kind of change that was taking place. Most corporations were taking a good look at their neighbors before formulating business plans. It is little wonder, then, that the result has been excessive competition.

But if most companies can still somehow manage to operate their new businesses more or less satisfactorily, despite the severe competition, there isn't a problem. In the past, whenever an abundance of companies entered a new market, the result was invariably the successful development of that market. One could conclude that the competition in product development contributed to market development and that the individual efforts of the firms to best one another enhanced the competitive power of them all. But the days of assured growth are gone. In today's economy, if the efforts of suppliers exceed the growth potential of a particular market, everyone does not end up winning.

In the materials industries most diversification ventures have not been successful. The collapse of the bubble forced many companies to withdraw from the ventures they were involved in at the time. One major reason why so few companies are succeeding in new ventures is timing—an aspect that is now of paramount importance due to the increasing speed with which new developments arise and markets change. An example of the dire consequences that bad timing can precipitate these days is the attempt made by a certain company to enter the workstations field. Because it debuted with merchandise that used Sun Microsystems' technology—the same technology being used by the computer makers already established in the market—its products turned out to be the same as those offered by Fujitsu and Toshiba. The company was unable to sell its workstations on the strength of differentiated maintenance services or software know-how, and the venture turned out to be something less than the company had hoped for.

On reflection, we find that keeping up with the Joneses is closely related to risk-averse decision making. When submitting a proposal to enter a new business, one is more likely to get it approved if it can be justified with the observation that "our competitors are preparing to do the same." Taking this tack to the extreme, a very convincing proposal would be one that says, "as our competitors are already in the market, we want to go in too, lest we be outdone by them." Should the venture fail, one can salve one's conscience with the excuse that "other companies have also failed."

What was once a spirited willingness to strive to outdo competitors has in many instances degenerated into a readiness to simply follow along and offer excuses. The statement "we do it because our competitors do it" was once the rallying cry of those who sought to enter the fray and best the competition, while today the same words are used either to gain approval for a copycat proposal or as an excuse to be offered up when a venture falls apart. Depending on how it is used, then, the same statement has two very different concepts underpinning it. The prevalence of the more recent usage is evidence that the mentality of Japan's business managers has become bureaucratic.

Externally Dependent Innovations

An important aspect of effective business diversification is determining which product areas to enter and what goals to set in terms of technological innovation. That is what makes a new business so attractive and interesting. In recent years, big business players—especially general assemblers producing finished products—have been spending more time and getting more interested in developing systems for making products that meet the needs of the market rather than developing key technology of their own.

As a result, we are seeing what almost amounts to a sea change in the relationship between assemblers and component makers. General assemblers are less and less adept at developing elemental technology. They are so busy developing systems and playing the role of arranger that they end up neglecting basic technology.

In the past, it was customary for finished-product manufacturers who understood the market to carry out technical innovation on a continual basis in response to the new needs that cropped up in the marketplace. That is no longer the case. Those best able to anticipate market needs and make a concerted effort at technical development are not the assemblers but the manufacturers of materials and parts on the upstream portion of the process. They are the ones who are more likely to come up with new innovations. Under the prevailing diversification strategy, assemblers often depend on the same component manufacturers, which means there is little difference between the products that the different assemblers offer at market. Under such circumstances, a successful venture becomes a difficult thing to achieve.

In not a few industries, certain key components have become so standardized that companies have no alternative but to follow along with the prevailing technology. In the area of personal computers, Intel's processors and Microsoft's Windows are widely acknowledged to be industry standards, and companies are very nearly forced to develop their products in accordance with those standards. While different companies offer different guarantees and services for their products, it seems almost a waste of time for them to spend time and money developing products that are essentially the same as those offered by their competitors.

The history of the hard disk offers an excellent example of the advantage that technologically endowed producers possess. The magnetic head is a key component of hard disks. Once the specifications for the magnetic head became established, all companies began to use the same thin-film magnetic head. Consequently, no producer of hard disks is able to establish a competitive advantage over other producers when it comes to the magnetic head. Any new product based on an improvement of this key component is dependent on magnetic head manufacturers. Over time, IBM technology developed a magnetic-resistant element and used this to develop an alternative product—the high-density magnetic disk. Because of the superior quality of the new disk, the magnetic-resistant element became a new key component of hard disks. None of the Japanese parts makers was able to produce this component to the same specifications as IBM. Because of that, superhigh-density hard disks are now dominated by IBM, which is the sole producer of one of the key components. While IBM might want to make money by selling that component, we cannot expect it to sell the component to its competitors, reduce its disk prices, and compete with them, in the same way that Sharp did when it developed liquid crystal. As this example shows, the gap between technologically endowed companies and those not so endowed can be huge.

It is not clear when the development of key components and materials began to be neglected. That firms were too busy vying with competitors in the area of product development to pay sufficient attention to basic technical development is no longer an acceptable excuse.

Management Plans Drawn in Sand

In addition to the practice of keeping up with the Joneses and the dependence on parts suppliers for technical development, one other factor that can make or break a new venture or a diversification program is how management planning is carried out. Generally speaking, a proposal for entry into a new business is presented to a management council or an executive committee for approval. And that is where the problem lies.

It seems to us that management plans are often built around profit and loss considerations. Such a strategy tends to focus on the projected outcome, with little thought given to choosing the methodology that would best see the venture through to success. In short, the plans and budgets for the investment of financial and human resources are not drawn up with meticulous care. Profit expectations are high, but the means of getting there warrant little discussion.

There is another important element here, and that is the question of who leads a project. In the past, people in the field would lead a new project. For example, at Canon, laser printers were, quite naturally, developed by engineers, and it doesn't seem that they were specifically directed to do so by their superiors. During the early stages of Sony's growth, Ibuka Hiroshi's hands-on leadership was the driving force behind the company's progress. At NEC, Kobayashi Koji and Sekimoto Tadahiro envisioned the corporate focus on computers and communications that has made that company what it is today.

Nowadays, however, the prosecution of new projects appears to be more and more in the hands of "planners." What is dubbed the formulation of management strategies or management plans by the planners and administrative people of corporate planning departments or project development departments involves the use of management consultants to draw up business plans and collect materials from outside the company. In the course of sorting out these issues, the planners and administrators contemplate the future direction of the company. When they decide on the new direction, they prepare business plans and send them down to the operating departments for execution. Of course, their grasp on future technological trends or future changes in market needs has not been achieved firsthand—with their own eyes and ears as it were. It is not the result of their own personal struggles with developmental work. Business plans are not sufficiently checked against operating-level expertise when projects are being developed and promoted. The resultant gap often means the projects don't work out as planned. This seems to be one of the fundamental causes of difficulties.

Future plans and business strategies drawn up by MBAs and other members of corporate planning staffs are like the papers handed in by honors students: they are all correct and meet the criteria established in advance. A business plan that scores 100 percent according to such criteria has no novelty or uniqueness about it. A favorable comment made about such a plan would be that it comes with a well-ordered set of numbers. But why would you entrust the future of your company to a business plan distinguished only by balanced controls and a set of numbers that jibe?

The essential cause of the failure to produce new business ventures of real substance lies in business planning by elite staffers and the absence of strong project leadership.

THE COLLAPSE OF THE COMPLEMENTARY SYSTEM OF PRODUCT ENGINEERING AND MANUFACTURING TECHNOLOGY

Different industries have taken different approaches to innovation. The question of technology management is something that an internationally competitive manufacturing industry cannot ignore with impunity. And lately, we have noted qualitative changes in the way technology is managed within the Japanese manufacturing industry.

One of the changes involves the relationship between manufacturing technology and product engineering. Japanese companies have traditionally been noted for the way that product engineering and manufacturing technology go hand in hand, each complementing the other. Designers go to the plant; plant operators feed back information to the designers; and together, they develop a product. When they conceive of a product, they are careful to take manufacturing methodology into account. When they manufacture, they do so with a view to producing a marketable product. This is the type of virtuous cycle that produces new products that are easy to manufacture.

Nowadays, elite engineers are not familiar with plant operations. They seem to lack an appreciation of key technologies. Although they can conduct planning using a computer, they do not possess sufficient hands-on manufacturing experience. To make matters worse, the progress of automation has so drastically reduced the number of technicians on the production floor who are knowledgeable in the area of manufacturing technology that the ability of plants to feed back required information has been severely curtailed. The interaction of engineers and technicians — or the relationship between product engineering and manufacturing technology, which has traditionally been characterized by good, complementary working relationships—no longer seems to be functioning efficiently.

For example, suppose a newly developed product is put on a commercial, mass-production line and the line cannot produce the planned yield. If the engineers are experienced in manufacturing they can go to the floor examine data from selected key control points, and adjust the process by making the changes that are needed to improve the yield. By contrast, in a company where the engineers are farther removed from the manufacturing floor they may have to undertake a whole new strategy of technical development or make a wholesale revision of the production design to meet the required specifications of the new product. As a result, such a company requires more time before it can launch a new product with a stable yield on a profitable basis.

The graduate school of Waseda University has an engine laboratory where the students assemble and disassemble engines. Few other universities give engineering students an opportunity to don greasy overalls and engage in this kind of hands-on work. This is a very important point. Not a few companies have lamented the fact that they have more and more office-bound white-collar engineers who are less and less inclined to work by the sweat of their brows and get personally involved in technology and production.

As mentioned earlier, engineers—particularly those in big companies—have eschewed efforts to develop elemental technology and have instead degenerated into arrangers who claim to be good at putting things together. They build systems and they integrate things, but they rarely go down to the plant floor. It is questionable whether this type of approach can really generate successful technological development.

The other problem relating to product engineering and manufacturing technology is the question of management. To be sure, Japan still retains a competitive edge in materials and components technology. But in terms of management capabilities questions are beginning to emerge.

A typical example is found with hard disk drives (HDDs) in computers. The combined market share in HDDs held by NEC and Fujitsu is no more than a dozen percent or so. Most of those companies having a greater share in this market are American firms that buy magnetic heads and motors from Japanese companies for assembly in Singapore or Thailand. Why is it then that American firms are successful in this business, while Japanese companies are not? The answer: new technology development. One of the causes of the failure of Japanese firms in this regard is they are now less capable of conceiving of and designing new products. It should be the business of the assemblers, if not of the suppliers of materials and components, to keep abreast of the market and take prompt action whenever required. Unfortunately, they seem not to be doing that.

In the past, personal computers and word processors were equipped with small hard disks with a capacity of some 50 MB. Nowadays, we require hard disks of greater capacity because the Windows software and its applications—not to mention graphics files—take up an enormous amount of storage space. This requires a new development effort to equip small personal computers with hard disks with a capacity of between 300 MB and 400 MB. Unfortunately, no Japanese firm has been able to come up with the new product specifications required. American companies—the leaders in the design of HDDs—study the market and develop new products, making use of next-generation technology. Japanese firms seem unable to anticipate the needs of the market; they lack the most important elements of design function because they lean on suppliers for components. As a result, Japanese companies, which are supposed to excel in mechatronics products, increasingly find they have become followers rather than leaders.

Undoubtedly, they are bumping up against the limits of their capabilities for product development and business diversification, thus bringing into sharp relief the basic problems facing Japanese corporations.

GLOBALIZATION THAT SPELLS PROFLIGATE INVESTMENT

One of the important items challenging Japanese corporations when it comes to structuring an effective agenda for the future is the question of globalization. The international environment surrounding Japan is increasingly severe, not only because of the strong yen but also because the nation is being buffeted by the surging waves of international politics. By dint of great efforts aimed at protecting the principle of free trade, the Uruguay Round of GATT negotiations produced agreements that resulted in the establishment of the World Trade Organization. That achievement notwithstanding, friction among nations over trade negotiations is still expected to intensify.

Japan is no longer able to simply manufacture products in Japan and export them. In addition, export-oriented firms, as well as many others, have found it is also no longer an easy task to carry on business strictly within the Japanese market. These days, even construction and retailing are on the agenda of trade negotiations. One cannot be assured of peace even when one is engaged in purely domestic operations.

Everything seems to have been put onto a global footing—the deployment of business operations, the pricing of stocks and bonds, the setting of interest rates on bank loans. So much so that very few business concerns can now afford to ignore the global perspective or the implications of international events when they conduct their business affairs. But taking on such a global outlook is much easier said than done. There are still many unresolved questions.

Fighting the Fire
One of the difficulties of globalization is the motivation behind it. Let us look at figure 3-1. This illustrates the relationship between antidumping litigation and transplants in Europe with respect to merchandise in which Japan has a strong competitive edge, such as videotape recorders, electronic typewriters, copying machines, microwave ovens, CD players, and printers. It is clear from this chart that as soon as the European Commission filed dumping charges, Japanese firms transplanted their operations to Europe to avoid litigation, regardless of whether they were actually found to be dumping and were charged dumping duties. In short, they chose to build plants abroad because they could no longer export products from Japan. We cannot help but suspect that they went forward without making a detailed study of what they were getting into.

When you open a plant abroad, you substitute local production for exported products. The size of the plant, therefore, is normally determined by the quantity of the exports to be displaced. But if you build a plant on the basis of the size of the local market, you cannot expect to have the economy of scale necessary to survive severe global competition. Your transplant is unlikely to be successful. Since these products are already considered to be "world merchandise," you should, once you decide to build a

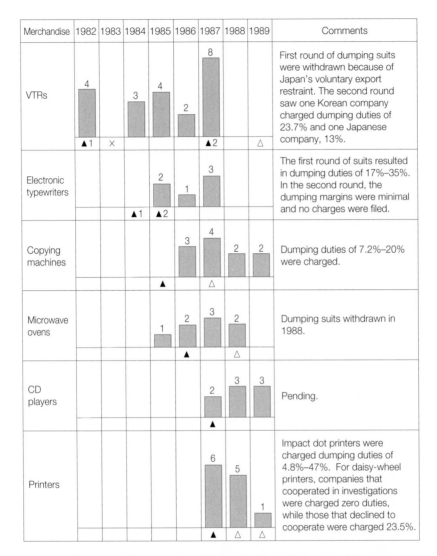

Merchandise	1982	1983	1984	1985	1986	1987	1988	1989	Comments
VTRs	4 ▲1	×	3	4	2	8 ▲2		△	First round of dumping suits were withdrawn because of Japan's voluntary export restraint. The second round saw one Korean company charged dumping duties of 23.7% and one Japanese company, 13%.
Electronic typewriters			▲1	2 ▲2	1	3			The first round of suits resulted in dumping duties of 17%–35%. In the second round, the dumping margins were minimal and no charges were filed.
Copying machines				▲	3	4 △	2	2	Dumping duties of 7.2%–20% were charged.
Microwave ovens				1	2 ▲	3	2 △		Dumping suits withdrawn in 1988.
CD players					2 ▲	3	3		Pending.
Printers					6 ▲	5 △	1 △		Impact dot printers were charged dumping duties of 4.8%–47%. For daisy-wheel printers, companies that cooperated in investigations were charged zero duties, while those that declined to cooperate were charged 23.5%.

Fig. 3-1. Dumping Filings by the EC and the Establishment of Overseas Factories by Japanese Corporations

Notes: 1. Prepared from *Conditions for Co-Existence of Japanese and European Machinery Industries*, an economic research report by the Japan Society for the Promotion of Machine Industry, dated May 1989.
2. The graphs show the number of factories that started production; dark triangles show dumping investigations started; white triangles show dumping duties assessed; and X shows dumping suits withdrawn.

plant in Britain, for example, discontinue your manufacture of such products in Japan and shift everything to the U.K. plant, turning it into your global manufacturing center for such products. In reality, however, these transplants only manufacture in the quantity equal to the number of units sold in Europe. With production capacities underutilized, they cannot hope to be profitable. We conjecture that almost all of these ventures are in the red. It begs the question: What is this globalization all about?

Only now have Asian transplants finally reached a stage where they are chalking up some profit. American plants are just breaking even, while European plants generally run in the red. What a sorry state of affairs is this globalization! In short, overseas ventures have been nothing more than a stopgap measure to avoid dumping suits.

In an exception to this trend, however, there is a European company that is turning a solid profit by producing dot-matrix printers that employ seemingly outmoded technology. A spin-off from Philips, this company has developed a product that meets current copying requirements (multiple printouts), and the firm has sold the makers of minicomputers and workstations on the product's ease of use and faster printing speed. It has now grown into a substantial business. As this shows, products based on old technology are nothing to sneeze at. Many Japanese companies are making similar products in Europe, but they are losing money. These companies import motors from Japan and elsewhere in Asia and procure other parts locally for assembly. They don't search out specific, segmented markets. In fact, they seem to be putting in no more effort than simply waiting for the end of the life cycles of their products. It is no wonder, then, that the performance of Japanese companies lags far behind the Europeans.

Deindustrialization and Technical Development

There is a widely held concern that the progress of globalization will hollow out the industrial base of Japan. Of late, this concern has become an important focus of macroeconomic study. It should be noted that in many cases when a plant is opened in Asia it induces the local market to expand so that the plant ends up producing more than it expected to when it went in. As a result, some argue, more components and capital goods will come to be exported by Japan for use in such plants, so there is little to be concerned about regarding the hollowing out of industry. Of course, it's hard to predict future developments, but the question of industrial hollowing out does not seem to us to be as simple as that.

Today, the majority view goes no further than expressing the hope that since the hollowing out of industry is inevitable in the long term, Japanese industry and Japanese firms have no alternative but to help build a nation of advanced technology in the short to medium term. This majority often cites the case of liquid crystal displays (LCDs), which became the target of dumping suits in the U.S. Many discussions on the hollowing out of industry seem to focus on the view that Japan should be developing strategic, technologically advanced products like the LCD in order to curtail industrial hollowing out.

The LCD is a product unique to Japan, and, like the VTR, it can be produced only in Japan. It is being acclaimed as a product that can beat the next rise of the yen, as well as an excellent vehicle for avoiding deindustrialization. However, on closer examination we see that LCDs do not consist entirely of Japanese components. The flat glass for the display is made by Corning; the liquid crystal, a hi-tech chemical, is a product of Merck. Both of these are manufactured at plants these companies have set up in Japan. In short, Western firms supply parts and technology in Japan, and the Japanese firms make the LCDs using assembly technology that is an application of semiconductor technology. The Japanese firms then market the product around the world. We dare say that the LCD is international merchandise, not a unique Japanese product, since it is manufactured with the cooperation of Corning and Merck. That is the unavoidable reality of LCDs.

These facts make us wonder about the competitiveness of Japanese firms. Of course, it is not only Japanese companies that possess the technical capabilities to make hi-tech products or that excel in competitive power. We might say that Japan has become a nation of advanced technology because of the concentration of the world's technology and competitive strength in Japan. Hence, a materials supplier finds that the effect of a technological development is greater if it is done in Japan because of the synergistic effect it engenders. As a result, a new development is commercialized in Japan and marketed from there as a new product to the world. Theory holds that technology belongs not to a nation but to individual corporations. Technological development that anticipates commercialization does not come only from the work of inventors or developers. The quality of the surrounding technical environment, as in the case of LCDs, forms an important social foundation, one that supports product development.

The behavior of Moog, an American manufacturer of hydraulic servo-mechanisms, is particularly interesting to us. It has a Japanese subsidiary, Japan Moog, which is working on the development of nonmilitary market applications for its products, such as hydraulic servo-valves for injection molding machines and items for the construction machinery. Essentially, Moog is a U.S. defense contractor, as it has manufactured servo-valves for rockets and aircraft. As military budgets have been slashed, the company, in order to survive, has had to turn to the civilian market as never before. The fact that the company has chosen to undertake product development in Japan may be an indication that Japan's competitive position engenders the desired synergistic effect, perhaps similar to the example of the LCD described above, but with slightly different dimensions.

Aside from the question of whether Japanese corporations are capable of technological development, for the time being it is highly unlikely that Japan's capacity to foster technological development will be drastically diminished. At the same time, we must ponder what really are the strengths of Japanese management and what this thing called competitiveness really is.

You will note that the globalization of Japan's automobile industry is similar, in some respects, to the entry into the EC of appliance makers and information terminals makers. Initially, automakers controlled the quantity of exports under voluntary restraint arrangements. Given these quantitative restraints, Japanese auto companies shifted their exports to higher-value automobiles to generate larger profits with a smaller number of units. Consequently, Japan's trade balance surplus refused to shrink. Then, acceding to the demand that exports must decrease in monetary terms as well, they had no alternative but to initiate the local production of automobiles and proceeded to open plants in the U.S. and Europe.

Initially, the transplants depended on imports from Japan for low-cost, high-quality components. As a result, while imports of cars from Japan declined, imports of auto parts did not. This gave rise to further criticism, which held that the new arrangement did not improve the fundamental employment situation in host communities. The next hurdle raised was local content requirements, and auto transplants were forced to use locally manufactured components. But when plants attempted to buy locally, they found the available components were built to different specifications and had a different standard of quality. Firms had to send in their designers to work with the local suppliers. In this way, Japanese auto manufacturers have not only localized the sale and assembly of finished vehicles and the procurement of components, they have also injected their developmental know-how. They can now rightly claim that their cars are of purely local origin.

In reality, localized development involves the redesign of the finished product based on the use of available local components. Macroeconomic analysts refer to this process as "the progress of techno-globalization." From management's point of view, the local auto manufacturer is saddled with higher-than-expected overhead costs and cannot turn a profit. The quantity of parts they buy from local suppliers is less than the quantity GM or Ford or Volkswagen buys from their suppliers. Consequently, the prices they pay for locally procured parts are higher, and the designers they must retain despite the small quantity of production also add to their overhead costs. Local production may have eased some political friction, but it has also rendered a bottom line that is less than satisfactory.

As can be seen, action taken to resolve international trade friction has turned out to be a drag on the bottom line. Companies expanded overseas, but they did so without having considered their long-term business structure, and they now find their performance gradually deteriorating. Very recently, however, the transplants seem to be improving their profitability thanks to the excessively strong yen and revitalized overseas markets, especially the U.S. market. It would be correct to say, however, that there is no guarantee that this good performance will continue through the long term.

We posit that the globalization strategy, much like the diversification strategy, has run up against a wall.

PART II

What Is Happening inside Japanese Corporations Today?

Chapter 4

The Fall of Managers
and Their Decision-
Making Function

Diversification and globalization have been the centerpieces of the
management innovation undertaken by many Japanese corporations. As described in the previous chapter, both have functional
problems and both have experienced a series of failures. We want
to look now at whether the cause or causes of these failures can
be traced to certain problems in the management system of
Japanese corporations. It may be possible to ascribe the failures to
changes in the business environment or to the weak-kneed government stance in trade negotiations. But are these the only
causes? What of the judgment of managers or changes in the management function itself?

THE ORGANIZATIONAL DETERIORATION OF JAPANESE MANAGEMENT

Every year—beginning in spring and running through the summer—companies listed on the stock exchanges go through their
traditional ritual of electing new directors. Many people no doubt
follow the events closely through reports in newspapers and other
mass media. From the disinterested observer's standpoint, the
change of directors these days is quite an intriguing phenomenon.
As we watch the resignation of directors who made mistakes by
investing excessively in financial assets during the bubble, and as
we witness the election of young, new directors, we know that
things are indeed changing in many fundamental ways.

At the same time, those executives who can make skilled decisions—those who could, if given the opportunity, be the driving force behind a company—do not generally get to be directors. Many companies appear to choose as directors individuals who are distinguished neither by superior ability nor an enterprising spirit, but rather persons who do their jobs reasonably well, but not spectacularly so. Those chosen for directorship are seen as well-balanced by their associates within the organization. Our sense of the situation is that more and more people of this type are being promoted to directorships today. Like the proverbial nail that sticks up and gets hammered down, a superior may consider an able subordinate somewhat uncomfortable to work with and may even suspect that he might one day jeopardize his own position unless he cuts him down to size. These are the misgivings we entertain as we review this annual reshuffle of board members.

Forgotten Field Operations—The Vitality Gap Between Head Office and Field Operations

The functioning of the head office is an issue that requires careful scrutiny. Generally speaking, the head office is considered to be the highest decision-making organ, a place where the elite management assumes the stewardship of the company, its operating divisions, and its functional strategies. In many cases, the staff that supervises an organization's finances, legal affairs, and personnel also work at the head office.

In reality, not many companies have their head office staff as the only occupants of the head office building. Not a few manufacturers locate their head office alongside their plants; more often, sales organizations are located at the same site as the head office. The head office of a big firm often includes operating divisions within it so that top management can be available for consultation.

Nowadays, more and more Japanese companies are pursuing management specialization. In such companies, the head office is supposed to function as the strategic focal point—where the elite staffers fully coordinate their incisive analysis and polished expertise. In many cases, however, reality doesn't quite measure up to this vision. In fact, as an organization grows in size, team systems are adopted to effect coordination among various organizational segments at the head office and decision making is done in conferences. These practices are becoming permanent fixtures. As a result, it is increasingly difficult to effect coordination among staffers who hold different views and have them arrive at decisions. It seems to us that—at the committee and conference level—too much importance is being attached to formalized procedures that have no substance and that this is spawning a bureaucratic climate.

More than ever before, the head office staff exhorts the operating divisions to, for example, prepare project plans, adjust their course in such and such direction, or set a target of x amount of yen for the diversification plan. Unfortunately, while the head office staff may be adept at thinking in abstract terms, it generally lacks information about what is going on in the field. As a result, when business plans go awry it tends to assume the role of critical appraiser vis-à-vis the people operating in the field, demanding to know "why the plan is not working and what you are doing about it." Since—from the perspective of the head office—each operating division is but one of many elements, the head office's admonition often takes on the tone of a disinterested third party. We see more and more management staff and management practices that resemble this.

In rare cases, companies do carry out only headquarters-type functions at the head office and do not engage in project operating functions. In many such companies, the head office has become a bureaucratic organization. Its members are so busy fighting turf wars, getting in each other's way, circulating proposals, and touching base that it is doubtful if such a head office contributes in any meaningful way to business operations. And the operating personnel are often left asking a lot of questions— "What is the head office doing?" "What should management staff be undertaking?" "What should be the relationship between management decisions and business activities?"—to which managers have yet to respond with clarity.

As strange as it sounds, the head office staff often see themselves as the company and look upon the field or operating division as nothing more than the means to the company's ends. For this reason, the relationship between the head office and the field or operating division tends to be at cross-purposes. It is no easy task to bring about a synergistic effect and get the company to function as an organic whole while they are getting in each other's way.

Meanwhile, many companies in the West are working hard to downsize their headquarters into a small head office. At the famous General Electric, Chairman Welch laid off many members of the business strategy staff of the head office. It is truly amazing that Asea Brown Bovery, a major heavy industry concern in Europe, should have only a few hundred people at its head office. When these companies are acclaimed for their innovation, it is no wonder that more and more Japanese begin to ask, "What are they doing at our head office?"

Loss of Management Function—Have We Lost Sight of Market Logic?
As illustrated in the case of hard disk drives (HDDs), Japanese companies seem to have lost the ability to understand the needs of the market, which is the most important factor in the design of a successful product. They no longer seem to know why a certain product sells. Generally speaking, it is not easy for a supplier to discern the needs of the market. But, for the manufacturers of machinery and equipment one of the first criteria by which to judge success or failure is how well they have been able to grasp the needs of the market. Measured against this, we must say that Japanese companies are in a very precarious predicament indeed.

Automobile companies believed that full-size cars would sell because of the so-called Thema phenomenon, the explosive popularity of the Nissan model. And they developed many large cars and produced them in large quantities. As now seems clear—in the cold morning light of the post-bubble period—these cars sold because there were a slew of people who had made extra money on stocks and real estate and were willing to spend it on automobiles. Those cars were certainly not priced within reach of ordinary people on a salary. One may be able to dismiss this particular case by saying that the car companies were simply taking immediate advantage of a short-term boon. But the case of HDDs seems to have a slightly different background.

There is a significant difference between Japanese firms' awareness of, and sensitivity to, new products, in the Japanese market—which allows only indirect access to information concerning changing market needs and new products, such as the Windows software—and American firms' awareness of what is going on in the American market, where players are on the cutting edge of new products and trends. And therein lies the cause of the declining vitality of the Japanese market.

In the Japanese market for telecommunications equipment, where the transmission of data and images is controlled by restrictive regulations, it is not surprising that the creative development of new products is thwarted. But we cannot accept the excuse that we lost our fight with the Americans in product development because we had to live under ignominious government regulations. When business is engaged in on the world market, it behooves companies to pay more attention to what each segment of the U.S. and European markets wants.

It goes without saying that you can no longer run a company by simply looking at the market, the products, and other factors from the perspective of the manufacturer alone. You would do well to develop the ability to evaluate a product from the standpoint of the customer. Companies must be able to evaluate new products from multiple viewpoints. But of course that is much easier said than done.

The fact that such a fundamental ability has been lacking at Japanese firms is evidence that corporations have become bureaucratic and inward looking. If this is indeed true, the dimensions of the problem go way beyond an inability to grasp the needs of the marketplace; we must presume that a more primal malaise is afflicting organizations.

Given the current situation of excessive decentralization of corporate functions, it is necessary to begin a reexamination of each function, trying to ascertain which elements are performing which tasks. Because of the extent of decentralization—whereby, for example, sales does nothing but sell and marketing does nothing but merchandise planning—there is no organized system of coordination. There is no system under which comprehensive study and planning are organized to find out what products customers want, how best to sell them, what merchandising is effective, and how to go about developing the products. Each function is so specialized and so segmented that it concentrates only on selling, planning, developing, or whatever tasks are assigned to it; management that should cut across the organizational structure to provide coordination and synchronization is not working properly.

Some observers have commented that the enlarged organization alone cannot account for the difficulties and that weakened leadership on the part of management is ultimately responsible. Of course, such an observation does not help resolve the problem.

It is often said that what is needed is customer-oriented management. The proposition usually posited as a way to achieve this is a system of producing varied types of products in small quantities, with many seeing this as indispensable to increasing customer satisfaction. It is somewhat questionable whether the production of many products would really meet the needs of customers. Auto companies, for example, may install CD players or stereo equipment in cars and call it their way of offering multifarious choices. We doubt that auto companies themselves really understand what is meant by segmentation of customers and what their needs are. Everything is made automatic in a car so that when it stalls due to engine trouble you cannot even open a window. The window panes in the rear only go halfway down. We often wonder if they really develop these cars with functional requirements in mind. These complaints are not limited to automobiles; we have similar complaints about personal computers as well.

Thus, the big question is: Do they truly know what the market needs? Sometimes their efforts fail miserably because they do not see the market. It is high time that firms reflected on the damage caused by their failure to keep an eye on the products and the market in a comprehensive way.

The Enlarged Organization—Does It Encourage Irresponsible Management?

A big challenge for management is recognizing a turning point for the business when one occurs. If management does recognize it, then the next question is whether management is designed to act properly in accordance with such recognition.

Of late, the market has stagnated and the strengthened yen has caused the shifting of production bases overseas. Faced with the resulting need to reduce personnel, companies decry the fact that there are too many managers and suggest that they be transferred to affiliates. When business expenses are run up excessively, firms go to the extreme of cutting back the budget for overseas business trips to zero, while leaving intact truly wasteful outlays. Do they think the divine wind will blow away their problems if they just wait long enough? We still see many instances of such a Japanese-style response to changing circumstances. Have we still not reached the point where such responses are no longer tolerated?

We feel that the decision-making function of management has become outmoded. The traditional method of decision-making involving *ringi* (circulating a proposal for approval) and *nemawashi* (touching base to lay the groundwork for approval of a proposal) has been viewed as the characteristic feature of Japanese organizational management. Although it used to function as a mechanism to ensure common ownership of information, it has lately degenerated into mere formality. As the organization becomes larger and more specialized, each segment expresses its approval or disapproval of a proposition from its own perspective alone, and in the meantime the organization as a whole is slowly losing its integrating function. When a proposal turns out to be a success, managers assert that they were among those who approved it because their signatures are on the proposal; when it fails, they disavow responsibility by claiming that they did nothing more than sign it.

With a view to restructuring the decision-making process, some companies have reorganized their business units into SBUs (strategic business units). But in reality they do not function as strategic organizations. When the reorganization was decided on, firms already had fixed notions of strategies about the market and products. Subsequently, the organization lacked flexibility and frequently failed to work properly.

Organizations may have, for example, a refrigerator SBU, a microwave oven SBU, etc. These designations are not necessary, but understandable. When the organizational demarcation sets apart the TV SBU from the audio SBU, it is not certain which SBU should commercialize, say, a karaoke system that utilizes multimedia technology. Both SBUs may go ahead with the developmental efforts in obvious duplication; or neither may undertake it, on the false assumption that the other unit is doing it. Laser printers and copying machines offer another example. Computers and office equipment target different market segments. But, given the similarity of the technological base, they might both work on the next-generation digital photo development technology, thereby increasing the risk of the dispersion of precious resources or mistimed market entry, both of which could have critical consequences competitiveness.

No matter how you structure your organization, you are bound to have strengths and weaknesses. Unless flexible thinking is exercised when dealing with business situations, the strategy— the S of SBUs—may become deadwood, and you can become entrapped in a web you have spun yourself. This is the sense we get when we look at organizations.

Another issue involved here is the inclination toward organizational redesign. American companies make no bones about changing their organization, redesigning them into efficient units, taking in the latest information technology, and downsizing into leaner, nimbler outfits. There are extraordinary people in America who are adept at designing and operating a whole organizational structure with a few talented individuals. Perhaps America needs such a superman, given the ethnic complexity of its people. In contrast, when we work on a similar organizational project in Japan, everybody gets involved as if it were just another administrative task. Some of the participants may think that they should let well enough alone. So, a Japanese company doesn't need anyone to design a whole organization. If someone dares to design a new organization from his personal viewpoint, he will certainly be rebuked for his ill-advised attempt. We see a vast difference in these two approaches. The inability of Japanese companies to design and execute comprehensive organizational reform has itself become an issue. When an organization has grown to a certain size, it should be subjected to review to see if it still serves its intended purpose. But Japanese companies have neglected to do so.

At least with major Japanese corporations, business diversification has resulted in the horizontal expansion of the organizational structure. The scope of business has expanded, horizontally, into different geographic regions, different products, and different functional areas, such as sales, planning, and marketing. At the same time, it should be noted that the organization has also expanded vertically.

The managerial staff who reside in the middle of this organization become multilayered as a result of the vertical and horizontal expansion of the organization. As they move up the hierarchy—from sales department planning to operating department planning to business division planning and finally to corporate planning—personnel are further and further removed from the field. Their tasks become those of control, detached from real business operations; the leadership necessarily changes in nature to the command-and-control type. The result is a system of lessening responsibility.

Additionally, we cannot lose sight of the fact that the emphasis on an advanced educational background is causing repercussions. Leaning on his illustrious educational background, every member of the staff has his own views, and decisions are hard to come by. In the course of decision making, friction occurs and conflicts abound. Staff members spend a lot of time arguing, and they are late in coming to decisions. Their decisions are, in fact, not much different from the decisions that a few participants could easily have arrived at. Going through the head office or its control department has become an inefficient, tortuous path of decision making. That is the problem.

We understand that for years some companies have had to deal with special interest groups, which exercise influence over the selection of their directors. Thus, it seems reasonable to assume that, in many respects, Japanese corporate organizations are coming to the end of their rope.

The Sinking Morale of Workers—Are They Being Properly Compensated?

In addition to the problems of directors and managers, the morale of the workers cries out for attention. In particular, varied forms of pressure are being brought to bear on people in the field, such as the institution of a fixed annual salary system or a compulsory retirement age for managerial personnel, if not outright layoffs. These days, the core employees of major corporations complain that the company has lost sympathy or that this is not what we expected of the company. Younger employees who know the feelings of their seniors are disillusioned with the company for the inadequate treatment of seniors despite their worthy contributions in the past. Those in higher positions within the hierarchy might grumble to those under them about their inadequate performance. But they did not all rise to the position of director or manager as a result of their accurate evaluation of skills or competence; some of them, in fact, climbed to their positions because they were judged to possess a sense of balance or simply because they were lucky. Because of this, you cannot expect all of them to be equally capable of making substantive decisions or taking functional command of operations. When their instructions to subordinates are excessively conceptual or abstract, effective communication breaks down. Friction heightens between the upper and lower echelons of the organization, and hierarchical relations suffer as a result.

And it is not just the older workers whose employment is at risk. As a reaction to the excessive hiring done during the bubble, companies have restricted the number of new graduates hired during the last few years, aggravating the job search for young people.

For a company, this is merely a matter of correcting excesses in its personnel policy; for young people, it is a very serious matter indeed.

One cannot ignore the effects of a personnel policy that sacrifices the weak, and it should be noted that the morale of many workers is now very shaky. In addition, there is an unacceptably wide gap between the actual lifestyle that Japanese workers enjoy and the lifestyle imputed to them by foreigners on account of the "high wages" of the Japanese. Appliances and automobiles with strong export competitiveness command a purchasing power parity of about ¥120 to the dollar, while that for food, housing, construction, and electric utility rises well above ¥200 to the dollar. Internationally competitive products sell cheaply, but those available only in Japan are very expensive. Wages may be high, but their value may be halved when you spend them. Regrettably, you feel that you can never improve your standard of living no matter how hard you work.

As a matter of fact, the Japanese have worked diligently and their wages have risen to the highest in the world, but the highest standard of living has eluded them because of the high cost of living in Japan. That very fact is evidence that our domestic structures are contorted. People on the production floor feel they cannot attain self-fulfillment through their jobs, and such a situation could in future lead to a vital loss of power on the part of Japanese industry.

SHAREHOLDERS AND CORPORATE DECISION MAKING

There are many problems to be resolved concerning the relationship between shareholders and corporate managers. The agenda includes a broad range of fundamental questions related to the cross-ownership of shares by Japanese corporations and the power of managers. We shall here discuss some of the more important problems in this area.

Soaring Agency Costs

Many studies have been made comparing the management of Japanese corporations with that of American corporations. One of the major arguments taken up in such studies is that Japan's business environment permits long-term investments, while American companies are in a financial environment that compels them to hold more short-term views. Perhaps it is time we put an end to such discourse.

Until only a few years ago, the trend in Japan was one of continually rising prices, be they of stocks or land. The principal factor behind that trend was the expectation of continual economic growth. It would not be wrong to say that the structure of today's Japanese corporations was built on expectations of long-term growth, as reflected in the relationships among shareholders, managers, and workers. Is it possible to assume that the same kind of continual growth can be sustained in our economy in the future? In America, they faced these problems some 20 years ago and worked to resolve them during the 1980s. Is it not correct to say that Japanese corporations are only now beginning to face these problems?

Let us for the moment put aside the issue of a business environment with continually rising indices and take a look at specific problems that have arisen because we have based everything on expectations of limitless growth.

Frankly, Japanese managers have been placed in, and influenced by, an environment without checks and balances for so long that the power of corporations tends to be concentrated more and more in management's hands alone. Corporate structures and decision-making processes that conform to the interests of management and not to the interests of shareholders are common in Japanese corporations today.

The result is a very high agency cost, according to the theory of agency in American economics. American managers see themselves as agents of the shareholders. When the agents act against the interests of the principals (shareholders), the principals incur damage, which is called the agency cost. On the basis of this theory, measures have been proposed in America to ensure that the interests of managers and shareholders are in agreement. These include giving managers stock options and determining their compensation on the basis of share prices. The effort to lower the agency cost by ensuring that managers share the interests of the shareholders has been made a top priority in many American firms, even though these arrangements do not always benefit the company.

What happened to American corporations as a result? Between one-half and three-quarters of American shareholders are institutional investors, such as pension funds and mutual funds. Institutional investors set the greatest store by income and capital gains from investments during each quarter, and they commonly demand increased dividends and higher share prices. Institutional investors welcome mergers and acquisitions and leveraged buyouts (in which a company is bought with money borrowed by mortgaging the assets of the company being bought), whereby the shareholders receive payments from the proceeds of stocks disposed of. They also welcome a company repurchasing surplus shares of its own stock in the open market. These actions are welcomed because they result in real cash being distributed to the shareholders. Since the interests of the managers of a company and the interests of its shareholders coincide—if not that of the company itself or its employees—managers' compensation goes up and dividends and other benefits to shareholders receive priority consideration. In a nutshell, the shareholders and the managers divide among them the take of the company with little consideration given to the future of the firm itself or the fate of the people who work there.

What about Japan? If we apply the same yardstick, we must conclude that the agency cost is indeed high. In short, the managers run the company as they please. The amount of compensation received by individual managers is not very high, in line with long-established standards. In fact, a comparison of remuneration for top executives in the U.S. and Japan reveals that Japanese managers receive far less than their American counterparts. But the real question is what these managers actually do.

We are not sure if it is truly in the interests of the company to simply grow quantitatively or to undertake diversification of questionable profitability. At least for the shareholders, these activities are not beneficial in many cases. In fact, some companies have suffered a decline in profits because of unnecessary diversification, while others have departed from the level of optimum profit when unnecessary expansion has resulted in overproduction.

Why Is the Diversification Strategy Being Corrected in the U.S.?
In Japan, the overall economy has grown at the same time as the agency cost has been kept high. Suppose managers keep expanding the scope of business in opposition to the interests of the shareholders. Under such circumstances, adequate dividends may not be paid. But, given a steadily growing market, a situation of overproduction can be corrected as demand catches up. This is the kind of life Japanese corporations have lived for a long time. Shareholders have not really had much to complain about. From here on, however, we cannot expect much in the way of growth. In the short term, in the next five years or so, for example, we might see a resurgence of growth; over the next 10 to 20 years, however, we are not likely to witness steady, continual growth. On the contrary, we should plan for declining growth rates. Despite this, corporations still have the same outlook they had during the high-growth period.

Right now, in America, business diversification is being re-examined. This matter is also touched upon in the American theory of agency. During the 1960s, American business tried all sorts of diversification strategies, including the formation of conglomerates. Those efforts broke down in the 1970s, and in the 1980s firms divested themselves of diversified businesses and slowed their pace of expansion. Whatever diversification they attempted was limited to affiliated businesses, and that became the way of American business in the 1980s. American companies that actively pursued financial restructuring in the 1980s moved on to portfolio restructuring, realigning their multiple businesses. They reined in the far-flung businesses into which they had diversified and refocused a limited number of them into areas of strategic importance.

In Japan, on the contrary, companies contend that the increased number of businesses that result from diversification helps spread the risk, which is necessary for the growth and viability of firms. But while expanding a company quantitatively, even at the expense of lower profits, may enhance the prestige of the managers or even create new positions for employees, it is not in the best interests of the shareholders. Such is now the common sense approach of American economics and business administration.

Against this American common sense, Japanese managers strive to maintain and grow their companies at the expense of shareholders.

The Compression of Free Cash Flow

We turn now to the capital market. Throughout the high-growth period, the principal source of funds for Japanese corporations was so-called indirect financing—namely, obtaining funds through banks. Many found fault with this practice, saying Japan was letting the banks dominate firms through their loans. Some commentators described the practice of indirect financing as the central feature of Japanese management.

As we entered the 1980s, there were signs here and there that this situation was on the verge of reversing itself, although this was certainly not the case with all companies. During the bubble, Japanese corporations took advantage of elevated stock prices and enthusiastically sold additional shares or issued convertible bonds or bonds with stock purchase warrants—so-called equity financing. (See figure 4-1.) They obtained low-cost funds with the expectation that the stock market would continue its upward trend. Securities firms encouraged businesses to resort to equity financing, at costs much lower than the interest rates being charged by the banks. For a time, there were many who predicted that Japan would eventually grow out of its proclivity for indirect financing and move on to direct financing. *A Scenario of the Year 2000*, put out by the Japan Management Association in 1990,

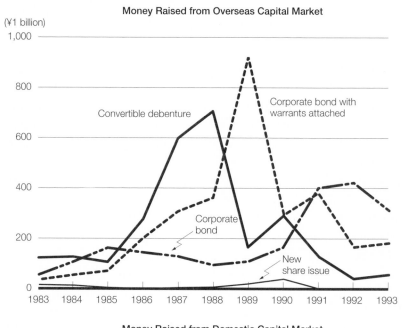

Money Raised from Overseas Capital Market

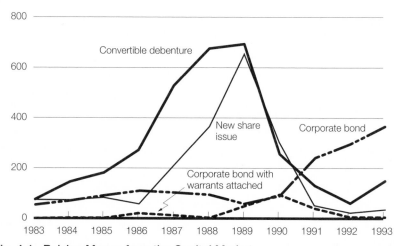

Money Raised from Domestic Capital Market

Fig. 4-1. Raising Money from the Capital Market

Note: Prepared from *the Economic Planning Agency's Economic White Paper for 1994*, dated August 1994.

2000, put out by the Japan Management Association in 1990, included such a forecast.

To be sure, the bubble made this equity financing possible. The important question is how the funds came to be used. Companies whose shares went up nonetheless decided to tap into equity financing anyway, to collect funds they did not need and had no plans to invest. There can be no denying this. In effect, they raised money without any idea where it might be invested. Equity financing may have made sense if, after reasoned judgment, the money was invested in a high-return venture. Instead, these firms simply issued convertible bonds and warrant-attached bonds on the recommendation of securities firms who assured them that "if your stock price is high, you can go to equity financing." There wouldn't have been a problem if they had used the money for necessary investments or to repay bank loans. But what they actually did was raise more money than they needed. And what happened? What happened is now the problem.

We don't know if companies repaid bank loans with the funds they borrowed. What is known is that a vast number of firms ended up with extra money—something business administration theory refers to as free cash flow.

When an American company has free cash flow it can quickly become the subject of a merger or acquisition. Suppose a company has $10 billion in free cash flow and its stock price is not very high. There is a good chance that somebody will be interested in acquiring it. There is, therefore, a sense among American businessmen that free cash flow is hazardous. The normal practice is to use such funds to buy back the company's own shares or to pay dividends. If managers choose to do nothing with it, institutional investors are likely to demand that dividends be paid. In short, there is no hoarding of funds as there is in Japan.

American steelmakers, for example, haven't done much in terms of putting money back into their business. Looking upon steel as a declining industry, they have invested little in equipment renewal. As a result, they end up with cash equal to the value of the depreciation taken on their facilities. That is often how American firms obtain free cash flow. Even US Steel became a target of Mr. Icahn's takeover bid. Not wanting to be bought out, US Steel acquired Marathon Oil at a price somewhat beyond its means. The message is clear: Unless you invest in something, somebody will buy you out. If you don't want to do that, you should pay dividends to your shareholders.

What did Japanese companies do with the free cash flow they reaped through equity financing? Not surprisingly, they used it to invest in financial assets. But these firms had no business dabbling in the manipulation of financial assets. If they had funds left over for such an exercise, they should have paid dividends and allowed shareholders the freedom to invest the money as they saw fit. Looking back now, we can see that strange things indeed were taking place.

We cannot help feeling that these firms deviated from the rules of capitalism—broke the strictures of a free economy. It was not, in the end, a question of American-style capitalism versus Japanese-style capitalism. In fact, many Japanese managers believed the extra funds raised through equity financing belonged to the company itself, and that they, the managers, were free to use them as they saw fit.

We were once given a tour of the headquarters of a brewery. On the walls we saw many paintings. The president—who claimed to be a connoisseur—was boasting to his dealers: "I didn't buy these paintings with proceeds from the sale of our company's products. I acquired them through my own resourcefulness." It seems most of the money raised by equity finance was in fact spent on expansion and renovation of the company's facilities, but there was still some left over. We believe that was invested in financial assets and used to buy famous works of art.

And that is wrong. We don't know how resourceful the president may have been, but the money he spent belonged to the shareholders. Japanese managers are not sufficiently concerned with the shareholders. During the long stretch of rising stock prices, advancing shares kept shareholders happy, even though managers made decisions with no regard for them at all. It is perhaps because that environment of rising prices persisted for so long that managers became oblivious to the shareholders.

When corporate social responsibility became an issue after the oil crises, many companies prepared statements outlining their social mission. In the course of preparing such mission statements, questions arose as to who the real stakeholders of a company are. Various groups were listed, such as consumers, employees, and others, but many firms failed to include shareholders. And the shareholders seemed little bothered by this—they simply followed along. The Japanese practice of cross-ownership of shares among companies was certainly a factor in this, as this strategy works to offset the power of individual shareholders.

Because we cannot look forward to significant growth in our economy in the future, the structure that served us in the past will no longer do. We must find more effective ways for shareholders to interact with firms, as well as decide which changes should be made in the structure of ownership.

There are now signs that foreign institutional investors are buying up Japanese stocks. They will have a lot to complain about in the ways of Japanese management. And it appears that some companies are beginning to agree with certain of the comments being made by foreign investors. As one manager said, "Our perception is changing little by little. After all, they are right."

Aside from the problems associated with business administration, we must also look at macroeconomic issues. The availability of surplus money in the economy as a whole without the possibility of reinvestment or the high liquidity of surplus funds coupled with an absence of discipline are both macroeconomic matters and require study.

In any case, whether guided by economic theory or the tenets of corporation law, when a company comes into such spare funds, these should be paid to shareholders as dividends.

DECISION MAKING IN THE LOW-GROWTH ENVIRONMENT

Revision of Spending Policy

As a premise for our discussion, we affirm that the Japanese business environment has changed enormously over the years. During a 10-year period beginning around 1960, Japan raced along with double-digit growth, much like South Korea did a few years ago and China is doing today. The oil crises dropped growth to about 5 percent. The economy is still growing today, at between 2 and 3 percent. We may plod through the 1990s with respectable growth such as this, but we can hardly expect to maintain that level of expansion into the twenty-first century.

The things in Japan that require attention are legion, including the creation of social capital and provisions for social welfare. However, undertakings of this nature are no longer large enough to have the dramatic impact on the economy they had during the high-growth period.

What Japanese corporations did in effect during the 1980s was develop export markets, and export drove our growth. Today, that driving force has been sapped of much of its strength. Japan's trade surplus of some $100 billion is extraordinary from the standpoint of what world trade should be. You cannot pretend there is nothing wrong in our continuing to sell products simply because we can. It is just not tenable that Japan alone should have chalked up such a huge surplus while almost all other advanced countries have run up deficits. Japan may be forced to adopt spending policies that will far exceed the cost of its overseas development aid. During its heyday, the U.S. had a number of spending policies, including the Marshal Plan and expenditures related to the Cold War. We do not want to see another huge rebuilding program on the part of Japan, which could well trigger another bubble. So we end up with the appreciation of the yen instead, which, unfortunately, we cannot avoid.

Unavoidable Deindustrialization and Fewer Young Workers
Until now, Japanese managers have worked diligently to build a corporate structure that can withstand the pressure of the stronger yen, and they have continued to steer firms in the direction of increasing exports. But as managers struggle to offset the effects of the surging yen they are left will little time to resolve other fundamental issues, and the expectation that the yen will just continue to appreciate has become widespread. A strong corporate struc-

ture is surely a welcome thing, but the enormous effort necessary to build it has resulted in things like longer working hours and the tragedy of *karoshi* (death from overwork), and in the end the real standard of living of the Japanese has scarcely improved. In the eyes of the public, such developments point to a problem.

The strong yen has caused wages to increase sharply in comparison with those of other nations. It should be said, however, that the Japanese standard of living and purchasing power parity tell us the yen is overvalued to about double its real worth. It must be acknowledged that we can neither avoid a certain degree of appreciation on the yen nor forestall the transfer of production bases overseas and a corresponding increase in imports. Deindustrialization is already under way in some sectors, and we should expect that well-managed deindustrialization will be further facilitated in the future. Through efforts such as these, we must strive to attain our essential goal—reducing the trade surplus.

Fast on the heels of the hollowing out of industry is the problem of the aging society, which naturally leads to questions about how we ought to be managing Japan's high-cost economy. At the same time as the populace ages, the number of young people in the labor force will drop, which means that the "productive" population will decline. The present number of infants in Japan is astonishingly small. Some people still cling to the hope that our population will continue to increase, albeit at a small rate, as in France. Don't bet on it. There may be waves of population increase every 25 years or so, but the size of these surges will steadily dwindle. By 2010, the population could be declining at a precipitous pace. It seems logical to assume, therefore, that as time passes the vitality of the Japanese economy will lessen.

Growth Strategy in a Low-Growth Economy

In American corporations, managers are given stock options and paid bonuses in accordance with stock prices to ensure that their interests coincide with those of the shareholders. This practice has a number of inherent problems. The shareholders and managers divide the profits of the company between them and think little of the viability of the firm itself or its employees. America in the 1980s was so enthused about restructuring that many firms pursued buyouts aggressively as a means of restructuring. They used leveraged buyouts and developed the technique of issuing junk bonds. As a result, many American companies found themselves up to their ears in debt. This is indeed a curious phenomenon. When a company wants to make new investments in order to grow, it goes public, that is, it gets itself listed on stock exchanges. The company raises money from the capital market, and growth is achieved by investing that money. During the 1980s, many companies that had grown in this manner—including some very large firms—disappeared from the securities markets. Included in that group were some 30 percent of the top 500 companies listed in 1990 in *Fortune* magazine. NCR and Nabisco retained their corporate names after being bought out, but they are no longer listed companies. Some erstwhile leading companies, like International Harvester and RCA, don't even have their names anymore.

Some of these acquisitions were paid for with the stock of the company doing the acquiring, but the most prevalent method during the 1980s was to use cash or bonds. Companies that had gone public, raised money, and had many shareholders, now borrowed money from the bank and paid off those same shareholders to turn themselves into private corporations—a strange transformation indeed. Instead of private companies selling shares to the public and raising money, which is the normal pattern of growth, we now had public companies going private and ending up debt ridden. Some later got on a roll again and went public, but they were rare. In this way, American companies moved from a system of direct finance to one of indirect finance during the 1980s. And that is a very serious problem.

When we look at that trend, what strikes us as disturbing is the fact that the companies themselves and their employees have been largely forgotten. At RCA, for example, there were obviously some lifetime employees who had taken part in important research and who had helped make the firm a commercial success. Even in America you find people who work at the same company their parents and their grandparents worked at—people who stay with the same company until they retire. They are perhaps fewer in number than in Japan, but they still constitute the majority of American workers. The problem with American companies is they have forgotten about these workers. Moreover, managers may have been installed in their positions only two or three years previously, with high compensation packages. They get the company to provide bonuses and golden parachutes to ensure their personal gain, but they give little thought to the workers. We wonder if this is a good way to manage corporations, which are, after all, public institutions in a society.

Of those companies that were not bought out, a good many of them—especially those in mature industries—reduced the scope of their operations by failing to reinvest in their own business, and eventually they disappeared from the scene. Their abandoned factories fell into ruins.

In the American steel industry, they talk about revitalization, but there is not a single U.S. firm that makes the steel mill equipment necessary to modernize a mill. Any steel company that would want to refurbish its production facilities—its rolling mills, for example—would have to turn to overseas suppliers for the equipment and its maintenance. We are concerned that a similar loss of industrial foundation caused by the life cycles of certain industries may be taking place in Japan as well.

Today, the Japanese economy is at a turning point in the sense that the rate of growth is slowing. As mentioned previously, the most we can expect from the market as a whole is growth of between 2 and 3 percent. Certain products are geared toward mature markets, while others are for consumption by growing markets. For the market as a whole, therefore, the best we can hope for is modest growth. Mature industry accounts for a sizable share. In the automobile industry, for example, they talk about having one plant too many and the need for retrenchment and for closing a plant somewhere. With the collapse of the bubble, it has become clear that no industry can afford to become single-mindedly devoted to capacity expansion. It appears that what happened in the U.S. in the 1970s is finally beginning to happen in Japan.

In America, the problem came to the fore in too drastic a manner. Many manufacturers of steelmaking equipment were bought by large conglomerates. These conglomerates—looking on their new acquisitions from the perspective of portfolio management theory—saw them as cash cows. And they milked them dry. Then they sold off the desiccated carcasses. There was no thought for the employees, and decline accelerated.

Irrespective of the results of such a strategy, some argue that, from a macroeconomic point of view, the United States is proceeding with a generational change of industry in a dynamic way. The American way is to leave the transformation of the industrial structure to the decision of shareholders. When a company is sold, the shareholders are paid what is due them with money borrowed from banks. In this way the shareholders—institutional or private—get their money back, and they can reinvest it in other companies. They may invest in the small but vibrant companies that are listed one after another on the NASDAQ. This is how money flows to new, vigorous companies from large, antiquated ones. Such a system gives birth to progeny like Intel, Apple Computer, and Microsoft. To the extent that money is circulated efficiently to hi-tech startups, the American strategy as a whole is well equipped to engineer dynamic transformation, albeit afflicted with individual problems.

In Japan, many companies took on hi-tech ventures as part of their diversification program. They melded traditional mechanical engineering with new electronics to produce the hybrid products of mechatronics. It was a positive situation, where traditional technical development gave rise to a virtuous cycle. It would be legitimate to ask if this was indeed the best way to catch up with American hi-tech industry, but on the face of it the effort led to the development of new technology and accomplished a transformation of the business structure through diversification. And the architects of the strategy were lavished with praise for following the trend toward structural reformation. Lately, companies suspect they have gone too far down the road of diversification and are reassessing their direction. But in Japan today, there is no mechanism at work that can replace the old strategy.

Certain things are taking place today that indicate that Japanese companies are up against it. If an individual with an entrepreneurial bent were to materialize at a Japanese company, his actions would be kept within the confines of the firm. Anything he wanted to try, he would undertake at the place he works and nowhere else. Since Japanese firms have no shareholders exercising definitive control functions, managers may well give him free rein. As this decision to let the would-be entrepreneur attempt what he wished might well be taken without careful consideration of the competitive situation in the marketplace—this being the way of personnel policy considerations in Japanese corporations, which are very much like closed societies—the company, based on the efforts of their in-house entrepreneur, may opt for diversification in complete disregard of the competitive implications. The result of such a venture can often be failure.

It seems to us that one reason diversification is not working well is that Japanese developers and managers cannot find any foreign precedents to use as models. In the past, Japanese managers—in steel, textiles, appliances, whatever—endeavored to catch up with and surpass the Americans and Europeans and, in the process, came up with new products and new businesses. It was a golden era. They would climb to the top of one mountain only to find another to conquer, and so they set to work scaling that. Then, all of a sudden, they got to the top and found there was nothing beyond—they had conquered the highest peak. Japanese managers then got either complacent or disoriented. It has finally dawned on them that they cannot repeat the things that worked in the past.

Another reason Japanese business reached its limits relates to the question of "seeds for diversified business." The industries and corporations that supported the high-growth economy matured in the 1970s. Managers today can instruct their people to try some new business, or can even set up an in-house venture program, but it is getting very hard to find the necessary "seeds" for new business. In fact, traditional large corporations have already deployed a large number of multiple businesses, turning themselves into general merchants. As they do so, however, they should remember that such a strategy led not a few American companies, conglomerates in particular, into failure. It became hard for them to find top executives who had experience enough to grasp fully the company's far-flung business resulting from excessive diversification, while the shareholders—who might have been in a position to support the company's multiple investments—could no longer comprehend the business.

If the top management of a company cannot grasp the current situation of each of the company's many business operations, the firm is in no position to diversify successfully. It is irresponsible for top management to say, "We are O.K. because we have left it up to division executives." This sort of "general store" operation is very inefficient. We dare say that as managers staked their prestige on the growth of the company, they diversified into businesses that had promising growth potential. But even if that sort of diversification program was successful, it only helped to turn the firm into a characterless corporation with an identity that was nebulous. So many companies fell victim to failed diversification that it is easier to count the successes than the failures.

JAPANESE-STYLE DECISION MAKING THAT HAS REACHED ITS LIMITS

Customer-Oriented Diversification

One of the major elements behind the failure of the decision-making function at Japanese corporations is an inability to see the market. The cause of this problem must be looked at from many angles, but after scrutinizing the corporate decision-making process and the reasoning of decision makers we come away with the feeling that the essence of the problem is management's propensity to find answers only on the basis of in-house reasoning.

Take, for example, a steel company that has made a foray into the semiconductor industry. In that industry, nonferrous metals firms, such as Mitsubishi Materials; manufacturers specializing in semiconductors; and chemical company subsidiaries, such as Shinetsu Semiconductors, are already firmly entrenched. Has the steel company fully investigated how it can best compete in the market and what technological or administrative advantages it can bring to bear on the effort to solve existing problems? A prudent approach would be to begin producing silicon—the raw material for semiconductors. It should be clear, however, that any effort on the part of the steel company to produce the semiconductors themselves will encounter significant obstacles. We wonder, in such cases, if companies really conduct serious and careful analyses to determine the kind of market that is out there, who the competitors are, what resources can be marshaled, and what special features can be brought to the market. Imperative here is the need to estimate the prospects of success in a thorough fashion and that such estimation be done before any final decision to go ahead is made.

Some diversification programs have resulted from the need on the part of companies to satisfy the demands of their customers, even though resources were limited. There have been cases where companies took up new product ideas that were advanced by their customers and—after successive efforts to meet customer needs— finally emerged with successful new ventures. It should be stressed, of course, that it is no easy task to grasp the needs of customers or the market. Recruit Co., for example, under the guiding hand of Mr. Ezoe, launched an information service business, proclaiming, "Our customers were our teachers. We entered this new business under the tutelage of our customers." Initially, the firm was highly praised for the move, but in the end the business failed. Caution is in order in such circumstances because the market and the customers could be, to put it crudely, merely egging you on. The market and the customer are fickle creatures, and it is by no means a simple matter to try to comprehend the true needs of either.

Recently, I had the chance to read *Sumitomo Memoirs* by Kawada Jun. The book was very absorbing, with the author reminiscing about the climate of the Osaka business community and the Sumitomo *zaibatsu* during the Meiji and Taisho eras. I could hardly put it down. One of the episodes related had strategic implications, and Kawada proudly recalls it:

Just after the First World War, Kawada was transferred from Sumitomo headquarters to Sumitomo Metal Industries and made the No. 2 executive there. Sumitomo Metal at that time was performing very poorly, making little or no money. The Japanese navy was its principal customer, and the firm dutifully manufactured one product after another to navy specifications. But since this meant producing many different products in small quantities, operation costs were high. Kawada—as he proudly proclaims in his book—was intent on changing this, and he did so by walking away from the navy and focusing instead on railroad companies, making them the firm's principal customers. He made sure to apologize to the navy for his decision to discontinue the relationship. The upshot of all this was he succeeded in reviving Sumitomo Metal. Kawada's decision to overhaul the entire business and subject even the company's most important customer to intensive reassessment turned out to be a very significant one indeed.

Not a few Japanese corporations in the latter half of the 1980s found themselves in a similar situation. Many had focused on meeting the meticulous needs of their customers, but in they end they discovered—just as Kawada Jun had scores of years before— that an overzealous strategy of producing small quantities of many different products just doesn't pay.

If some of the choices they have made are any indication, it is questionable whether companies today even know what it means to be customer oriented. Management must reexamine—from the bottom up—any supposedly common-sense judgment that involves a formal scheme of producing small quantities of multiple products. Management must decide whether such a strategy is in fact really a customer-oriented one.

Diversification to Maintain Employment

Diversification proceeds in different directions: horizontally, vertically, diagonally. One statistical analysis of these various tangents concludes: "Generally speaking, the diversification efforts of Japanese corporations have been successful." Of course, your take on diversification depends on how you approach it. It is important to ask what exactly is meant by diversification. The diversification that is undertaken in the food industry, for instance, does not involve movement into other industries. Competition in the area of distribution is very intense in the food industry, with new supermarkets popping up all the time. Manufacturers find it increasingly difficult to control distribution and arrange for their merchandise to be offered to customers. Instead of developing and marketing their products and working through wholesalers to get shelf space at retailers, they think it makes sense to take over other companies and use the acquired firms' distribution channels to sell products. This is horizontal expansion. But we are not sure if we should even call this diversification. Perhaps the term may need to be redefined.

This type of diversification into related business is said to be reasonably profitable. The contrary strategy—moving into unfamiliar territory and doing something you likely have no knack for—is difficult.

When diversifying, managers and corporate planners often claim: "We cannot expect our present business to grow. If we do nothing, positions like that of general manager and deputy general manager will disappear. Let's move into new business, diversify, and find our path to happiness." This approach presupposes that a firm has achieved efficiency in its existing business and will assign surplus manpower to diversified business. The question is who will be assigned to subsidiaries created as part of diversification efforts. Even the most talented individuals in the company may not quite be able to cut it in the new business, in comparison with competitors who have been in the field for a long time. At the very minimum, they will have less experience. Knowing that, firms often send out second and third contingents to the new business. And as the story so often goes, even these additional people are unable to make it work.

Perhaps it wouldn't work no matter what the strategy. It doesn't work when things are left up to the new people sent in, and, if the parent firm wants to control it, it doesn't work because the firm and its people don't understand the key points of the new business. You cannot expect a person who has dealt previously in merchandise expressed in tons to handle merchandise expressed in microns. A fertilizer company cannot turn into a fine chemicals company without first experiencing a great deal of hardship.

The Malaise of Large Corporations and Excess Hiring

In connection with restructuring, we want to share with you what we were told by a steel company executive. Steel companies are under pressure to reform their cost structure—something, incidentally, that is sorely needed in other industries as well. The challenge is to lower fixed costs so that steel firms can be more flexible regarding operating rates. In Japan, fixed costs include depreciation, which is a principal element, and labor costs. If you want to lower fixed costs, you cannot invest in new equipment as much as you'd like, making it necessary to continue using old equipment. If you want to exclude this from your considerations when looking for ways to lower fixed costs, a specific option might be to reduce manpower. In fact, steel companies are committed to reducing manpower by 20 percent to 30 percent. But the fact of the matter is they already went through a period of retrenchment during the 1980s, and as a result their plant payrolls were cut to the bone. Other industries may find themselves in a similar situation. In essence, on the production floor costs have already been reduced as much as they can be.

The remaining challenge concerns white-collar workers—namely, how to go about reducing their number. Up to now—whether Parkinson's Law was in play or not—white-collar workers have tended to increase in number whenever firms found themselves with a little extra leeway. As operating people must account for profit or loss at the plant level, they are very cost conscious, especially with respect to personnel, and they try to shunt off surplus people to the head office. The head office accommodates them, creating work for them to do, which means of course that they end up doing something that is not really needed. In this way, surplus manpower accumulates willy-nilly at head office. Such extra personnel are perhaps the appropriate candidates for a decisive reduction in the work force. It seems inevitable that firms will eventually cut back these staff department white-collars at headquarters.

Active shareholders at American companies delegate the authority to run the business to management. Being accountable to the shareholders, management takes actions in full exercise of that authority. No such external control function exists in Japan, where persons who did well while in the ranks are often promoted to senior positions. When a company isn't profitable, such people are asked to resign or accept transfer to a subsidiary. Since no justifiable reason exists for such termination or reassignment, bitterness increases within the company. In this way, companies do force personnel reductions, and these can cause serious problems.

That's why firms often choose to keep people working at superfluous tasks that have been created just to keep them busy, as mentioned above. In this sense, even among the directors of a company, there may be a few who could be classified as "in-house unemployed." A director with a chauffeured limousine and other perks may cost a firm more than ¥20 million annually. If you can shed five such people, you save ¥100 million, perhaps enough to turn red ink into black. There is the somewhat tongue-in-cheek story of one company that reportedly calculated that the removal of the chairman and president would save the firm some ¥200 million in expenses per annum. Realizing that the departure of the two executives would leave no one to run the company, management laughed off the short-lived suggestion. In many big companies, however, it is costing a bit too much to keep the big shots in their lofty positions.

This question of white-collar workers is a serious one. They cannot be fired without good cause. On the other hand, it is hard to make a case for keeping so many of them around when their benefit to the firm is slim. Suppose a large firm decides that a conference is needed to discuss a certain subject and that three participants are sufficient to mull the matter over. But because this organization is finely segmented into departments and each department has its cadre of professionals, it turns out that such a conference will often need to be attended by five or six people. Everybody at the meeting knows his own mind, and the gathering gets bogged down. Advance *nemawashi* is also time-consuming. In a company such as this, decision making is a slow, inefficient process.

This is the malaise of large firms. Companies are getting used to the culture of procedures. We believe the real cause of this is the excessive number of managerial and white-collar personnel. In a company steeped in tradition sometimes a whole day is wasted in conducting *nemawashi* to touch base with all those who need to be honored with advance consultation or briefing.

The reason firms have so many white-collar workers is similar to the situation surrounding capital investment and long-term planning discussed earlier. Companies got excited during the high-growth period and outdid one another with capacity expansions. At the same time, they hired too many people. They have stopped hiring now, but the surplus personnel are already in place. What should be done? You can sell off excess equipment, but you cannot sell off surplus people. The response by firms has been to ask mid-level employees to quit and to get younger ones to stay. Obviously, this makes mid-level employees very unhappy. Even when a company asks such employees to go to subsidiaries or to accept transfers to outlying posts, the veiled wish that the employees will take the hint and quit is often evident in the way the firm handles these personnel adjustments.

Past mistakes are coming home to roost. Companies undertook diversification beyond their means to give proper treatment to mid-level employees. They believed that even if they weren't growing now they would eventually do so and would therefore need more people. In the meantime, the firms reasoned, these employees would busy themselves doing something. In most cases, it is big companies that are wrestling with this question of surplus personnel.

The Social Prestige of Large Corporations

Working men and women will have to take a different attitude toward companies—they will need to cultivate a different awareness as employees. In the past, when a section chief left a company to join one of its subsidiaries, he went there as general manager of a department. When a departmental head moved from the parent to a subsidiary, he became one of its directors. All of this was expected, and new careers were provided for in this manner. But this is no longer being done. Subsidiaries and affiliates resist when the parent company wants to impose its people on them. Available positions having been filled, a section chief of the parent company now moves to a subsidiary as a section chief. Perhaps it is a measure of the significance of the changes that have occurred that such a transfer is now accepted without much opposition. People have lived the company life, riding on the big name or social prestige of the parent firm—"I would rather be the tail of a lion than the head of a fox." To work for a big company was to enjoy social prestige. Such a structure is not right.

With higher salaries and better benefits, employees of big companies enjoy higher real income than others. Executives in large firms receive salaries that are on average more than double those received by similar executives in smaller companies. Compensation differs greatly from one industry to another. With smaller bonuses now being paid by securities firms, banks are the only employers who have maintained employee salaries at an elevated level and who have made no move to cut back. Remuneration at trading firms has not risen much since about the time of the oil crises.

Japan is a society dominated by corporations and is so structured that money is accumulated by these corporations. Money that should properly be paid to shareholders as dividends is retained by companies and spent in a wasteful fashion. Such waste is caused by bureaucratic inefficiency and the inflated salaries at some of the larger corporations.

Field Orientation and Elitism

From now on, working men and women will have to have a different awareness about their work. If they are only interested in advancement and assume they can climb the corporate ladder faster if they have a college diploma, they may not find self-fulfillment on the job. During the Meiji era, only a few choice individuals had a college education, and therefore giving them special treatment presented no problem. Today, however, almost everybody finishes college, and there just aren't enough positions to go around. Maybe we are returning to the days when one's ability was what really counted. We don't want to sound like we are lecturing, but we feel you should decide on your profession as early as possible, concentrate on it, and let destiny take you where it may. Of course, people will have to continue educating themselves.

In terms of in-the-field experience as it relates to diversification, if able individuals of a company endeavor to run a diversified business with which they are very familiar they are less likely to fail. When they tackle the new business, they will be utilizing experience and how-how they have acquired while working for the company in the field. On the other hand, in the case of the steel industry, for example, every firm is moving into computers and semiconductors simply because the other steel firms are getting into them. In Japan, a company's entry into a new business invariably spurs its competitors to follow suit. If a *ringi* (proposal seeking consensus) to approve entry into a new business is passed around that attempts to justify the move by saying the venture is promising because nobody else has done it, rejection will almost certainly be the result. If, on the other hand, the move is justified on the basis that other competitors have already made it, the likelihood for approval is increased. In the end, it can be said that the decision-making process for diversification has become obsolete.

If a company expands into another business just to keep up with the Joneses but lacks the experience necessary to succeed, then it cannot hope to build solid field operations. In the end, that company cannot be field oriented. In the past, there were good things said about being field oriented. Somehow those words seem to have disappeared. Being field-oriented was one of the characteristic elements that supported Japanese management. This went on the skids over the past 10 years or so, however, as Japanese corporations—bloated in size and wallowing in world fame—started to grow complacent. But the old structure has not changed entirely. We still have companies, that emphasize field orientation. In such companies administrative departments don't meddle in field operations. We observe, however, that in an increasing number of companies the corporate planning departments pester those in the field: "What do you think you are doing? Don't you think you are wasting money?"

Every industry has its share of elitist companies—firms that hold MBAs in high esteem. Many MBAs, trained abroad or in Japan, join corporate planning departments and once there form a power structure. They prepare strategic charts without so much as a glimpse at the field operations. From the standpoint of business schools, it may be a welcome development to see their graduates come to power. But do we really need a set of specialists who are only versed in business administration? Such qualifications are perhaps desirable in business commentators, management auditors, and outside directors, but can those who formulate plans and manage a company do their jobs without understanding the capabilities of the company's plant operations, the current situation at the company, and the market it serves? It is indeed questionable whether they can effectively carry out their responsibilities without an understanding of what goes on in the field.

If we may make a general observation on American MBAs, we believe they are too intent on achieving personal success—which is measured by the amount of annual compensation they earn. In one sense, a market for business managers is being formed. Business managers within that market move from one company to another. In Japan—where there is an emphasis on the field—those who have risen from among the ranks in the field become managers. Frankly speaking, these people can only hope to ascend to management within their own company, and that is perhaps why such managers concern themselves only with the company and not with its shareholders.

In any case, a handful of elite "managerlings" can be usefully put to work checking functions. But a company should never allow an elite group of employees, far removed from the field, to occupy all staff positions, including those involving planning and business management.

Chapter 5 | # Changes in the Business Environment and In Japanese Strategy

A MORE RESTRICTIVE BUSINESS ENVIRONMENT

One problem that recently came to the fore and that requires particular scrutiny relates to the changes in the quality of the various power structures that involve managers and corporations. In particular, it is suspected that the power structure at big corporations has been on a runaway course, showing little regard for the wishes of the shareholders, employees, and other interested parties. This is being addressed as a matter falling within the domain of corporate governance, which includes the relationship between shareholders and managers.

We also point out that changes are taking place in the fundamental conditions surrounding the relationship between financial institutions and business corporations. In particular, the readiness of banks to provide financing on unrealized capital gains has diminished, making it impossible for corporate managers to paper over the wasteful decisions they have made.

Still more significant changes are taking place between consumers and corporations. Japanese consumers have always had a sharp eye for products in terms of price and quality. They are meticulously discerning. Until recently, there was a fear that this discernment encouraged the celebration of high-priced items and that corporations as a result attached little importance to offering low-priced, quality products. It is clear today, however, that consumers have had their fill of such corporate practices.

We cannot help but feel, then, that many of the conditions in the business environment that have traditionally supported

Japanese management policies are beginning to change and that things are increasingly moving in a direction that is less and less advantageous to the ways of the past.

Less Vigilant Overseeing of Financial Institutions

In terms of the monitoring of financial institutions, Japanese banks have traditionally kept an eye on the investment activities of those corporations to which they extend credit to uncover any marginal, profligate decisions. These days, however, the vigilance with which such monitoring is carried out has been in decline. Shareholders' meetings and corporate auditors function in name only. When auditors become a mere formality—when they are chosen by a firm's personnel department to give certain employees a chance to embark on "a second corporate career"—no true auditing function can be expected, no matter how much the auditors' authority may be augmented by the Commercial Code. As external supervisory organs to Japanese corporations, Japan's financial institutions have played a significant role. Today, it appears as if they have abandoned their watchdog responsibilities, perhaps because the banks themselves currently have plenty of their own problems to deal with thanks to failed investments and mismanagement.

Financial institutions wrestling with bloated personnel ranks find it necessary to second older employees to companies receiving their credit. Banks are no longer able to exercise effective supervision over those companies because of a reversal of their own positions; the banks now have to solicit their clients' cooperation in securing jobs for employees. The fact that many managers now act on their own and in rampant fashion may be the result of such attenuated supervision. If shareholders do not take managers to task for their failures, serious problems are bound to surface. That is how the decline of control over corporate management has come about. And it represents a serious change in the business environment of Japanese corporations.

Bloated Financial Management

An international comparison of corporate finances reveals that many Japanese companies are beset with serious financial problems.

During the bubble economy, many firms procured considerable capital from abroad and invested these funds overseas. When they didn't invest abroad, they bought real estate and stocks in Japan, the value of which has now declined substantially. Funds raised for the purpose of investment must now be repaid, and companies are repaying them out of the financial reserves they have diligently accumulated over the years. It is not just business corporations that find themselves in such dire straits. Certain financial institutions are in even worse shape. Under a strategy of equity financing—a method used to raise quasi-equity capital—the capital that was raised turned into debt when stock prices collapsed. In their desire to dig themselves out of a tough situation, some companies dabbled in derivatives and went even deeper into debt.

The yen is overvalued today. Currency, along with securities, has become a speculative commodity. Some argue that the basic cause is the trade surplus. From the point of view of investors, the P/E ratio of Japanese stocks is 100, compared with an average of around 20 in the U.S. and Europe, meaning that the average return on Japanese stocks is a miserly one-fifth or so of that on Western stocks.

At the yen's current excessive level, very few manufacturers in Japan can survive, barring some special fortuitous happenstance. There is no question that the foreign exchange market has become a purely speculative one. Firms that anticipate the further decline of the yen may be thinking that now is the right time to buy large quantities of dollars and invest these abroad. But playing at the back of their minds is the memory of how they have been burned in the past by imprudent overseas investments. Japanese financial firms are always the first to withdraw any extra funds. The money doesn't get circulated to start-ups, however, and that may be adding to the pressure on the yen.

Differential in the Value of the Yen in and out of Japan

Another problem that is closely related to the foreign exchange issue is the value of the yen inside Japan versus its value outside. The stalled rise in real income has demoralized wage earners. Related to this are the high costs of Japan's political system and tax rates, which are fairly high given the relatively small defense budget. From the business management side, there is the difficult issue of reinvestment value—namely, there is a difference in the value of reinvestment depending on where you reinvest. The difference today between the value realized through investment in Japan and that realized through investment overseas is so great that it is no longer profitable to invest here. When you purchase a lot in Japan and put up a building, you can expect only a small return. Under such conditions, it seems obvious that funds would flow to foreign lands.

Additionally, many individual consumers and households—residing in a nation where incomes are supposedly the highest in the world—live from hand to mouth, burdened with the high costs of housing and education. This is brought about by the price differentials between domestic and overseas markets. No matter how difficult or painful it may be to correct the situation—and even if some financial institutions are put in jeopardy as a result of corrective measures—we cannot avoid crossing that bridge. It is inevitable. Even if the government were to implement policies that led in the opposite direction, it would be to no avail. There is no denying the inexorable trend that prevails in an open, international economy.

Thus, from an international perspective we must conclude that the business environment surrounding the activities of Japanese corporations is beginning to show its limitations.

Policies Without Leadership

Many of the strengths that supported the growth of Japanese corporations have become weaknesses in the wake of the burst bubble. There are, for example, inherent contradictions between financial policies on the one hand and trade and industrial policies on the other. The core of a company's management structure is more and more a matter of formality and increasingly bureaucratic. An information disclosure system that is incomplete, a financial system that prevents capital from flowing to healthy corporations, and numerous other macroeconomic and public policy problems that are beyond the scope of this book all need to be addressed.

In the old days, the Japanese political system and business corporations cooperated with each other—like two wheels of the same axle—and they made a success of it. However, things took an unexpected turn with the implementation of the easy-money policy designed to offset the high-yen recession after the Plaza Accord of 1985 and then Prime Minister Nakasone's plan to revitalize the private sector. In light of BIS rules, financial institutions began to attach great importance to profits, and the resulting excess liquidity was directed to the purchase of real estate and stocks, leading to the formation of policy-induced markets, which was a very contradictory development.

Once the bubble had stretched to a certain point, it had to be punctured with a sudden tight-money policy. But the lending policies of financial institutions have been tightened so much that even worthwhile projects don't receive the funding they deserve. Moreover, the soaring yen has so weakened the competitive edge held by such Japanese exports as automobiles, appliances, and electronics equipment that manufacturers have been forced to shift production overseas. We see this development as proof that our political system has malfunctioned.

Changes in the financial climate have had serious implications for corporations. During the bubble, they employed equity financing in Japan—floating convertible debentures and selling new stock issues on the market—while overseas they issued bonds with warrants attached. With the bubble's demise, however, equity financing was no longer possible, and they now find themselves saddled with increased common debentures and bank loans. The banks have their funds tied up in nonperforming assets and cannot finance worthwhile investments. Firms that shouldn't be going bankrupt are. The immensity of the disaster fomented by policy decisions taken during and after the bubble is mind boggling.

The Breakdown of Hidden-Asset Management

Heretofore, management has been able to retain and manage hidden assets—unrealized capital gains (or losses) from corporate assets—and this provided a sort of haven that could be used to gloss over managerial blunders. In fact, the management of such assets may not have been without its problems. Some listed companies maintain that their interests would be well served if they were obligated to provide information concerning unrealized capital gains/losses in the course of their normal disclosure practices.

In this connection, we must examine the matter of consolidated financial reporting. To be sure, an improved disclosure system would be of benefit when you consider cases where subsidiaries are used to retain hidden assets or keep unrealized losses from being made public. It should be noted, however, that at that point in the process no taxes have yet been paid by Japanese corporations and no capital raised on a consolidated basis. Even if consolidated statements were published, it is clear that the information released wouldn't come close to telling the real story because the only thing that would have changed is that disclosure would now be on a consolidated basis.

We cannot just assume that consolidated statements reflect the reality of a particular business. As long as taxes continue to be assessed on corporations, ways will be found to offset a subsidiary's deficit with proceeds from the sale of the parent's assets; it is not impossible to use one subsidiary's profit to offset the deficit of another. If each subsidiary were to raise its own capital, it would make its own financing decisions. If you subscribe to new share issues or purchase warrant-attached bonds on the basis of information in published consolidated statements, you will find it very difficult to ascertain how the proposed use of those funds balances with the amount of funds procured. In sum, consolidated management cannot lead to well-balanced overall management unless it includes consolidated taxation and financing as well as a consolidated settlement of accounts.

In certain cases, unrealized losses (as well as unrealized gains) have become an issue. Companies with poor results can often control profits by making use of their affiliates to declare dividends.

Others may manage by sleight of hand to stabilize ordinary profits in order to support share prices. The know-how and techniques involved in the settlement of accounts such as these may well be the result of a system that deals with unrealized capital gains. If, at the end of the day this system proves untenable we may eventually end up with something much closer to the American system, which emphasizes earnings and dividends for the current quarter, resulting in management with a short-term perspective.

In addition to hidden-asset management, there is one other factor that has made it possible for Japanese firm's to commit to long-term investment—namely, their relationship with financial institutions. The fact is that even as Japanese corporations were raising capital from stock and bond markets they continued to consult with their banks—which were also their shareholders—and, in the end, they obtained substantial capital through indirect financing, which committed them to long-term investment. Given the currently depressed prices on securities markets, there are limits to what you can obtain through direct financing. On the other hand, it is no longer as simple as it was to obtain ample indirect financing because of the financing curbs banks find themselves under. Because of this, the climate for long-term investment is no longer favorable, a situation exacerbated by the slowdown in market growth. In this sense, the strategy of long-term investment, which has been one of the principal features of Japanese management, finds itself with its back against the wall.

DISCREDITED PAST SUCCESS

The business environment in Japan has changed, and conditions that in the past supported management have gradually become restrictive. This development has started to have a significant impact on the strategies corporations employ. Management is undergoing a series of transformations. Let us review some of those changes here.

Management by Long-Term Investment

Regarding the specific factors that in the past helped make Japanese management successful, certain features of the manufacturing industry are quite distinctive, such as an emphasis on field operations, companywide cost-reduction campaigns, and a focus on exports. In addition, one would certainly have to include the stance on long-term investment when listing the reasons behind the past success of Japanese corporate strategy. Japanese corporations were able to make investments with a long-term focus. However, as was evident in the case of the HDD, Japanese corporations do not seem able to emulate their American counterparts in terms of vitality, due principally to Japan's regulatory rules on information and telecommunications and to the influence of organizational and behavioral customs with respect to advanced information. We see many instances of Japanese companies lagging in their market access functions and coming out with products that lack a competitive edge, despite the companies' strengths in components and elemental technology.

Notwithstanding questionable technical development capabilities, success did come the way of Japanese corporations in the past. But this success in many cases was not attributable to the specific business strategies of the corporations, but rather resulted from the fact that investment was sustained over a long period of time. An investment that may be excessive in the short-term can be sustained over a long period with the help of financial institutions in such a way that, after an initial period of inactivity, the time eventually comes when equipment begins to operate profitably. In the end, such an investment proves its worth to the business and is not wasted.

Another characteristic of Japanese management is the disinclination to identify the specific individuals responsible for executing a project. While in the U.S. or Europe a project is likely to be led by the executives and management staff of a company, the same project in Japan might well be executed by people in the field. The field is the site of development and production, and decisions here are presumably made by people closer to the action, rather than by senior managers. At the development site, you find engineers dreaming of new things to create, while at the production site cost-reduction efforts are carried out autonomously by the people there. This is advantageous and helps to strengthen the organization. But Japanese products have lost so much of their previous competitiveness that we wonder about these supposed advantages.

The most fundamental strategy of any corporation is the one directed toward the product market. But it seems that effective strategy formulation in this area is being replaced by bland assertions about the company's ability to comprehend the needs of the future market or about the company's ability to best the competition in offering products to meet those needs. Any new strategic planning project drafted and promoted by management that does not tap into the firm's know-how in the field runs the risk of being merely an armchair theory. Strategic discussions are carried out in the bureaucratized head office with no awareness of the technical trends in the field and of changes in consumer sensitivities. And yet such brainy plans—based on nothing more than common sense, prepared with the help of management consultants, lacking in creativity, and weighed down by theoretical thinking—are held in high regard. And they are becoming increasingly prevalent.

Changes are also taking place in production plants. It used to be that when the resources of the whole plant were marshaled to achieve the goal of cost reduction, for example, the system worked very well, involving everybody in the plant and pushing each employee to do his or her part. The result was achievements such as automation, manpower reductions, and resource saving. Today, however, corporations—and this is especially true for people in the field—have lost sight of the end-use market. They don't know where they should go, and they can no longer marshal all their resources to any one particular end.

When everybody has lost sight of the market, what can be done to make it visible again? In the past, a long-term business plan would, for example, make public a goal of, say, a 20 percent cost reduction and provide guidelines for actions designed to achieve it. Today, however, a long-term plan is only a formality—it contains no substantive guidelines or directions and is motivated first and last by the need to make sure that all the numbers jibe.

Necessarily, in the absence of any directives for specific action a system that marshals the power of all employees has no chance of getting started.

In marketing, the goal in the past was export oriented: ship products to the world market. But as international economic friction intensified and as the value of the yen soared, Japanese firms were forced to globalize their production bases. It seemed that everybody went overseas. As business operations, most of these global projects turned out to be failures. When that happened, it was not possible to revert to exporting. Firms wavered while trying to decide which direction was most likely to lead to growth. One solution was to increase prices, and some chose this path. But such decisions, driven as by management considerations alone, cannot hope to produce long-term vitality. The focus seems to be a preoccupation with clever calculations in the fundamental areas of business activities and product development.

Amid these developments, however, a turning point for business management is in sight. Solid, promising, medium-sized companies and start-ups brimming with entrepreneurial fervor should be able to replace big corporations. But their growth has been nipped in the bud by constraints on financing in support of investment strategy and by problems with financial structure. The vitality of Japanese corporations as a whole is on the wane, making us wonder: "What have they been doing?" and "What were their strengths really?"

New Product Development

The huge capacity of Japanese corporations to develop new products was one of the factors behind the unrivaled competitive positions they built around the world. Today, however, that ability for technical development has become outdated.

Japanese shipbuilding surpassed all others because, for one thing, it excelled in the production of high-quality engines, the development of various kinds of auxiliary equipment, and the design of ships. Japan's camera industry never stopped producing high-quality, low-priced products. In electronics, Sony's Walkman and Victor's camcorders were examples of new-concept products created by engineers with vision. Technological prowess bolstered competitive strength, as exemplified in the case of the high-density recording method called helical scan. It is questionable how much of that old-time challenging spirit is left in Japanese corporations. We must examine why companies no longer seem able to focus on specific technical trends or goals to discover whether firms have lost the courage to look into the future or whether they are no longer able to grasp what the real needs of that future will be.

The reality is that cutting-edge products like LANs (local area networks), microprocessors, new operating systems, networks and high-speed modems, routers, and gateways are made almost exclusively in the United States. Now that we are on the cusp of the advanced information society, what has happened to the Japanese technological prowess related to these markets? We are concerned. In fact, we feel a sense of crisis over this waning of Japanese competitive strength in the area of technical development. It seems possible that Japanese engineers are simply no longer able to feel the pulse of future market or technical trends.

Serious problems have emerged in the collaboration of engineers and craftsmen. Many hi-tech products embody the melding of the skills of craftsmen and the technology of designers. In many areas, such collaboration in the past supported the practicability of products, such as in the grinding of metal molds, the polishing of nonspherical surface lenses, the grinding of superhard objects, and the polishing of precision magnetic heads. Because craftsmen in the field exercise their skills beyond the realm of engineering or built-in controls, collaboration with them in the operation of equipment—such as temperature controls in the removal of single crystals from crucibles and devices that handle ultrafine powder— helped to ensure the stability of product quality. Today, the aging of technicians and a formal personnel system that gives priority to college graduates threatens to impair the exercise of crucial technological prowess.

Indeed, there are many who wonder if there is any longer such a thing as production engineering in the field. With respect to the equipment used in the manufacture of semiconductors, Japanese companies may hold a superior position in areas that utilize optical technology, such as steppers, but they do not necessarily have a competitive edge in product areas based on fundamental physical phenomena, such as chemical vapor deposition devices and ion injectors. In the latter area, American-made equipment reigns supreme. In the development of key technology indispensable for the next generation of semiconductors, Japanese companies do not have the upper hand in all areas. Crisis seems to have overtaken even this Japanese industry, once so widely acclaimed for its strength in manufacturing technology. Some companies have degenerated into mere users of technology and components from outside sources.

We are worried that the strengths of Japanese manufacturing technology have been forgotten. We suspect that for some companies in such industries as shipbuilding and steel, which have in the past enjoyed superior international competitive positions, the only thing they had going for them was an advantageous location. Some have observed that the markets for Japanese automobiles and appliances grew because Japanese engineers exercised superior management skills, or had autonomous product development capabilities, or produced quality differentials due to well-organized manufacturing technology. On the other hand, others have argued that, in the area of automobiles, the Japanese went ahead of the Americans only because the Big Three became complacent and neglected the development of new engines—a view that cannot be dismissed.

At a time when increasing importance is being attached to telecommunications, computers, and information technology (IT), it is in fact the Americans who are making headway in the development of multimedia. When the U.S. developed new technology to transmit images through networks, Japan was effectively barred from such business because of its laws governing communications and broadcasting. Government officials may well try to rebut this, saying, "there were no legal restrictions," but the fact is they nipped the emerging industry in the bud with excessive administrative guidance. And, to our dismay, they have done little in the way of soul-searching over their misguided actions. Electronic data interchange (EDI)—the exchange of information between companies—may well fall victim to the differing policies of the Ministry of International Trade and Industry and the Ministry of Posts and Telecommunications over the issue of technical standards, possibly resulting in another critical disadvantage vis-à-vis the West.

In particular, our backwardness in computer software and telecommunications is a serious problem. The U.S. leads in open system interconnection (OSI), while we are totally dependent on the Americans for software in areas such as communications protocol and network operating systems. In the area of image transmission, Japan's business infrastructure is the stumbling block, including the shortage of coaxial cables due to delayed investment in ATM switched networks as well as delays in the spread of cable TV. Database software is developed by Oracle, Sybase, and Informix—all American firms. The only thing Japanese firms can do is wait and see which products become the industry standards.

The software and know-how used by banks in their international finance endeavors are imported from the U.S. financial products called derivatives, such as futures, swaps, and options, are the result of American and European know-how. The truth is Japan is no longer able to lead the world.

Competition on the Basis of Price and Economies of Scale

Along with long-term investment, another characteristic factor that supported Japanese management in the past was its enthusiasm for price competition and economies of scale. Today, the various fixed costs in Japanese organizations are so high that they cannot compete on the basis of price and economies of scale, even in a globalized world market. Due to political friction, economies of scale cannot be fully taken advantage of. The excessive investment companies engaged in is now obvious to all, and, bloated with equipment, they are performing poorly. To compete on the basis of price and economies of scale has traditionally been the characteristic means by which Japanese corporations implemented their strategies, but this no longer works.

It was Matsushita Konosuke who said: "I want to provide consumers with an inexpensive and convenient life." Such pride seems to be absent in today's managers. It may be necessary for us to begin anew, with a reexamination of what ought to be the philosophy of business managers.

Competing on the basis of price and economies of scale would be possible if Japanese firms would view their business structure from a global perspective, including Asia. But when they persist with operational bases in Japan only, it is inevitable that a change of course will be required at some point. Related to this is the fact that Japan has yet to produce managers who can manage from a worldwide perspective. If, on the other hand, a firm wants to maintain both competitiveness and high prices, it will have to radically shrink its operation, becoming a small company with high productivity. It can be done. The question is whether companies will decide to go that route.

Network-Type Industrial Structure

The system of subcontractors that has supported Japanese corporations and spawned a network-type industrial structure is beginning to come apart at the seams. One aspect of the *keiretsu* system has been to assure a supply of components of stable quality through established channels. The other aspect has been to assure organized, industrywide development efforts. The latter aspect is achieved by the implementation of a "design-in" methodology, which involves the collaboration of assemblers and makers of components and materials.

Let us look at automobiles, an industry in which *keiretsu* transactions have been a cause of trade friction between the U.S. and Japan. In America, automobile companies make components in-house, a system they call captive production. In Europe, assemblers and parts makers are independent of each other. Accordingly, in Europe a small automobile company can manufacture cars by buying components from parts companies. In Japan, there is a vertical relationship, with the parts makers accommodating the assemblers, who do nothing but assemble. That is the Japanese-style network structure.

If a Japanese automaker wants to produce in Europe or America, it cannot obtain parts and materials there. Consequently, it must buy them from Japan. But it can only do so subject to the constraints of local content rules: the percentage of parts procured locally. It is no wonder then that firm's cannot succeed. Many automakers are able to maintain their operations in Japan because of the existence of the industrial structure described above. It is clear that, thanks to this type of industrial structure, new products can be introduced in a relatively short period of time.

On the question of distribution, marketing channels led by automakers have become an issue in trade talks. The resolution of trade friction is being sought by leaning on Japanese dealers in the *keiretsu* system to help sell Ford and GM cars. But it should be noted that Europe has a vertical automobile distribution system similar to Japan's. Why is Japan's distribution system being singled out for criticism by the Americans? Is our government to blame for its inability to counter their attack, or is the industry to blame for its inability to provide appropriate materials for negotiations?

Excessive Competition

Japan's industrial society has one characteristic of which it is justifiably proud: excessive competition. It is important to remember that all industries in which Japanese companies maintain international competitive strength, including automobiles, electric appliances, telecommunications equipment, and semiconductors, face excessive competition right here in Japan.

Within this industrial structure, Japanese companies are engaged in intense competition and must constantly strive to improve themselves. American auto companies have been amalgamated into the Big Three and operate as an oligopoly, and in Europe a similar grouping is making headway. In Europe, in the areas of electric appliances and telecommunications equipment, corporations can operate without worrying about competition. In contrast, Japanese corporations encounter constant competition, causing them to hone their competitive edge.

The current discussion is on the level of an introduction to the theory of industrial structure, and Japan's is a textbook case of intense and stimulating competition. In Japan, industries that do not face competition continue with their old-fashioned ways, unaware of competition and snug and comfortable under the protection of government regulations, much like American automakers or European appliance makers. These companies without exception are wanting in competitive edge. There is no question, therefore, that the maintenance of an industrial structure marked by excessive competition is extremely important.

Self-Indulgent Domain Theory

It has been pointed out that to promote diversification projects and ensure long-term corporate viability, a corporation must recognize its role or function and conceptualize this so that it can be understood by society. Such conceptualization involves questions of corporate domain and a definition of functions.

When we discuss the necessity of pondering these questions, the case of American railroad companies is often cited as an illustration. American railroad companies saw themselves as being in the railroad business, not in the essential business of transporting men and materials across the continent. That is why they were left behind when automobiles and airplanes came upon the scene.

In contrast, Xerox has always seen itself as a document company, not just a maker of copying machines. Consequently, it worked on the development of fax machines and laser printers; developed Ethernet, a network technology related to the computerization of office operations; and is now working on the commercialization of LANs. Such management measures to prolong corporate life have attracted attention, and they have been undertaken by other firms in Japan as well. However, they are not necessarily easy. Many companies have attempted to define their own domain but have been unable to do so. On the contrary, in their enthusiasm many managers have tried to define corporate functions that were beyond their grasp, and they ended up becoming smug, laboring under a domain theory that was self-indulgent.

One of the motivations behind the effort to get firms to conceptualize their corporate domain and functions is the fact that many companies have gotten so big and their range of products so broad as a result of diversification and globalization that they no longer have an integrating influence. In the past, even if a Japanese company were able to define the nature of its business activities it was not used to considering either the architecture of the organization or the system that runs it. Consequently, firms focused on questions such as "What is the company's mission vis-à-vis society?" The important domain theory only ended up providing fodder for discussions on the company's corporate identity, logo, and publicity.

One of the highly acclaimed examples of Japanese corporations in this context is the C&C of NEC Corp. Kobayashi Koji and Sekimoto Tadahiro, the architects of the resurgence of NEC, defined the purpose of their business as the development of products befitting an age witnessing the melding of computers and communications (C&C), and they carried out a successful strategy on that basis. True to the character of Japanese corporations—which must keep up with the Joneses—a certain company soon trumpeted its new E&E, another announced I&I, and still another came out with U&U—all of them a familiar echo of NEC's C&C. But these carbon copies were nothing more than cut-and-dried billboards, summarizing what business the firm is in. It is important to note that C&C was originated by engineers in the field—the name came after. One must be careful with names, as they sometimes reveal little and can even be downright confusing—"Urban life industry" and "Value creation corporation" being two examples. With such sloganeering, many firms seem satisfied that their mission has been made clear or the direction of their business clarified. Stewardship of a company will be in uncertain hands if such self-complacent managers take the helm, their smugness apparent in their preference for forms and appearances.

Casio is no longer a mere producer of calculators. When its corporate identity guru suggested a change in the corporate name, Casio's management rejected it by saying: "Our company's logo is Casio and there is no need to waste a lot of money to change the formal name of our company." It was refreshing indeed to hear of such a decision.

JAPANESE STRATEGY SHOWS ITS LIMITATIONS

The business environment that had supported Japanese management saw its strengths turn into weaknesses after the bubble. At the same time, the characteristic features of decision making by Japanese management began to wear thin. When a corporation is going through change, it can run up against an invisible wall, which often means that it has not only changed functionally but that internal corrosion has progressed and the organization is ill. On reflection, Japan is in an advantageous position, being the only advanced country with a trade surplus and the rest of Asia on its doorstep. Did Japanese management become undisciplined because of a complacency brought about by this advantageous position? Did managers run up against the wall when the consequences of sub-par global management know-how and experience finally came home to roost? Did their bloated, bureaucratized organizations lead to decision making based solely on in-house reasoning, causing them to lose sight of the market? These questions require examination.

In fact, the surrounding environment is in effect a death knell for strategies employed by Japanese management in the past. If Japan lacks the ability to sell the world on unique Japanese systems and mechanisms—making them standard practices around the world—what are we to do? The answer is obvious. We must take another look at the system of management that we have labored to build up over so many years. Within Japan there is a variety of contradictions at work, as seen in the interactions between our political system and corporations, in the relationship between the financial system and business corporations, in the relationship between corporations and shareholders, and in other areas. We Japanese are now under pressure to revamp these systems on our own.

Let us pause here to summarize some of the principal limitations of the Japanese strategy that have been addressed so far.

A scheme of producing multiple products in small quantities was hailed as being consumer oriented. It is questionable if the intention really was to provide individual consumers with the products they needed. One wonders if it wasn't to sell pricey merchandise differentiated only by mere add-on options and accessories under the guise of meeting the needs of the consumers. One could characterize these products as sham. Questions also remain as to whether the manufacturers really grasped the needs of the market and engaged in competition on the basis of such recognition. Why did they not concern themselves with the essential functions of a product, preferring instead to make money by simply adding options? Arguably, the maturity of the market and excessive competition had an impact. In the past, the market and competition went hand in hand, competition serving both to catch hold of the needs of the market and to give rise to new needs. The market grew and fostered further competition, with each feature complementing the other. Today, when the market has ceased to grow, the only feature that remains distinctive is excessive competition.

On the question of globalization, we expected that those managers who failed to achieve the internationalization of their business operations would learn from this and redouble their efforts to advance global management for the next generation. On the contrary, manager mentality and decisions reveal vacillation in this area. Lately, managers seem to be making a greater effort to engage in cross-cultural exchanges, but it is not easy to train managers to exercise leadership and run an organization while employing people with different cultural backgrounds and values.

The diversification programs that corporations have carried forward along with their internationalization efforts have ended on a distressing note for many. When you diversify into a new business area, you must learn and understand the reality of that business. You must be aware that the risks are high at least until you have gained experience in that field, which takes time. Instead, we have seen many instances of simple-minded decisions that led to developments that failed and necessitated withdrawal. We often wonder at the performance of the managers in such cases. They have high expectations for their projects, but they seem to pay scant attention to the attendant risks.

We also question the hiring of excessive numbers of people as well as excessive investments. Pressured by labor shortages during the bubble period, big corporations struggled to best one another in grabbing new hires. No amount of soul-searching will resolve the issue of excessive employment. We wonder, though, why firms were not able to hold fast to the long-term perspective they displayed in the area of implementing capital spending when it came time to recruit new personnel.

The changing financial reality no longer permits a long-term, random investment strategy. An extensive review is required of this issue.

Product engineering is withering. We are concerned that, in too many large corporations the technical focus has shifted to network technology and system technology, with elemental technology relegated to secondary importance. In essence, central technical development in Japanese companies has moved from the area of elemental technology, which they are good at, to the area of system technology, which they are not good at. We are afraid that this change will cause our inherent technology to fade away. It is possible that the Japanese strategy that put new technology to full use and introduced new products one after another—and reinforced the business foundation in the process—may not work anymore.

In the course of cataloging these concerns, we have come to realize that obsolescence and decay are eating away not only at the basic business structure that has supported Japanese management but also at the Japanese corporations themselves. If management is maintained in its current form, it will be by dint of resources accumulated in the past. And if the present methods and mechanism are left as they are, the future will not be a bright one.

Chapter 6 | Japanese Management Is Being Tested

What on earth could have caused the withering of Japanese corporate management that became apparent after the bubble collapsed? American firms during the 1980s were absorbed in mergers and acquisitions; as a result, many large corporations disappeared, while others recovered their vitality. We don't yet know what judgment posterity will pass on the American management of the 1980s. European firms—many of them locked in competition with Japanese companies and not faring particularly well—are working hard to rebuild themselves with the aid of government protection under a system of oligopoly, but they still have a long way to go and are in no position to relax.

In this way, many corporations throughout the world are running up against a similar wall. The Americans and Europeans have endeavored to rebuild their economies and individual firms without the benefit of growing markets for at least the past 10 years. They have an advantage in this regard, having been at it for a long time. Japanese management, on the other hand, has not yet had a test of sufficient length.

A GROWING MARKET AS THE SAVIOR OF JAPANESE BUSINESS

The success of Japanese firms up until now is ascribable to the fact that they have been riding a wave of economic growth. Those companies that missed the boat have seen their market share dwindle. But the individual successes were not necessarily achieved by dint of effective strategy. It appears that success more

119

often than not came to companies laboring under irresponsible management that merely followed what their competitors were doing and made one extravagant, almost wanton, investment after another. This overinvestment was only saved by the prodigious growth of the market. Investments were not initiated on the basis of a clear perception of the market. Due to an emphasis on the production floor, management tended to limit decision making within the parameters of what they could see clearly. Moreover, the company-centered and employee-centered approaches that are typical organizational characteristics of Japanese business have created a structure that seeks only stark solutions for the company and its segments. Such a decision-making structure—by not keeping an eye on the market—may well have allowed for excesses in diversification, globalization, and investment strategies. If that is true, it is no wonder that they failed.

How did all this come about? When you delve into the causes, you find a structural defect that permitted managers—who are not subject to outside supervision by shareholders, auditors, or anyone else—to make stark moves and get away with them. With this decision-making structure as a backdrop, the decisions made gave priority to in-house reasoning. In time, Japanese corporations expanded in size and spent huge amounts of money. Occasional failures did not set off any alarms. Today, of course, everyone realizes that massive blunders were made, and the risks that were taken are evident for all to see.

Admittedly, this observation may be overly critical. If, however, this view is even partially correct, then the mechanism that caused the situation has to be changed, and greater caution must be taken when making investments.

When a market matures, three major responses are normally in order. The first is a revision of the management agenda. The consequences of expanded size and profligate investments will be resolved in time. But if we believe such resolution will take a long time to achieve, we should begin soon. It is imperative that decisive action be taken to correct the imbalances caused by excessive R&D personnel, excessive sales costs, and production overcapacity.

The second is a revision of management objectives. If the expansion of the scale of operations is the goal, it can induce additional, wasteful investment. Failure will succeed failure, and no matter how often you replace managers you may never reach your goal, and friction within your organization is sure to proliferate. In short, you will have to change your business objectives, moving away from size expansion or further growth to more tightly controlled management that emphasizes sound efficiency, profitability, and ROI (return on investment).

Last, you would do well to change the rules and standards of decision making. When you have low-profit, noncompetitive products and high-profit, highly competitive products, you can do better than just taking to task the division making the low-profit products. Instead of exhorting them to work harder, you might decide to withdraw from such problematic business areas and put your resources to work in areas where better results can be expected. You will be praised for your decisiveness.

These actions on decision-making standards, business objectives, and management problem solving must be carried out hand in hand with one another. In this sense, the traditional decision-making system, process, and content must be changed from the inside out. During the bubble, some managers did have an inkling of what was coming, but they kept at it, went just a bit further, and eventually failed. Today, we are wrestling with the consequences of those failures.

POLICY AT A TURNING POINT

Management structure is changing, and with it the business environment and structure. The important thing now is to get managers to wean themselves from the old ways. They must transform themselves. Unfortunately, they don't seem to be sufficiently sensitive to the need to do that. Nothing will happen until they realize that need and muster the will to answer questions like: "What sort of new structure should be created?" and "What should our basic policy be in the future?"

Already at issue is what is to be done about the control function over managers. As time passes, the financial structure cannot help but change under the influence of internationalization. Foreign investors come to Japan when they please, and they will continue to clamor for improvements of the control function over management for a variety of different reasons. For example, they already suspect that insider trading goes on in Japan. It behooves us to clarify a set of standards that are understood internationally and to proceed with deregulation to achieve our intended purposes.

The control of management is perhaps the most pressing and difficult problem we face. Unless the system of cross-ownership of shares among Japanese companies is changed, the power of shareholders will remain weak. We suspect, however, that the situation will not alter until a true mobility of capital brings to Japan enough foreign shareholders who will cry "this is wrong!" Today, some of the shares held under this system are being sold in the market to pay for the mistakes of overinvestment. We are anxious to see what the outcome of such action will be. In the end, it will be necessary to create a system where the wishes of the shareholders—acting as a control—are reflected in the actions of management.

As pointed out in the earlier discussion on diversification, the steel industry invested in semiconductors when the industry had reached maturity and had no further prospects for growth in steel. The jury is still out on whether their semiconductor foray will be a success or a failure. For employees, however, this diversification has the definite merit of securing their positions, and that is why many companies are intent on diversifying come hell or high water. It is being done for the sake of smooth sailing on the personnel management front. We fear, however, that failure is almost preordained when investment is carried out in this manner.

Before a decision is made to diversify, any and all shareholders must be allowed to express disapproval. At Cemedyne, for example, the owner-shareholders sued the managers for their failure in a U.S. investment. Shareholders may be perfectly happy to curtail the company's growth as long as profitability remains high.

In Japan, managers just go ahead and diversify without regard to profitability, and the employees follow dutifully along. In Japan, unlike the U.S., managers and employees appear to have shared interests. In the future, however, it is doubtful whether employees will always follow where their managers lead. Managers who want to dabble in many things are likely to cause unrest. We may even begin to see employees filing motions of non-confidence. Things of this nature are already happening. At Isetan, the employees invoked their veto power over investments overseas, hoping to counter a share buyout.

In like fashion, the future may see more employees in revolt against management decisions. Of course, the managers may still proceed with their plans for diversification or overseas investment, believing that what they are doing is good for the employees. When they do this, however, they are not likely to have the interests of shareholders uppermost in their minds. That they would be able to proceed in the face of employee opposition indicates clearly that the ownership structure of Japanese corporations is out of whack.

Used continuously since around 1961, the cross-ownership of shares is a Japanese process of building a breakwater against the inflow of foreign capital. As mentioned above, this mentality is not likely to change soon. Managers gain confidence in one another under this cross-ownership scheme, and quite naturally little in the way of a control function can be expected in this situation. The managers are intimate associates—including on the social level—to the point where economic organizations in the business community have become like fraternities.

To be sure, the ownership structure of corporate shares differs greatly between Japan and the U.S. and between Japan and Europe. But these walls may one day tumble under the juggernaut of internationalization.

If it should develop that the Japanese management structure is proven more efficient than its counterparts, then our confidence in its methodology will be bolstered accordingly. But today, we find ourselves at a crossroads. And we believe that the Japanese structure is likely to be found lacking. Leaving it unaltered will result in continued poor corporate performance.

For example, financial corporations and business corporations once shared the same interests through their one-on-one relationships. Corporations borrowed from banks to invest in plant and equipment, sold products overseas, and earned profit. Banks received repayment and lent those funds to others. This mutually complementary relationship has continued. But when investment opportunities dried up, corporations turned—unwillingly or not—to stocks and real estate and lost decisively. In the meantime, the yen soared. At the current level, small and medium-size manufacturers will no longer be able to survive in Japan. Instead of buying parts from domestic makers, they may start buying them from abroad. How will that change the industrial structure? Will it be possible to sustain a system where a wide variety of parts are readily available and companies are engaged in competition with one another? Japan's industry and Japan's corporations face a critical turning point.

As a result of the interrelationship between the level of the yen and the level of stock prices, the interests of financial companies and business firms no longer coincide at all times. As long as the entire economy is growing, a company—should it run into problems—can expect its bank to grant it more time, and in this way it will eventually be able to pay back the loan principal as well as the interest. If the bank is confident of such an outcome, it will wait. Currently, however, it seems that no matter how long you wait, real estate and stocks do not increase in value. In this situation, banks have no alternative but to cut firms off cold, as in fact has occurred in a number of recent cases. In short, when no prospect exists for continued growth, the rules change.

But it is not only the behavior of banks that has had an impact in this respect; the effort on the part of individuals to protect themselves has also had a significant influence. Japan has become affluent, and at first glance the nation's disposable income seems high relative to the international standard. But the cost of living is also high, with inflated rates for public utilities and high-priced consumer goods. That's why Japanese consumers are good savers.

It's not that they are stingy and don't want to spend money. It's that they are concerned about their old age and want to provide for it and therefore don't spend money on unnecessary things. Some economists believe the high savings rate in Japan is detrimental to the nation economically. They should be aware that Japanese people save as insurance against their old age, for the purpose of self-protection. We believe that if they trusted the government, the Japanese people would gladly spend more.

There were times in the past when, if you worked hard, you were sure to become better off and could eventually afford things like a refrigerator or a new television set. Today, as the yen continues its upswing, there is uncertainty about jobs, and the price differentials between domestic and foreign markets are not expected to shrink anytime soon. Unfortunately, more and more people say that their jobs are not fulfilling and that they do not expect their lifestyles to improve.

PART III

What Changes Are Needed?

Chapter 7

Japanese Management
—What Was It All About?

The purpose of this book is neither to praise Japanese management nor to uphold the status quo. Rather, our intention is to take a hard look at the current state of Japanese corporate management and explore ways to open up a path to its improvement. Therefore, we are not laboring under any premise that holds that Japanese corporations have a "Japanese" way of functioning and that those characteristic features ought to be maintained.

Lately, the management of Japanese corporations has changed considerably. Many companies are in distress and performing poorly due to the burden of bureaucratization and imprudent, excessive investments and reckless financial management by elitist executives. As a result, so-called restructuring and the practice of *kata-tataki* (the "tap on the shoulder" that tells someone he is no longer needed) are being resorted to as means of getting companies out of dire straits. Is it not time that we thought long and hard about just what the essence of business management is? To address this question, we will look once again at what Japanese management has traditionally been all about and at what it should be in the future.

THE CHARACTERISTICS OF JAPANESE MANAGEMENT

The phrase "Japanese management" immediately calls to mind the so-called three "treasures" of Japanese management: lifetime employment, a seniority wage system, and enterprise unions. But we have long entertained doubts as to whether those are really the essence of Japanese management. If one argues that Japanese-style management has been the motor that has driven the nation's economy to the level it currently enjoys, then it is clear that the cause of that success is not restricted to the three treasures. We could enumerate several other causes, including (1) employees who consider themselves entrepreneurs; (2) investment done from a long-term perspective; (3) investment done with an eye on the world market; (4) constant effort toward improvement; (5) valuing the production floor; (6) technology-oriented strategies typified by the phrase "a nation driven by advanced technology"; (7) a company-centered approach; and (8) an employee-centered approach.

Each of those items can be said to express certain features of Japanese management. In a nutshell, the essence of Japanese management may be summarized into the following few points.

The Company-Centered Approach and the Employee-Centered Approach

We have a theory that sees the eight factors enumerated above as being interrelated and forming a structure. This is illustrated in figure 7-1.

While it is perhaps true that the company-centered approach is the basis for the seniority wage system, lifetime employment, and enterprise unions, we can also place the employee-centered approach alongside it.

A mosaic of welfare benefits, including company-owned housing, recreational facilities, lifelong in-house training programs, and even chauffeured limousines for executives, have traditionally been basic components of Japanese management. The employee-centered approach and the company-centered approach were superimposed on one another to produce a synergistic effect whereby employees worked for the company and the company looked after the employees. This mechanism was one of the bases of Japanese management.

At this point, we would like to look at the upgrade that Matsushita Electric carried out at its Okayama factory for video recorders. At the time, video recorders were widely sold in the U.S., Europe, and the Middle East, but the market—which catered

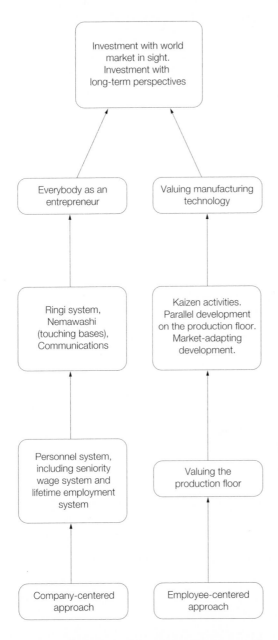

Fig. 7-1. Structure of Japanese Management

to high-income consumers—had run up against a wall. After the upgrade, the Okayama factory had a manually operated assembly line on one side and a new, almost fully automated line on the other. The demand from high-income citizens of Saudi Arabia and other Mideast countries had been satisfied for the time being, and growth in the market had dried up as a result. The factory had already been upgraded, but with few new products needed it was not economical to start production in the new section. In a case like this, the normal course of action would be to fire the part-time workers on the manual line and just run the fully automated side. There is no question that such a strategy would lead to greater efficiency and cost reductions. Matsushita, however, chose to maintain the old line and not start up the new one. Subsequently, when a popular new video recorder came out and spurred market growth, the company used the employees it had retained to triple, or even quadruple, production in one fell swoop.

Matsushita is known for dam-type management, a strategy characterized by thoroughgoing preparations for periods of growth and jumping right in when the right time comes. The plant that retained the part-timers produced splendid results in the end. Let us leave aside whether or not the firm's action is an example of the employee-centered approach, or whether it was based on a medium-term plan, or even whether it illustrates that Matsushita is possessed of an enhanced sense of entrepreneurship and superior insight. Be that as it may, there is no question that Matsushita's move appeared nonsensical at first sight.

Let us cite another case involving Matsushita. Because of the soaring yen after the Plaza Accord of 1985, Matsushita Electronics Parts Co. was on the verge of bankruptcy. In response, managers were willing to try anything that would help keep the employees on the job, and the company began producing printers and floppy disk drives, ignoring the short-term profitability of the investment. Under the prevailing climate of the strong yen, the pressure was on to move the manufacturing of most of Matsushita's products overseas. What was the firm to do? A sagacious staffer might well have studied the possibility of transferring employees to other jobs or plants, thereby avoiding more drastic measures. Matsushita decided that all employees, including engineers, would be retained and that the firm would embark on new business ventures. As a result, it reduced by 50 percent the price of the computer terminals it produced under an OEM arrangement. Undoubtedly, this action indirectly contributed to supporting Japan's competitive position in today's terminal market.

It is, of course, possible to consider Matsushita's action in terms of labor relations. It is clear that Matsushita's determination to preserve jobs above all else energized its employees and led to better results than anyone expected. We don't know if that esprit de corps is still alive at today's Matsushita, but this sort of response is a characteristic feature of Japanese management. It seems that these actions were possible when the company-centered and employee-centered approaches came together, joined perhaps by the mentality of valuing the production floor.

Because of this philosophy, the employees acted with the company uppermost in their minds and had no desire to form a union. The employees came up with suggestions for improving operations, and they didn't mind working at night, if that was required. Designers and development people worked on weekends and stayed overnight at the company when the need arose. Such conduct can be said to be the quintessence of Japanese management. We may be waxing somewhat sentimental here, but there is no question that when a company takes care of its employees it galvanizes those employees and sustains itself. Unfortunately, we find too few of these laudable anecdotes in labor relations today. It is perhaps because the Japanese have become too affluent, or maybe the reason is there just aren't very many projects that reward such heroic efforts with satisfying results.

Heretofore, Japanese industry has kept pace with the best in the world; it knew when a firm in the U.S. achieved lower production costs, or when such and such a product hit the market. Everybody in Japan was confidently focused in one direction and took appropriate action where it was needed. Perhaps because of the small differential in pay between managers and employees, everyone on the production floor was excited by their jobs. As a result, an unstinting challenge to improve was always in place, and the actions that Japanese firms took on the world market—which was viewed as one market—bore much fruit.

In the case of the Japanese home appliance industry—which came to dominate the world—one could argue that the intense competitive conditions in Japan did not allow all firms the luxury of only doing business in Japan. It necessitated their entry into the world market.

Strategies of Competition and Investment

The mosaic of factors revolving around the company-centered and employee-centered approaches as discussed above represents one group of factors that helped underpin Japanese management. The other group of factors revolves around other, relatively functional aspects of Japanese management.

Japan's precision equipment, from cameras to copying machines; heavy industry, from steel to shipbuilding; and consumer durables, from home appliances to automobiles—all of these achieved a dominant presence in the world. How was Japan able to dominate the world market in these industries, albeit only for a short while? On reflection, it seems strange that it ever happened.

It does not seem to follow that in each of the above industries Japanese firms were able to stay focused on the world market and their competition at all times. But in each of the respective industries there were always some manufacturers in America and Europe that could be looked up to as models, firms that stood at the summit of the industry. Japanese companies were able to make decisive investments that emulated the actions of those advanced companies. They could invest in plant and equipment in a decisive manner because the market expanded to the extent that they were able to best the competition in cost and quality. Their ability to make such long-term investments derived from the financial characteristics of the Japanese economy. It was also facilitated by the support and leadership of the Japanese government, which promulgated the Law on Technology and Capital and guaranteed the payment of fees for foreign technology imported by Japanese firms. Thus, through a combination of the government, the financial structure, and corporate investments Japan's industry strengthened its international competitive position. It is the inter-action of the eight elements listed previously that made it all possible.

The employee-centered and company-centered approaches, which represent the organizational side of Japanese management; and long-term investment, the nation's financial system, and the interaction of government and industry, which represent the func-tional side of it—these two groups of factors comprise the elements that have traditionally supported Japanese management. If we were to broadly categorize them, it could be said that one group comprises a set of special characteristics pertaining to cor-porate behavior, including organization, personnel, and management, and the other comprises the working-level invest-ment activities and investment strategies that support the first group. For example, when steel companies were outdoing one another in building blast furnaces, they anticipated that the mar-ket would expand, and they incurred inordinate risks, as is clear in retrospect. The timing of the aluminum and chemical industries was bad in terms of the maturity of the international market and the changes in their respective environments, and as a result they did not do as well as the steelmaking firms. But for a long time they were busy putting up plants in the Kashima and Setouchi industrial belts. We submit that these are the things that support today's Japanese economy and characterize Japanese management.

Japanese Management Brought Forth by Environmental Factors
By what process, and when, did Japanese management come to be? It is, to be sure, a controversial subject. There is, first of all, a question as to what is meant by the word Japanese in this phrase. Is the management style rooted in the culture of the Japanese peo-ple, or did the term simply arise because specific economic conditions in Japan justified its use? Some contend that when a cross section of economic progress at a particular point in time showed that American and European firms had already matured while Japanese firms were still growing, it enabled Japanese com-panies to adopt behavior that was different from the foreign firms.

It is true that there are certain attributes that are characteristic of Japanese management. But it is difficult to pinpoint how these attributes came to the fore. For instance, in the area of personnel management lifetime employment also exists in the U.S. and Europe. In fact, a good many workers at Philips in Europe have parents and grandparents working there as well. And they love their company. Often, when we cite what are supposedly the unique characteristics of Japanese management, we hear responses like "No, you'll find them elsewhere too," or "It used to be like that." It is perhaps too great a stretch to look at today's cross section and describe it as an example of Japanese management.

As a matter of fact, Japanese scholars of business administration and corporate management only became aware of the existence of Japanese management in 1958. *The Japanese Factor—Aspects of Its Social Organization*, by Dr. J.C. Abegglen, was published in that year. It pointed out that the principal feature of Japanese management is lifetime employment. Everybody accepted the conclusion and resolved to uphold lifetime employment as the basis of Japanese management. That's basically how things went.

Strictly speaking, it is questionable whether the lifetime employment system described by Dr. Abegglen really existed in Japan. It is said that about the time of the First World War, the textile, machinery, and shipbuilding industries had to train or raid from other firms skilled workers, and the companies in those industries developed a type of all-expenses-paid employment practice to retain skilled workers or train them in-house. Some argue, however, that these things really happened after the Second World War.

As a matter of fact, there is a great difference between labor relations before and after the Second World War. Before the war, relations were built over top of the feudal system of social ranking and had a distinct hierarchical structure, one that is unimaginable today. After the war, of course, everybody was hungry. Local communities—even close-knit communities of kinship—were in turmoil. Indeed, the only "community" one could turn to was one's company. Soldiers back from the battlefield went for help to the companies they had worked for before hostilities broke out. They did so because they had nowhere else to turn. The companies and the plants receiving them housed them and looked after their every need. That apparently was the genesis of the practice of generous welfare benefits given to employees. Wages were at subsistence level; they were not a reflection of an individual's skill. It was a time when no employer could afford to pay more than the minimum required to live on.

Afterwards, during the time of the Dodge deflation and the recession following the Korean conflict, people were laid off, and most companies fell into dispute with the unions who opposed the layoffs. Executives who handled labor relations during those tumultuous times and survived eventually made their way to the top of corporations by the mid-1960s. It was immediately after the disputes over layoffs that Dr. Abegglen met with Japanese managers, and they told him emphatically that it was their duty to protect the workers and their families. Dr. Abegglen must have been impressed with such claims. In fact, those managers who went through the layoff struggles were determined that it would not happen again. We believe that they embraced the concept of lifetime employment at this time, concluding that it should be maintained.

In the beginning there was no such thing as Japanese management. It probably developed gradually to conform with changes in the business environment. In this sense, there is nothing absolute about Japanese management; it is a product of the business environment changing over time.

Japan's Cultural Climate and Japanese Management

Although it is clear that Japanese management has been fostered with the nation's economy as an influential backdrop, we cannot assert that it is totally unrelated to Japanese culture. Since it is believed that a very severe feudal system of social rank was still in place before the war, the post-war democratic changes and people's growing allegiance to democracy must have provided the foundation upon which was built the personnel system, labor relations, and the "valuing the production floor" mentality that are now characteristic of Japanese management. Despite the claim that a constant effort to improve was the essence of Japanese management, we are told that the Zero fighter—considered the ace machine during the early years of the Pacific War—was never improved upon by the war's end.

It is possible that being company centered is related to Japanese culture. If one had to choose between horse-mounted nomads or agricultural settlers, one would choose the latter as being characteristic of the Japanese. The idea of staying put in one location and cultivating the land intensively is bred in the bone, and this concept remains strongly influential at today's corporations, especially among the technical people. In contrast, U.S. firms are more like mounted nomads—when a business fails, the people running it move on to the next one without a second thought. Likewise, employees think nothing of moving on to another job if they are not happy with their present one. These are distinct differences.

In addition, we should point out one particular concept that was fostered under the feudal system of the Tokugawa era and still remains strong among the Japanese today. During that era, Japan had clans and lords that formed communal entities. It was a political system as well as a system to sustain the livelihood of the lords and their subjects. Everyone was strongly committed to safeguarding the system. On could argue that that attitude has, over time, led to the present-day desire on the part of employees to protect their companies for the sake of their own livelihoods.

How much influence have labor laws, the tax system, and various other systems established after the war had on Japanese management? How should we view the existence of small and medium-size companies? It seems that those systems that happen to have functioned effectively in the post-war environment have come to be recognized as characteristic attributes of Japanese management. When one views the history of change that Japanese management has undergone, a new perspective emerges, however. The essence of Japanese management seems to be that when the business environment changes, management changes with it.

The Quintessential Cultural Characteristics of the Japanese

Does it follow that the functional and economic aspects of Japanese management—such as corporate behavior centered on long-term investment and an export-oriented business structure—will change in compliance with contemporaneous demands from society and changes in the market environment? The personnel system is changing under the influence of changes in the labor market caused by slower growth and an aging society. Does that mean then that all attributes of Japanese management are relative in nature and change in response to changes in the business environment?

We believe the answer to that question is no. And if it is true that some of the attributes of Japanese management are indeed rooted in Japanese culture, those characteristics may perhaps be its fundamental elements—things that are not affected by changes in the business environment and do not alter over either the short or long term. Identifying such unchanging elements is an important task; it touches on management philosophy and relates to a fundamental aspect of business management.

One of the fundamental elements is the company-centered approach. We believe that what lies at the base of this is the spiritual tendency of the Japanese people to value their workplace, their company, the group their company belongs to, their industry, and all the organizations around them. This attitude supports those behavioral patterns that are the very essence of what is called the company-centered approach.

Second, Japanese society is characterized by certain types of interpersonal relations and relationships among colleagues. In particular, the relationships between colleagues on the job seem to be different from those in other nations. In terms of family relations and friendships, there seems to be little difference with other nations—friends trust each other as much in Japan as anywhere else. Similarly, parental and filial feelings in the world's nations resemble one another for the most part. There are, of course, certain cultural differences in this respect. The average Japanese may well display a lesser family attachment than certain other peoples. When it comes to family members helping each other, we see much closer ties among the Latin peoples in Europe and among Jews. But when it comes to the workplace, the Japanese are more likely to establish greater ties of trust with their colleagues. Often, interpersonal relations within a Japanese company are as close as those within Japanese families. We refer to this as corporate familialism.

It is a unique characteristic of large Japanese corporations that such familialism extends to personnel and labor practices. Neither the seniority wage system nor lifetime employment are offered by small and medium-size companies. It is often said that these smaller companies, buffeted by severe competition, cannot afford to adopt such an employment system. In point of fact, however, even the employees of a small company are more likely to to stay with the company for a long time, to be happy working for it, and to cherish the company than their counterparts in other countries. This is perhaps due to the influence of Japanese culture.

What we want to point out here is that the Japanese have a different human nexus on the job than Americans or Europeans. It is certainly natural to want to strengthen functional relations on the job to improve the efficiency of the organization, but Japanese always seek to establish, and they presume the presence of, relationships of trust in such a situation. It is characteristic of Japanese to assume a relationship akin to friendship in this functional context. Europeans and Americans seek to make their on-the-job relationships distinct and separate from all others in their lives. While Europeans sometimes seek to bring family relationships into the realm of corporate personnel relations, Americans in general try to leave functional relations separate. Of course, they aim at smooth communication, but they do not consider friendships or bonds of personal trust as a prerequisite for achieving that.

In a nutshell, the U.S. is a multiracial nation with people from a wide variety of ethnic backgrounds with different value systems and distinct lifestyles working together in a complex human environment. We surmise that in Europe—where different social strata are in evidence, strictly speaking—any occupational relation- ship that crosses over into another stratum would remain purely occupational.

The Japanese have been able to maintain their unique concept of labor and labor-management relations as discussed earlier because they see themselves as a homogeneous nation. Since the company is, above all, the place where employees perform their jobs, it is natural that the functional aspect of human relations is given great importance. The Japanese seek to inject an aspect of personal trust into their on-the-job relationships. This is a characteristic unique to the Japanese.

We don't know if that is a good thing or not. Examples of the negative repercussions include employees being coerced into drinking parties after work to cultivate personal relationships that could have been left at the functional level or, in extreme cases, vying against one another to curry favor by sending gifts to the executives of the company.

On the other hand, it encourages employees to pledge greater loyalty to the company, to strive to stay with the firm as long as possible, and to help one another to safeguard jobs and continue in their prescribed work. Perhaps because of the existence of stronger personal bonds, employees want to help one another, being unable to constrain themselves within demarcated functional parameters. In Japan, universities try not to fail students with bad scores. This is perhaps how the system of *amae* (dependence on the generosity or indulgence of others) got started. Doi Takeo writes in *The Concept of Amae* that the relationship between a doctor and a patient is not a functional one, but one in which the patient wants to be indulged. The author is astonished to learn that patients would ask doctors to indulge them, but they do. Japanese culture makes manifest this psychological trait.

This trait sometimes surfaces when Japanese do business with foreigners. In June 1982, the Federal Bureau of Investigation undertook a sting operation while investigating a case of industrial espionage at IBM. The FBI arrested six Japanese working for Hitachi and Mitsubishi Electric. The Japanese employees caught in the sting had worked with American consultants, had drinks with them, and thought they were friends. But the Americans made no bones about betraying them. The Japanese were flummoxed that their trusted "friends" had sold them out.

Wherever the Japanese go, be it to the U.S. or Southeast Asia, they conduct morning exercises, sing company songs, and sponsor events like company track meets. If they don't do that, they stress, whenever possible, that everyone is in the same boat. It is conceivable that such emphasis on togetherness may increase confidence in the Japanese managers. But when managers depend on the indulgence of their employees, they could be let down.

THE TRANSFORMATION OF JAPANESE MANAGEMENT

It is becoming more difficult today to maintain the special features of the Japanese system, such as lifetime employment and seniority-based wages. We believe that a cornerstone of Japanese management is starting to give, but it would be premature to suppose that there will be a transformation to a totally different style of management. Let us now review which of the various features of Japanese management we have discussed can be discarded and which cannot.

Global Operations and Japanese Management
As Japanese businesses make headway in globalization, what has attracted significant attention is how Japanese-style human relations and employment relations have been introduced and maintained at their overseas establishments.

If the Japanese method of human resource management lifts the morale of employees and enhances their loyalty to the company, resulting in increased productivity, it should be introduced at the overseas establishments of Japanese firms. However, reality has been somewhat different. When foreign operations were first established, many firms certainly worked hard to introduce or transplant Japanese management strategies. As time passed, however, they began to realize that it was not that simple a task to achieve, and they started to adopt a variety of different labor relations policies. It appears to us that, for the most part, the U.S. subsidiaries of Japanese companies have studied and taken their cue from American business management; European subsidiaries have taken their lead from the practices of European business management; and Asian subsidiaries have studied the management methods of the particular countries they are situated in, as well as the culture and institutions of those countries, and have, on the basis of such study, severed on-the-job relations from personal relations.

The Japanese Employment System under Criticism
Of the various features of Japanese management, the Japanese employment system in particular is buffeted by the strong waves of environmental change and is being subjected to critical reassessment. When the oil crises pressured firms in the materials industry to restructure, they found it difficult to continue operations in Japan. Many shifted their production bases overseas in search of lower-cost energy. When the aluminum and chemical and synthetic fibers industries shifted production overseas, they were compelled to adjust employment at their domestic operations, giving rise to a plethora of pink slips. The downstream firms in the petrochemicals industry were also placed in a very difficult situation. Similar employment adjustments are going on today in assembly industries affected by the strong yen. What is taking place is the so-called hollowing out of industry.

While restructuring has been going on, younger workers have been able to observe that their seniors are not being given sympathetic treatment, causing them to feel disillusioned about their work and the lives they have built around the company. We are sure that companies did their best to reassign older employees elsewhere or, if they were forced to dismiss them, tried to find new jobs for them. That notwithstanding, the Japanese employment system, built on the foundation of lifetime employment and commanding absolute trust, is now in a precarious state (figure 7-2).

Drastic adjustments in employment have had a profound impact on the progress of internationalization. The oil crises exposed the weak international competitive position of Japan's energy industry and made it impossible for energy firms to continue business in Japan. Even with today's strong yen, they are forced to move operations to Southeast Asian countries like China. In this sense, the globalization of the business environment

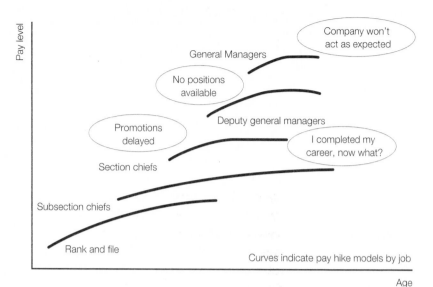

Fig. 7-2. Limits of Japanese Personnel System

can be said to have significantly shaken up the Japanese employment system.

This globalization question should also be viewed from another perspective—that of international adjustments in the labor environment—and not merely from the perspective of a changing business environment. We would point out that at the time of the oil crises this issue was taken up by the Federation of Chemical and Synthetic Fibers Labor Unions, one of Japan's strongest unions. Federation members claimed that when business crosses national boundaries, not only management but unions as well have to cultivate an international perspective. They insisted that international coordination among the labor unions of advanced and developing countries was imperative. At that time, some companies in Taiwan and South Korea, as in the Japan of older days, had 12-hour workdays and pay scales that violated minimum wage laws—all of which added up to a wretched work environment from the standpoint of the unions. Japanese labor leaders were concerned that Japan's materials industry and chemical industry would lose out in competition with developing countries unless these problems were dealt with. They stressed that if Japanese labor unions focused only on improving domestic labor conditions—such as the strict enforcement of an eight-hour workday—without also working for adjustments in international labor practices, Japanese businesses would not survive. And they held seminars and conferences with foreign labor unions to discuss ways to achieve concrete adjustments in labor conditions.

While this sort of question is left unattended, the waves caused by internationalization are lapping at our shores. As business conditions get tougher, we can no longer expect permanent job security.

Job security or the maintenance of lifetime employment is no longer an issue for blue-collar workers alone. As positions for middle-aged and senior employees grow scarce, companies can no longer afford to look after the white-collar elite in perpetuity. In fact, white-collar employees are the ones bearing the brunt of retrenchment efforts.

Many companies find it increasingly difficult to swallow the costs associated with maintaining the in-house unemployed, and they are being put out to pasture. Japan will no longer be able to boast that the heart and soul of Japanese management is the maintenance of employment. When you think of it, it is natural enough that changes in economic conditions have compelled the Japanese system of personnel and labor relations to change. The traditional system can just no longer be maintained.

Those who have been put out to pasture must have been filled with hope and vigor when they joined the company fresh out of school and started their lives as full-fledged citizens. But as time passed, they may have made mistakes, they may have had bad luck, they may have lost out in the competition for promotion, or they may have had tiffs with their bosses and therefore were not looked upon favorably. Clearly, those who could be general managers are not fit for ordinary clerical work. To say that it is only proper that those who are not fit for the position of general manager should not be made general managers and that the company cannot bend over backwards to accommodate them is to admit, it seems to us, that companies lack resourcefulness in dealing with their personnel. We Japanese would do well to acknowledge that our personnel system has regularly fallen victim to this kind of shortcoming.

We know that in addition to the tragedy that has befallen some elite employees many others are in a state of disarray; we cannot help wishing for the arrival of the true elite—ones who can really manage companies in the manner required. Yet the fact is that many companies continue to pursue formality, filling a good portion of their staff positions with graduates from certain universities or with MBAs.

The Strengths of Japanese Management Are Being Lost

A natural consequence of a company's inability to maintain employment is that its employees no longer feel any allegiance to the company-centered approach. Indeed, who should be expected to devote themselves to working for a company when they are subject to dismissal at any time for the sake of the company's profitability, as is the norm under American labor-management practices? Who can blame employees if they are more interested in self-protection and self-improvement?

Will Japanese corporations change and become like American corporations? The authors would answer that query in the negative. There are a number of reasons why we believe this will not happen. One is the fact that in the course of striving to achieve corporate objectives, dividends to shareholders and job security are given different priority by Japanese and American firms. We don't know about the distant future, but in the short term it is impossible to imagine Japanese companies changing so much that they begin to behave like American firms, going so far as to discharge employees to maintain dividends to shareholders. Then again, you never know what actions Japanese managers might take if foreign shareholders increase in number and persist in their demands for a higher payout.

Let us set aside the question of where this will lead us at the end of the day. It is clear that Japanese management is facing a crisis because employees' work ethic and the high morale that is attributable to their allegiance to the company and which constitutes an integral part of Japanese management are about to collapse, along with the company-centered and employee-centered approaches that supported them. Precisely because Japanese management is now changing, we believe we should be asking ourselves this important question: "What are we about to lose?"

One of the strengths of Japanese management has been its emphasis on substance rather than formality. Its representative manifestation is, as mentioned, valuing the production floor. That means that Japanese companies have in place managers who understand the working-level operations. Their attitude is in sharp contrast to the economic bureaucrats, who are not above disregarding the factory floor when they make decisions and blaming the people in the factory for their own lack of competence should failure ensue.

It is said that the Japanese are more likely to respect craftsmen than do foreigners. This tendency is thought to date back beyond the Edo period. It has long been a tradition with the Japanese to respect the blacksmith who makes guns and value the potter who makes ceramics. It may sound paradoxical, but Japan was not steeped in the Confucian culture of Asia, as was the case in China and Korea. Everything about Japan may well have been eclectic. The Japanese may never have taken the whole of Confucianism to heart and therefore they valued crafts in a very practical and functional way. As times changed in the shift from Meiji to Taisho to the present day, the Japanese respect for craftsmanship that has been nurtured throughout the years has come to be conferred on the engineers in plants.

After the war, this mentality led to operational improvements in the factory and to valuing the production floor. Of particular note is the fact that the system of social rank disintegrated. Through extensive education, Japan has embraced democracy as taught in textbooks much more than the Western nations that gave birth to the concept. Because managers had so much confidence in blue-collar workers, when the QC methodology was introduced in Japan no one had second thoughts about making it the job of the people in the field because they were fully capable of doing it. In the United States, where this methodology was developed, QC was the exclusive domain of engineers and managers, whereas in Japan it was assigned to the workers. It is a reflection of Japanese management's respect for their skills and their intelligence.

Because the production floor was so important, white-collar workers descended to the shop floor, had drinks with the workers, and discussed the problems of the company and the work place. In this way, designers heard the views of the people on the production floor before they proceeded with their work. Thus was maintained smooth communication across all job classifications. Unfortunately, this seems to have been lost. But recently it has been reported that, for the purpose of cutting back on the costs of production, firms are again realizing the importance of design work that takes the manufacturing workplace into account. We should reflect on how we let the vital functions of our system deteriorate while we took it for granted. Do we truly understand the strengths of Japanese management? We wonder.

Japanese manufacturers who once considered innovations in manufacturing technology as one of their prime weapons have been awakened anew to the importance of such innovativeness. They are realizing all over again the importance of truly valuing the production floor. This may be evidence that people who can actually design and make things are being given renewed respect, rather than the armchair theories of elite engineers detached from the production floor.

Western Firms Learning Japanese Management

A representative case of valuing the production floor by Japanese corporations is TQC. The representative techniques of scientific management developed in the United States include industrial engineering and quality control. In American and European firms, QC has been seen as a way of exercising control in the production field or as a way of measuring the economic balance. Since QC was introduced in Japan, it has been firmly established as a method of autonomous management in the workplace or as a method of improving activities in a scientific manner.

Japanese automobiles are still given high marks by American consumers for their superior quality because of the minimal trouble they give their owners. Acknowledging this fact, American automakers have dedicated themselves to studying QC all over again. In the process, American automakers have been astonished to find that the Japanese on the shop floor are carrying out improvements in a scientific manner. The difference between QC and TQC is not just the *T*, it is the way in which workers in the field come to grips with the task of improving operations.

There is an episode that we know of involving a Japanese subsidiary of a Western firm that is conducting improvement projects and TQC. The Japanese subsidiary received periodic audits from its American parent. It was pointed out at each audit that the QC activities and their execution were left to the shop floor and that the true objective of QC—which is the auditing function—was not being performed. "QC's purpose is to oversee and check operations in the field; the people who do the work cannot supervise themselves. You have a totally different concept of QC." These were some of the comments heard. Thus, the subsidiary was at odds with the parent company at every turn. On the other hand, Fuji Xerox—a U.S.-Japan joint venture located in Japan—recently received a request from its American partner, Xerox Corp., to re-import *kaizen* (improvement) to the States, which it is now trying to do. It appears that Americans are coming around to the view that since QC results in a bloated organization and increased control costs if set up as a control function, it would be better for all concerned if it was used as a tool for self-management.

There is a vast difference between Japan and the West in the approach to interpersonal relationships and the concept of organizing work. When QC was sown on different cultural soil, it brought forth different fruit. Japan expanded QC so that everyone in the company could be engaged in improvement activities. If we had adopted QC as the disciplinary QC of the West, costs would have gone up, autonomous improvement activities on the factory floor would not have developed, and we would have been beset with other problems.

When we visited the famous 3M (Minnesota Mining and Manufacturing Corp.), a mid-level manager came up to us and said that he had studied Japanese management. On closer inquiry, it developed that he had attended a one-week seminar on TQC. 3M's management is well known for its democratic ways; workers in the field are involved in improvement activities. This gentleman's answer must have been a persuasive one within 3M.

Chapter 8

The Changes Needed

WHICH PART OF JAPANESE MANAGEMENT NEEDS CHANGING?

"An organizational and personnel system characterized by life-time employment and a seniority wage system" and "a company-centered approach"—such descriptions have come to symbolize the principal characteristics of Japanese management. But the relationship between companies and their employees that is represented by these phrases is now under pressure and facing overhaul due to the economic environment of low growth and a rampantly overvalued yen that has resulted from the collapse of the bubble economy. And this is not something only managers feel—it is an awareness shared by all.

Companies that find themselves in dire straits are revising their seniority-based wage schedule—something that has hereto-fore formed the very foundation of Japan's wage system. Reductions in personnel and furtive recommendations for resig-nation directed at middle-aged and senior employees are coming to the fore. Some argue that lifetime employment—that most Japanese of employment practices—has in effect collapsed. This is not to say, however, that there are no companies struggling hard to maintain this practice—many are, believing it to be the heart and soul of Japanese management.

Practically speaking, many companies with operations abroad have already found that the Japanese employment system cannot be applied to their overseas establishments with respect to wages or compensation paid to non-Japanese personnel. Indeed, one of the most important items on the agenda of such firms is finding ways to reconcile an international management style with Japanese employment practices to ensure the sound progress of the company.

In this chapter, we shall take up questions related to personnel organization and discuss how the ways of the old system have run up against a wall and are under pressure to change.

Bloated Organization and Diminished Authority

Nissan Motors recently reviewed its organization because earnings had deteriorated sharply under the enormous impact of the strong yen. The company found that its organization had become bloated beyond imagination and job functions minutely divided beyond necessity. Managers became aware that the strategy that had supposedly melded production technology and design engineering was not in fact functioning as intended. Taking advantage of new information technology, such as CAD and CAM, which aids design work, design professionals were completing their work and sending down finished designs to the plant. Plant personnel would then take these and manufacture the products. Of course, if the designers and production people had gotten together to compare notes they would have been able to reduce costs and secure greater stability in terms of quality. In other words, optimum designs might have been achieved. In fact, they were not. Regrettably, the type of lateral communication across the organizational structure that has traditionally been a strength of Japanese corporations had ceased to function at Nissan. And the cause was the bloated organization. These problems seem, more or less, to afflict large corporations in particular.

In a Japanese plant, it is said that quality is built into the product at the plant. Throughout the production process, each worker checks the quality within the area of his responsibility. The result is a quality product emerging at the end of the line to be delivered to the customer. This has been the preferred method of quality control. But the exercise of this system—which Japanese corporations have prided themselves on—became perfunctory at Nissan as a result of the bloated organization and the excessive number of models offered.

We heard of a similar story at Fujitsu, a computer manufacturer. Fujitsu wanted its sales department to stay close to customers and expanded its sales force for that purpose. But it divided sales areas so minutely by geographical region and by type of business that when the firm formulated a new companywide plan to increase sales it found that, while each salesman in his assigned territory knew exactly what his customers' information needs were and when those customers planned to replace their current equipment, salesmen were unaware of how to achieve additional sales for the firm as a whole. For example, one of the users of computers is the retail industry, which is expanding into ever-broader geographical regions. With the entry of agricultural cooperatives into supermarkets, for example, computer networking is a burgeoning business that looks to increase business tie-ups to achieve greater interchange between regions and take advantage of economies of scale. To build such a network, there is a need for certain information that goes beyond the requirements of individual companies. This information cannot be identified by individual salesmen contacting individual customers. What is needed are salesmen familiar with the progress of information technology who are able to take a broad view of customer needs as well as their relations with their own customers and propose a new information system that cuts across the industry and connects several companies. Also required is an organization and personnel who can make recommendations on the needs of broad-based systems that go beyond the needs of individual firms.

These examples would seem to indicate that the mere enlargement of an organization to keep pace with expanded business will not enable a company to deal effectively with changes to its environment.

A similar case can be made with respect to trading companies. Mitsui & Co. reorganized its headquarters into various product divisions. The aim was to integrate the organization to ensure a more dynamic allocation of business resources. It seems that with the old organization of departments and branches, financial and human resources were limited, and the company had difficulty responding to big projects. Even though a trading company as a whole handles a large volume of business, it contains departments staffed by only 20 or so employees. The basic problem was that the subdivision of the organization had progressed to such an extent that individual departments were powerless to do much of anything.

Diminishing Lateral Communication
Changing subject slightly, we will now take up something that relates to diversification. When we compare the successful examples of diversification in the materials industry with the failures, we find that the successes involved companies that valued their manufacturing technology and carefully screened proposed diversification alternatives to select new business areas that would fully utilize that technology, and they built their diversification projects on the basis of that technology. Mitsubishi Materials, for example, wanted to get into ferrite materials, failed once, and withdrew at an early stage. But it persisted in its desire to enter that business. It tried but failed to break into the market, which is dominated by TDK and Alps Electric, with their magnetic heads, magnetic media, and various other products. The firm then changed course, deciding instead that it would make motors, which also use magnetic materials. Of course, it is tough for a materials maker to take up the business of manufacturing motors, and as expected it took Mitsubishi Materials a long time, scouting engineers and accumulating technology. Today, however, it has made a success of it.

In the materials industry, many companies look to expand into the same product areas at the same time. The engineers of large corporations in the materials industry are proud and confident and are anxious to get into new markets, believing there is nothing they cannot do if they set their minds to it. But because their manufacturing plants lack competence or know-how, firms are forced to come up with answers on the basis of product engineering alone. In fact, they should start by improving their own manufacturing technology and producing their own products. Failing that, they should go back to the design of materials. In addressing a problem that should normally be handled with production technology, they are forced to rely on materials design. This is just one example of the many failures of diversification at materials companies, which lack competence in areas other than their own basic technology.

When viewed from a functional perspective, good communication within companies—said to be another feature of Japanese management—has played a specific role in the melding of manufacturing technology with product engineering and the linking of elemental technologies within firms. It ought to be a universal principle that such functional communication be maintained at all times within an organization. The basic cause for the deterioration of a company's performance may be its bloated size and bureaucratic ways. But if, in addition, effective communication within the organization has also diminished, it is in serious trouble indeed.

The organizational features of American companies and their Japanese subsidiaries are vastly different from those of Japanese concerns. Particularly in American corporations, official roles are so clearly defined that communication that cuts across functional areas or across business divisions is relatively awkward. At a certain precision machinery manufacturer owned by foreign capital, each business division develops certain fundamental technology independently. Because these divisions should be cooperating with one another in this regard the result is depleted efficiency. When marketing has to be coordinated among the various divisions of this company, there are problems, and managers make no bones about reaching decisions that are self-contradictory when viewed from the standpoint of the company as a whole. It is apparent that the firm's managers are not likely to promote internal communication on their own initiative. To improve the situation, formal changes within the organization will be needed.

Some years ago, we visited DEC Corp., a computer maker near Boston, just after it had restructured itself along the lines of a matrix organization. The reason for this change was that the firm's traditional organization did not facilitate the smooth execution of project development. In the old system, the printer department, for example, was unable to conduct discussions on technical coordination and interfacing with the computer department unless it went through the department heads. We were astonished to find this incongruity in America, but we were told that after the switch to the matrix organization people were able to communicate directly with appropriate people in other divisions without having to go through their superiors.

In the sense that lateral communication has worsened, we are afraid that Japanese companies have reached the same point as American companies.

The Reality of the Long-Term Investment Strategy
It has been pointed out that one of the principal characteristics of Japanese management has been to conduct investment from a long-term perspective and that therein lies the great difference between Japanese companies and their Western counterparts. But can we be sure that Japanese companies really forecast the market trends, assessed the competition, and made investment decisions from a long-term perspective? Although it is questionable if investment decisions were backed by justifiable reasons, it is at least true that on the face of it Japanese firms made investments under the assumption that the payback period would be a very long one.

Japanese companies expanded plants and bought equipment before the high-growth period began, and many of those investments were prudent ones. But it is difficult to know whether managers had a clear outlook on the future when they decided to invest. When the steel and automobile industries made large investments in 1955, nobody except those involved in the decisions thought the investments would pay off. Mr. Ichimanda, president of the Bank of Japan, uttered his famous remark concerning the blast furnace program of Kawasaki Steel's Chiba Works: "I'll see to it that the plant site is covered with weeds." Similarly, when Sumitomo Metals, a nonintegrated steel producer, merged with Kokura Steel in Kitakyushu—which had blast furnaces—to establish itself as an integrated producer, it met with ferocious opposition from the Ministry of International Trade and Industry.

In 1955, it was impossible to imagine that Japanese automobiles would ever gain a share in the world market or rival American and European cars. While the engineers who joined automakers at the time were hopeful that Japanese cars would get better, the authors, who were students at that time, did not believe such a scenario would ever come to pass. Today, people involved in automobile projects in Thailand and the Philippines believe they can develop and foster their auto industries to the point where they become competitive players in the international market. We doubted that Japanese automakers would ever make it, in much the same way that many now doubt that these Asian auto projects will succeed. Japanese economists at the time were predicting a depression in the aftermath of overinvestment and overproduction. There are even indications that Japanese government officials wanted to inhibit such investment. From 1961 to 1965, politicians on three occasions submitted to the Diet A Temporary Measure to Promote Designated Industry, a bill designed to reduce the number of companies. Their efforts are fictionalized in the book by Shiroyama Saburo entitled *The Bureaucrats in the Summer*.

Honda's desire to produce passenger cars precipitated an altercation between Honda Soichiro and Sahashi Shigeru of MITI. At that time, MITI officials wanted to promote mergers of existing automobile companies in order to maintain the industry's international competitive position. MITI's strategy was not realized, but in the end Japan's auto industry did become very competitive internationally. Because of severe competition, the steel and automobile industries have been successful to this point in time in terms of their international competitive position.

This long-term investment strategy emerged with renewed vigor during the bubble. The steel industry continued to operate blast furnaces that had been scheduled for shut down, and the automobile industry built a number of new plants in Kyushu and Tohoku. Ethylene producers defiantly made massive capital investments when it was doubtful that investment in plants in Japan was really needed to secure a base for the industry. The results require no explanation. To pay the price of the ensuing overcapacity and surplus manpower, the industry has had to shut down old plants, transfer employees, and submit to their unions' plans to reduce payrolls. These backward-looking measures continue today. One company took immediate steps to redesign its plant, in line with its reduced scale of operations, while another had to build a parts plant of its own to take up the slack resulting from its supplier's refusal to increase capacity. That company is now suffering due to the low production capacity of its parts plant.

Japanese Management Living On in Asian Countries

Many express the view that Japan must build its future on technology. To this point, Japanese companies have produced products for export on the strength of technology. While Japan has not produced the geniuses who in Western companies are put on a pedestal as champions, there are many engineers who deserve medals for the hard work they have done to make new products possible. After the war, Shiraishi Yuma of Japan Victor became interested in image transmission and dedicated himself to developing a recording formula. When RCA (now part of GE) announced the development of the video recorder, it decided at once that the device was for commercial use and did not lend itself to popular use by consumers. Mr. Shiraishi continued to devote himself to the development of videotape recorders for home use and finally came up with a method called heliscan, which records images diagonally on the tape. Without this technology, it would have been impossible to record inexpensively images containing a large amount of information. This example shows how the commonly held view that Japanese corporations are only good at copying and commercializing Western inventions is wrong. The truth is that an obscure technology such as heliscan was developed by the Japanese and has helped open up a large market.

Something similar happened in the shipbuilding industry. Japan once dominated the world in shipbuilding but is today rivaled by South Korea for the top position. The reasons why Japanese shipbuilding swayed the world are very clear. One is its technical development. With research aid from the Japan Association of Shipbuilders, development was focused on designing the most efficient hull possible. One result of this was the commercialization of the bulbous bow, a rounded bow designed to reduce the effects of wave resistance. More recently, counter-rotating propellers have also been commercialized. The first invention embodies technology that originated with researchers in the U.S. and Europe in the nineteenth and early twentieth centuries and was then transformed and applied for mass production, while the second involves the development of new technology in the production of gears and bearings.

Japan's steel industry is in no position to be laid-back about competition from South Korea and other steel-producing nations. If the thin-slab and strip-casting technologies now under development are commercialized on a mass-production basis, Japan's steel industry may regain its dominant position. Of the steelmaking technologies developed in the past, a good many were turned into commercial, mass-production technologies by Japanese firms that took them up while they were still at the "ideas" stage and worked to develop them further. And while it is true that those ideas may have resulted from fundamental research done in the U.S. or Europe and patented there, it is also the case that if they had been left simply as ideas they would never have been put to any practical industrial use. It was Japanese production technology that translated them into practical applications. The Japanese should be rightly proud of the manufacturing technology they have developed on their own and which is just as valuable as the product engineering of the West.

Japan has scores of academic societies, and corporate engineers are always glad to present papers there outlining the latest developments. And those who hear the new ideas presented at these societies become inspired and strive to emulate them and improve upon them through new approaches. It is in this way that engineers have learned from one another; inspired one another; polished their skills in Japan's traditional cultural climate, which cherishes manufacturing; and helped build the industrial base of today's Japan. It is imperative that this tradition be upheld.

A new product is born only when there is a new technology to support it. An idea on its own does not make a new product. It has to be worked on by product engineering and manufacturing technology before it becomes a marketable item. A new product thus goes through many processes before it is launched. It is a widely held view that Japanese manufacturers are only good at copying, and—with the support of superior labor and financing—they rush into mass production in order to dominate world markets. Nothing could be more wide of the mark. This is not to say that some companies do not behave in this manner. And we do not deny that after the war there was a time when Japanese firms disassembled products—American products in particular—in the course of performing maintenance and gradually learned to manufacture the same products and that that strategy built the basis for today's industrial position. But that alone would not have been enough to create the current Japanese economy.

In addition to developing our own technology, we Japanese have carried out active investment programs with an eye on the world market. It is thanks to such efforts that we have acquired our competitive position.

Today, South Korean manufacturers are expanding their businesses and deploying internationally in the same way that Japanese manufacturers did in the past, and they are making a success of it. It seems to us that this is one way for developing countries to catch up with advanced ones. South Korea and Taiwan are no doubt aware of what Japan did in the mid-1960s, and they have learned from it. They ought to be applauded for the daring entrepreneurial spirit embodied in the large-scale investments they have made in their effort to crack the world market.

A plastics manufacturer in Taiwan introduced the world's most modern manufacturing equipment and came charging into the market, fully intent on exploiting the company's economies of scale. It is now the world's top producer of vinyl chloride. A South Korean competitor discussing this development at a meeting some 10 years ago was heard to remark: "That's the way to chase out Japanese business." Addressing Japan's success, Indonesian Prime Minister Mahathir once declared: "Japan's presence is a great encouragement to us." Japan's emulation of them shows just how strong American and European companies were in competitive position and command of technology and markets. We think it is true that Japan's success—achieved without the benefit of natural resources—has inspired the Asian NIEs and ASEAN countries.

However, these countries do not employ the same methods. Taiwan has many small businesses, and the nation's computer industry is bursting with vitality. South Korea is coming to grips with the advancement of its industry and is utilizing the power of *zaibatsu*. In their own way—not in the Japanese way—these countries have acquired advanced technology, analyzed competitive factors, and engaged in competition.

To be sure, this spirit now seems to be widely ingrained in the minds of Asians. Pohang Steel in South Korea is a typical example of success. The diversification efforts by the South Korean *zaibatsu* have been similar to those of Japanese corporate groups during the mid-1950s. During that period, the Japanese had a great deal of anxiety about the future of their industry. This apprehension, of course, turned out to be misplaced. But in the case of the South Koreans, we wonder if they might not be overdoing it, might not in fact be overproducing. So far, however, problems seem to have been resolved as they have emerged. In November 1992, antidumping suits were filed against South Korean semiconductor firms, and they were forced to discontinue export shipments to the U.S. That did not stop these firms from manufacturing them, however, and they were not hurt by the excessive inventory, as the world's supply and demand balance worked in their favor and helped to completely exhaust the inventory.

It seems clear that the strategies of capital investment undertaken by Japanese corporations after the war—whose design was at times conscious, at times unconscious, and which sometimes even seemed reckless—are now consciously and steadfastly being emulated by South Korea, Taiwan, and the Asian NIEs. They are alive with entrepreneurship and full of the spirit of challenge. We have not seen comparable strategies or enterprising initiatives being pursued on the part of Japanese managers since the collapse of the bubble.

The Company-Centered Approach Doesn't Work

Recently, we had the chance to talk to mid-level employees at a number of companies. Here are some of the things they told us: "Our seniors did so much for the company, but it's not repaying them. The company is firing them so casually. Is that right? We thought we'd have a good life if we made it to general manager, but our department head isn't much different from us. With this kind of pay, we wouldn't be able to afford a home even if we worked until retirement." It makes you wonder what has happened to the idea of loyalty to the company that Japanese workers are famed for.

It would be understandable if certain individuals in the corporate hierarchy who had lost out on promotion were distrustful of the company. But the reality now seems to be that many employees no longer have a guarantee that if they work hard they will be better off and taken care of by the company. As a result of this lost guarantee, things that were unimaginable in the past are now happening. We are concerned that the relationship between the company and its employees is growing more distant. We are apprehensive about the developing chasm in the company-centered and employee-centered philosophies—a rift that seems to be widening all the time.

Until the 1980s, Japanese companies, including small and medium-size ones, had only one day off a week. Everyone came to work on Saturdays. Against this backdrop, a typical salaried employee's life revolved around his company. Many people took it for granted that the company would take care of everything —gifts for newlyweds, help during time of illness, and life after retirement. We know of one man working as an assistant superintendent at the Monsanto Chemicals plant in Yokkaichi in 1965 or thereabouts who said that since joining the company he had been absent from work only four or five days. The only vacation he had ever taken was for his honeymoon. We thought that his being off for four or five days meant that he had missed that many workdays. On further inquiry, however, we learned that since joining the company he had reported to work every day, including Sundays and holidays, except for those four or five days.

In the past, there were many people like him. Today, however, anybody so involved in his company's affairs as to ignore his personal life would be condemned for a lack of virtue. We know of another man—an executive at a pharmaceutical company—who was much the same. When he got up in the morning on Saturdays and Sundays, he would go out for a walk and end up at his office. Nowadays, however, firms are closed two days a week. And because they now work less, people should be able to have a more detached view of the company they work for.

Nure-ochiba (wet fallen leaves) is a phrase that refers to a retired person who can't do anything other than the work he did all his life and therefore sits around clinging to his wife like a wet leaf stuck to a shoe. There are a good number of people who are at a loss as to what to do. Stopping by a coffee shop in the Marunouchi district around 11 a.m., we often see old men who look like retirees sitting alone at tables, sipping tea, and reading the newspaper. Some retirees miss their company so much they seem to unwittingly end up close to their old workplace. We feel sorry for such individuals, and we are tempted to find fault with the company for letting it happen. It makes us sad. If this is the life of the erstwhile warriors of Japanese corporations, it may be inevitable that the company-centered approach will crumble.

A Personnel System That Values Generalists and Denigrates Professionalism

To be sure, up until about the mid-1970s it was considered a virtue in Japan—to one degree or another, depending on the individual—to sacrifice individuality for the sake of the company. Since then, the social environment and the living environment have improved, work hours have been reduced, and people are now able to spend some time pursuing personal interests. We should, as result, be living more leisurely lives, such as Europeans enjoy, spending weekends with family. But we are not doing this. Perhaps Japanese society moves along at too fast a clip, and workers and salaried employees are incapable of making a switch in their traditional practices. The rise in the value of the yen elevated the living standard of the Japanese to one of affluence if viewed in terms of international statistics. In fact, the cost to the family budget for children's education has soared—thanks to money spent on cram schools to help children get through the "examination hell" imposed by an educational system devoid of substance. Food is very expensive, rents are high, and if you want to take a trip your hotel bill will be exorbitant. Moreover, we Japanese cannot spend what little we have saved because we are uneasy over our pension benefits, which do not include cost-of-living adjustments, and we don't trust the present government to do anything about it.

After employees have devoted themselves to a company, what does the company do for them? The answer to this question is something we are quite interested in. At the same time, we also know that very few employees are ready to answer the following question honestly: With what degree of competence do you as an individual and as an employee contribute to the company?

People need to ask themselves this question. Some respond by saying the important thing is not that they may lack specific professional skills but that they work hard for the sake of the company. Only a few respond in specific terms: "I have superb financial skills." Only I can deal with such and such a problem. The contribution I have made to the company cannot be disputed by anyone. I developed this part of this technology. And therein lies the problem. What type of employees should firms be producing? The answer requires that we take a hard look at the philosophy of labor.

The majority of the elite staff at firms have been trained as generalists, not specialists, under the Japanese system. Such training means they are subjected to frequent job rotations, and in the process they often lose whatever degree of specialty they may have acquired. Typical cases of lost specialty can be found in trading companies, which are staffed by college graduates. Many know the sorrow of executives—once members of the elite, graduates of XYZ university—who now receive the pay of a general manager but do not work as one. Almost every company added to its roster of college graduates and managerial positions during the bubble. Now, they have to take care of them through restructuring and re-engineering. It leads one to wonder just how much Japanese companies value people.

If they truly valued people, firms would train them when they are young so that they develop into useful individuals with a specific specialty; ask them in what capacity they want to contribute to the company and give them greater flexibility in selecting a profession and then nurture them accordingly; and help them enhance their professional capabilities so that they can move seamlessly throughout the field. In this sense, firms should focus more on career development programs and personnel development programs that give participants an opportunity to choose. Companies should move away from the agenda of traditional personnel management—which places all decisions in the hands of the company and assigns work at its discretion—and toward a system of personnel management that cultivates specialty in employees. People will be happier if they can work at their chosen specialty, and they will cherish such work.

The notion of specialty discussed here includes the professional business administrator. It is important to value functional specialties, such as those involved in legal affairs, wage administration, marketing, and production technology. But people in those areas must be sure to give consideration to other business management skills and try to foster those. It seems to us that decisions made by managers lacking in professional skills brought about the overinvestment of the bubble period.

Managers whose task is the stewardship of a company must possess business management skills. Firms must ponder what is meant by such skills and how managers can best acquire them. But skills alone may not be sufficient; there are certain attitudes and postures appropriate for managers. Heretofore, the personnel system in Japan has not recognized any difference in the managerial layers of an organization and has made job assignments in accordance with this lack of recognition. We believe the time is over for giving ostensibly equal treatment to all employees, developing everyone as a generalist and requiring nobody to develop professional abilities in specific fields.

JAPANESE CORPORATIONS REQUIRE A CHANGE IN STRATEGY

Crumbling Invisible Assets

The international competitive position of Japanese corporations is recognized as being very strong. Among the basic reasons for this strength are two networks: a materials network, which provides required parts and materials promptly, and a technology network, which combines necessary technologies quickly.

To be sure, the oil crises and the appreciation of the yen after the Plaza Accord brought the Japanese economy face to face with changes to the business environment greater than any it had ever seen. At each such critical juncture, the Japanese economy was compelled toward globalization, and corporate structures underwent considerable change. On each occasion, the overseas business activities of Japanese corporations were invigorated. In the aluminum industry, Japanese engineers went to Asahan, Indonesia, and provided technical assistance ranging from smelting to ingot production, and products from there are now imported into Japan—a real change in the pattern of overseas production. Macroeconomic changes in the business environment have made it impossible for many industries to sustain domestic operations. The oil crises caused the upstream operations of the materials industry to move overseas, while the period of the strong yen after 1985 compelled the assembly industry to shift operations abroad—a move that continues today.

Compared with American and European firms—which see off-shore operations as a convenient means of reducing costs—Japan's domestic industry has maintained its characteristic ability to produce a broad range of products. Japan has an infrastructure that provides products tailored to all requested specifications, ranging from production materials to parts to equipment. If we amateurs go to Akihabara, we can buy all the necessary parts to assemble a TV set—if we don't mind the prices of such merchandise. Few other countries offer such convenience.

Not only is it easy to obtain materials and parts in Japan, the country also has an industrial infrastructure that enables it to develop new technology quickly and come out with new products to meet the changing needs of the market. Japan also has a vast number of academic societies, and researchers take part in their activities and exchange information with other colleagues. Japan has university networks that are separate from the world of business. The alumni of the aeronautical engineering faculty of Tokyo University continue to stay in touch with one another, sometimes 20 years after graduation. Even after they retire from business or government service, they work together or exchange information with their old school chums. This is the kind of environment Japan has nurtured.

One of the strengths of Japan's economy is the presence of an environment that is geared toward the development of new products. While its benefits may not be apparent on a day-to-day basis, this environment—along with the factors discussed above—goes a long way to supporting the competitive position of Japanese firms. In short, the strong infrastructure for supplying parts and materials and an environment that facilitates the development of key technologies work together to form the backbone of the Japanese economy. It is evident that Japan's environment for product development is superior to that of other advanced countries, and it is essential that we examine how this has come about and what is likely to happen to this environment in the future. But whatever that future may be, it is clear that the current situation in Japan allows for the domestic procurement of all the elements—from materials to parts—needed to make any product, precipitates the skillful development of technology, and brings new products to market smoothly and quickly.

In Japan today, under the impact of the supercharged yen small and medium-size companies are finding it extremely difficult to sustain their production of specialized components. We are afraid that, due to the effects of the yen, the environment that has long supported the development of new products and which represents the real strength of Japan's economy will eventually disappear. We are concerned that by the time we realize it is gone, it will be too late; it will be impossible to go back. During a discussion we were involved in at an American think tank about the revival of the American steel industry, a representative of the Japanese steel industry remarked: "The U.S. no longer has a steel-making equipment manufacturer." We remember how an American researcher who was present sighed when he heard that. We only hope that Japan never finds itself having to reflect on lost ground like that.

As Japan progresses along the path of internationalization, it would do well to keep in mind the origins of the nation's competitive strength. Japanese automakers, for example, began production in Europe to avoid the political restrictions of countries to which they were exporting cars. They later began to buy components from local manufacturers, such as Bosch, to meet the local-content requirements of the host countries. The volume of production at Japanese transplants is smaller than that at long-standing local producers, such as Volkswagen, and this results in higher prices for the parts they buy. In the end, Japanese firms are unable to purchase low-cost, quality components, which is a serious matter, as such components form the very foundation upon which Japanese auto firms have built their reputation for quality. Many well-designed Japanese cars produced at transplants have not sold well, which leads us to wonder just exactly what edge Japanese cars are supposed to have in international competitiveness. It is clear that, once they have internationalized Japanese car makers do not necessarily maintain their competitive strength. They are at a loss to know which systems or arrangements will enable them to maintain their competitive position in a global business. It is doubtful that these firms possess the management know-how necessary to run a global business effectively.

Just exactly what was it that gave Japan the competitive edge that allowed it to do so well in the international export market? Did this edge derive from a business infrastructure that facilitated a supply of low-cost components—the *keiretsu* system? Or was it because Japanese firms had access to a network-type business environment that included suppliers of materials and components, and not because individual firms were possessed of any kind of superior business know-how?

To be sure, industrial structures are not built overnight. The captive production system of the United States and the lateral relationships of parts makers and assemblers in Europe (comparable to the Japanese network system) have their own history of development. In post-war Japan, as we struggled to reconstruct our industry we did for a certain period copy the advanced practices of the West and work to replace imports from the U.S. and Europe with domestic products. During the time when our foreign exchange reserves were low and material goods were in short supply, it was part of the national agenda that we should strive to produce things in our own country. In *zaibatsu* groupings, some companies were charged with producing certain goods not then available in Japan. Some of those efforts resulted in the growth of industries of international renown, others did not. Among the industries that do not currently find themselves in a superior position are the chemicals industry and the pharmaceutical industry.

Even liquid crystal displays—one of the most representative examples of hi-tech industry in Japan—were only able to establish a competitive edge by using flat glass from Corning and liquid crystals from Merck. We cannot lose sight of the fact that a high concentration of firms, including foreign ones, has supported Japan's industrial structure. It is important to remember that hi-tech concerns—foreign-owned and domestic—form the industrial infrastructure that supports the liquid crystal display industry.

When key technology moves overseas, there is a danger that the whole industry to which it is directly related may move with it. For example, when a Japanese manufacturer of microwave ovens transferred the production of magnetrons—a key component of microwave ovens—to a South Korean maker, the South Koreans increased their international competitiveness rapidly. The result has been that the production of microwave ovens has slipped in Japan as it has increased in South Korea. We are not debating whether such technology transfers are good or bad. The point is that the availability of parts within Japan is an important support to a firm's international competitive position.

Key technologies are being transferred to more and more countries all the time. Castings are no longer available in ample supply in Japan. (It is, of course, debatable whether this involves a key technology, but the point is still valid.) It is an industry fast being relocated to Indonesia. What changes will be wrought because of the transfer of this technology? Will we conclude that it is only natural that this industry—with a foundry environment that is perceived as dirty, demanding, and dangerous—be moved to developing countries? Or will we conclude that with the move the industry has abandoned any chance of developing pressure-type hi-tech castings with ultrathin walls that can compete with those made by the injection method? We will have to watch developments further before we can answer these questions. But what is clear now is that a simple transfer of technology without due consideration to the future path of technical development is very likely to cause problems in the future.

Japan's synthetic fibers industry in the 1960s absorbed Western technology and produced nylon and polyester fibers and expanded business during the high-growth period. The way Toray and Teijin entered the Asian market at that time is of particular interest. In fact, it was taken up as a case study at Harvard University. The move has something to teach us as we reflect on the recent failures of globalization. In each host country, the two companies started with downstream operations, such as spinning and sewing; next, they established upstream operations, first fiber forming, then the production of synthetic fibers; later, they attempted to dominate the industry in each country and lobbied the respective governments into prohibiting the importation of a number of products. In the end, they were swamped by waves of localization, with local capital coming in and gobbling up all the equity. Eventually, the companies were forced to withdraw. In recent years, they have re-established old networks and are engaged in new business tie-ups.

The story is similar to the situation in Japan at the time of the Second World War, when the country nationalized the production bases of foreign manufacturers, and these later developed into some of the giant manufacturers of today. These include GE-Toshiba, Western Electric-NEC, Siemens-Fuji Electric, and many others. In this sense, then, perhaps we should conclude that the synthetic fibers industry did not fail in its effort to dominate Asia but rather succeeded in aiding the industrialization of developing countries.

It is clear that Japan's industry is firmly supported by the network that supplies parts and materials and the existence of a large number of corporations, which enables an effective melding of technology. And are these things not important national assets that should be cherished? Were they to disappear as a result of transfers to Asia, we fear that a very serious problem would result. We are not saying there should be no further technology transfers to Asia. On the contrary, Japan ought to make an active contribution to the development of Asian countries. But at the same time, we should do all we can to maintain the supply network in Japan, as it is indispensable to the development of new technology and products.

Can We Sustain Local Industry?
Turning now to an issue with different dimensions, we propose to examine whether local industry can continue to operate in Japan.

The bicycle parts industry, for example, still operates as a local industry, centered on the city of Sakai in Osaka Prefecture. Bicycles were first imported from England around the beginning of the century. During the First World War, Japan was unable to obtain replacement parts to make repairs. Building on the gunsmithing tradition of days gone by, the production of bicycle parts began in and around Sakai. This industry came to thrive in the years leading up to the Second World War, and after the war it was one of the first to be rebuilt. It was due to competition among local firms that Shimano (formerly Shimano Industrial) was born. Today, Shimano is a world leader in the bicycle parts industry and has established several plants overseas.

Certain local industries have thrived as independent concerns—scarves in Yokohama and eyeglass frames in Sabae are examples. Many others—the hi-tech-related industries of Tokyo's Jonan and Kawasaki, for instance—support larger industries. These local firms are generally poorly capitalized and cannot respond readily to the skyrocketing yen by going global. They are also being buffeted by the onrushing waves of change.

Some have asserted that there is little to worry about. At one point, the American bicycle industry was thought to have vanished. But several new companies have emerged, and they believe the industry offers some excellent opportunities: the Americans are back in the game. The American enterprising spirit is truly impressive. They have developed mountain bicycles, with new, carefully considered designs, and are exporting these to Japan.

The *Financial Times* a few days ago carried an article that said that the U.S. has twice as much potential as Japan to create employment and five times as much as Europe. The gist of the article was as follows: "Population increases in the U.S. at a faster clip because of immigration, but America still maintains an unemployment rate of about 10 percent. How did the country create so much employment?" In the U.S., as soon as new business opportunities present themselves there are new firms to seize them. This vitality is very important.

The American semiconductor industry was thought to have yielded the memory chip market to Japan, but Motorola and Texas Instruments (TI) are back in the game with new, cleverly designed products. The former has chosen the route of a joint venture with Toshiba, while the latter has entered into agreements with Hitachi and Kobe Steel. Although TI had at one time consolidated all its manufacturing bases in Japan, it has now restarted memory chip production in the U.S., which just goes to show that it is a shaky position to believe that once an industry has lost its competitive edge it will never get it back. It is important that Japan do all it can to get the nation's small and medium-size companies to muster the courage and vitality to re-enter promising markets they have left.

American Rationalism Is in for a Second Challenge
Since long before the Second World War, skilled workers have supported Japan's strength in parts and materials. Lathe operators of legendary skill, parts workers of renowned workmanship, unequaled camera lens polishers—such craftsmen have been great-

ly respected in Japanese society since the Edo period. Before the war, Japan lacked the industrial base necessary to mass produce tanks of the same quality as American tanks. Japanese tanks did not have interchangeable parts, and repair required masterly skills. There is no question that the collaboration of engineers and craftsmen propped up Japanese products for a long time.

A long time ago, I read an amazing war story called *The Cave War of Peleliu Island*. It is the story of how Japanese troops engaged the American army when it landed on Peleliu Island with tanks. Using guerrilla tactics, the Japanese would attack the tanks and withdraw into the caves. After successfully attacking all 10 tanks that had come ashore, the Japanese thought there were no more. But the next day, they found another eight tanks coming at them. The Americans had interchanged parts and repaired the damaged tanks. The Japanese solders were astonished. I, in turn, was astonished that the Japanese soldiers would have been astonished. At the time, the U.S. industry functioned on a mass-production basis and produced interchangeable parts. That's why when one tank was damaged in one place, another tank damaged in another was able to supply parts to fix the former.

After the war, Japan came to see the rationality of the American mass production system. Japan invited American scholars to visit here so we could learn more about industrial engineering, quality control, and other techniques to help enhance productivity. Many books were also translated, and managers attended endless seminars. In this way, quality control, work control, and the American-style rationality that lies behind these gradually found root in Japanese corporations, accumulated there as organizational know-how, and eventually helped form the basis of today's production system.

Some 15 to 20 years later, Japan sharpened its production technology to facilitate small-quantity production of multiline products, in keeping with the multifaceted needs of the market. We would posit that in the process the Japanese system of production became flexible—it developed multiskilled workers, operated a large number of machines, and evolved mixed-flow capabilities.

Unfortunately, however, the stratagem of the small-quantity production of multiline products soon shed its inherent rationality, turned itself into a slogan, and came to be enforced willy-nilly. Today, production lines are being retrenched under a rallying cry of maintaining the competitive edge and reducing costs.

Recently, at an NEC-sponsored seminar on wireless LANs, I learned that NEC is producing wireless LANs as an OEM of NCR. This is the very same NEC that is famed for its communications prowess—the one that produces telephones, communications equipment, and computers. Only two products—one by Motorola and the other by NCR—have satisfied the Japanese standard for wireless LANs, and Japanese makers are now selling products they have OEM'd for these two foreign firms. This says a great deal about the reality of today's Japan. We are supposed to have a strong competitive position internationally, but in fact we seem to be lagging—even in the information industry, an area the nation is striving diligently to make itself a success in.

In communications, Erickson, Alcatel, and Siemens of Europe all have strong competitive positions. Northern Telecom of Canada is a leader in software and many other areas. It is probably a good idea, then, that Japan not blithely claim to have a competitive edge in this industry. In countless areas—including wireless LANs, communications equipment, LAN connectors, and items such as network operating systems, EDI, protocols (transmission procedures), and E-mail—Japan's international competitive position in information, supposedly a growth industry, is in a sorry state indeed. We were amazed to learn that many of the products in this area are developed by American start-ups. The U.S. complains that the fattest section of the trade deficit with Japan is in communications equipment. In fact, the culprit in this respect turns out to be facsimile machines, which the U.S. does not produce.

How did all this come about? Is Japanese industry losing its technological edge? To be sure, when the Japanese are overestimated by others—described variously as good at semiconductors, the world leaders in semiconductor production, the bread and butter producers in the hi-tech industry—they are liable to get on their high horse. Some even claim that Japan boasts such an over-whelming level of high technology that its trade surplus will never disappear. We are not so sure about that.

One of the factors that should be taken note of is the revival of American rationalism. This is going to pose a serious challenge to Japan—indeed, it has already started to rock Japan's highly productive industrial base. There is a very pronounced American counterattack taking place in the machinery industry, for example, as well as in the automobile industry.

For example, the Americans (1) have introduced TQC and *kaizen* activities; (2) are introducing automation and robotization, after carefully studying Japanese manufacturing equipment; (3) are making efforts to reorganize the production floor to respond more flexibly to multifaceted products; (4) are researching ways to shorten the development period for new products, with a focus on all aspects of engineering; (5) are showing very real interest in the kind of streamlined management evident in the *Kanban* system and other lean production organization systems; and (6) are fostering collaboration between parts makers and assemblers in the process of new product development, using an information database called CALS (Continuous Acquisition and Life-Cycle Support), a computer-aided, integrated system melding design, parts procurement, production, and service. In addition, American firms are building industry networks and carrying out research aimed at achieving more efficient development. And the above list is far from exhaustive.

Japanese manufacturing on the other hand—finding itself under attack from America—seems unable to decide on a new direction and seems to be vacillating when it comes to striving toward the development of the next-generation technology that will be the key to bettering the Americans. Which leaves us, yet again, wondering where Japan's competitive edge has gone.

It is probably correct to say that the success of Japanese auto companies was a wake-up call for the American automobile industry. The United States resorted to various political means to press for redress on the one hand, and studied Japanese ways on the other. The quality differentials between American and Japanese cars have narrowed, and the yen's appreciation has reversed the price differential. As a result, the advantages that Japanese cars once enjoyed have suddenly evaporated, and salesmen are having a tough time selling them. Some companies are piling up huge inventories. It is easy to see from such developments just how seriously the rise of the yen has affected Japanese industry.

Public Policy and Corporations Digging Their Own Graves

The yen is now sky-high, and the gap in purchasing power parity is getting larger. When one can buy something for $1 in the U.S. and the same item of merchandise costs ¥150 in Japan, the purchasing power parity can be expressed as $1=¥150. Purchasing power parity expressed for a specific group of goods represents a weighted average of those goods. In the areas of housing, construction, and energy, purchasing power parity now stands well above ¥200. It is only on goods with an international competitive edge, such as home appliances, that parity is at an appropriate level—about ¥120.

If the current inflated exchange rate for the yen continues, it is clear that many domestic items will be replaced by ones from abroad. Things made in Japan will be priced so high that their competitiveness will wither. And if Japan is not then inundated by imports, the U.S. government will waste no time in charging that Japan is blocking foreign products by retaining trade barriers.

This situation can be corrected either by an overflow of imports pushing down purchasing power parity—which would result in prices approaching a level in line with the present exchange rate—or by the exchange rate returning to the level of, say, ¥160 to the dollar. The relationship between foreign exchange rates and purchasing power parity is a very delicate subject and can cause no end of economic friction.

The exchange rate situation acts as a backdrop for the hollowing out of Japan's manufacturing industry. A reversal of this hollowing out can come about either through a correction in the exchange rate or the lowering of wages and consumer prices. This situation needs to be observed closely, involving as it does both politics and macroeconomics.

While some bemoan the current exchange rate, others say the most important thing to do now is exploit the strong yen to improve the standard of living in Japan. Although things like inexpensive fruit juice and imported beer are the talk of the town of late in the distribution industry, there is a swift-moving effort afoot to bring in more and more imports. For many manufacturers, the high exchange rate remains a significant problem (figure 8-1). Why is the yen so high? The answer is simple: There are more purchasers of the yen than there are sellers. Which begs another, connected question: Why are Japanese stocks so attractive to foreign investors? Some respond to this by pointing out that the high stock prices attract an unceasing flow of foreign investment into Japan. Some even hold that the high stock prices result from manipulation by the Japanese government or the Ministry of Finance.

The mostly widely accepted view, however, seems to be that the huge trade surplus is the problem. While we don't believe the answer is quite that simple, there can be no denying that Japan is

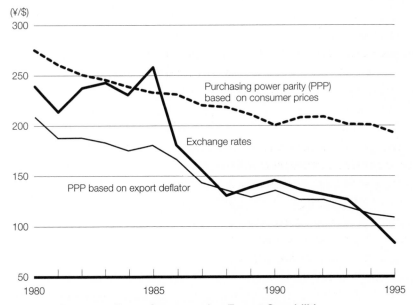

Fig. 8-1. Exchange Rates Overpowering Export Capabilities

Note: Prepared from Miti's *Trade White Paper for FY 1995*, dated May 1995.

the only advanced country with a massive trade surplus. It is not good for world trade that Japan alone should have amassed such a huge surplus while most other nations of the world are in the red. Japan does not retain all of the funds it earns, recycling a large portion of them by investing in securities overseas. In addition, Japan now has a number of financial institutions that are hard-pressed to repay loans borrowed offshore during the bubble.

That is not to say that all of our securities investments abroad have been money losers. Some are beginning to earn returns in the form of dividends. Having said that, however, it must still be admitted that many more have turned out to be duds. Typical examples are real estate investments made in the U.S. Almost all such investments are now in the red. Similarly, cases abound where the acquisition of companies or the building of factories in the U.S. reaped losses. The problem with these investments is they were not the result of strategic decisions by individual companies, but rather were prompted by the perceived need to keep up with the Joneses, or by unofficial requests from the government.

The value of corporate investment in bonds and treasury paper has definitely diminished due to the rise of the yen. For instance, the value of American bonds has declined in accordance with the diminished value of the dollar, leaving holders with an unrealized capital loss. It is natural that people will want to sell their holdings if the yen rises still further. But even though they know they would be better off selling the foreign bonds, repatriating the proceeds, and buying and holding bonds in yen they are afraid of the capital loss that will result when they translate dollar-denominated assets into yen-denominated assets. To put it more technically, if long-term assets incur latent capital loss due to the strong yen neither the present tax system nor disclosure requirements provide for a re-evaluation of those assets in accordance with the current foreign exchange rate. Such a situation is not without its problems, of course, and relates directly to the question of the international harmonization of accounting principles.

Life insurance companies that actively bought American bonds may perhaps complain that they were forced to buy them. It is in fact questionable how much independent judgment and self-discipline Japanese financial institutions exercised when they invested in the U.S. It is doubtful whether they carefully evaluated and weighed the consequences of acting on behalf of their clients while making decisions that satisfied the wishes of the government.

The appreciation of the yen—said to be a reaction to Japan's persistent trade surplus—is severely damaging Japanese industry.

Perhaps this subject should not be dealt with in this book, but here it is. The role of government, government-to-government negotiations, and other macro influences are increasingly influencing the business environment, and it therefore demands our close attention. The Japanese government is engaged in difficult negotiations with the U.S., which brandishes Japan's trade surplus as a weapon to press its demands. We are not alone in wondering if it would not perhaps be better for the Japanese government to insist that negotiations be conducted in some other way.

The U.S. is, for example, trying to force Japan to accept numerical targets to improve the trade imbalance. In the past, however, while engaging Europe in trade negotiations at a time when it was running a trade surplus with the Continent the U.S. insisted that the most important item was the current balance, rather than the trade balance, maintaining that "we should be satisfied if the total flow of funds balances out." If the current U.S.-Japan negotiators were to add the capital account balance to the balance of payments—as the U.S. did in its negotiations with Europe—it would involve adding the balance of payments on patents, transportation, travel, images, and computer software to merchandise trade, and the total balance would show a Japanese deficit in the tens of billions of dollars per year against the U.S. The trade balance doesn't reflect these numbers. And when you think about it logically, it seems somewhat anachronistic to count only trade in merchandise at a time when the service industry is rapidly on the rise. Japan should formulate and present a new concept of the international account balance, which includes tertiary industries, and persuade the U.S. to accept it.

Changes in the way the government and corporations interact with each other are having a serious impact. The ongoing trade negotiations between the U.S. and Japan are addressing voluntary import goals. During the dispute over semiconductors, the negotiators are said to have exchanged a letter that said in effect that the foreign producers' share in the Japanese market would be at least 20 percent. In the event, with the contents of the agreement nowhere near being firmly established, the Japanese government apparently pressured Japanese firms into buying American semiconductors. Taking a broad view of the situation, Japanese corporations have supported the government position and cooperated with it. That sequence of events gave rise on the part of the U.S. government to the idea that a result-oriented approach is the best way to improve the trade balance and pry open the Japanese market.

That idea threatens to escalate into a bigger problem. In the case of Motorola car phones, news leaked out that the Japanese government had written to the U.S. saying it would take all possible measures to facilitate the installation of Motorola antennas. Some in the government are of the view that Japan should do everything possible to avoid friction. It seems to us that American negotiators believe the most effective method of improving the U.S-Japan trade imbalance is to get the Japanese government to compel Japanese firms to do America's bidding. In line with this, the Americans threaten Super 301 action and press for the establishment of numerical import criteria.

In the same way that the government's handling of negotiations leaves much to be desired, the inclination of Japanese management to just go along with the government's wishes is also a problem. Given the business-government relationship in Japan, it is doubtful that Japanese negotiators can effectively reject the U.S. demands by claiming that corporations are independent and that the government is powerless to make commitments. The U.S. expects Japan to make efforts to improve the trade balance, and it is clear that many Japanese citizens value the country's relationship with the U.S. and hope that the trade imbalance can be improved.

The U.S. has threatened to cite Japan as a nation engaged in unfair trading practices under the provisions of Super 301 if the two sides cannot agree on quantitative import goals. Why has it come to this? What went wrong? It is easy to blame the Japanese government for its weak-kneed stance, its lack of policy, and its inter-ministry discord. Indeed, all of those items are contributing factors. But the corporate strategies of following whatever administrative guidance the government offers and disregarding the interests of shareholders, employees, and others involved are also a big part of the problem.

There is a lot the U.S. ought to be doing at home before it looks to restrict imports from Japan. American multinational corporations—in a move that exacerbates the U.S. trade deficit— are increasing investment in Europe and moving factories to Mexico under the aegis of NAFTA. Shouldn't the U.S. government seek to restrain such moves before pressing demands on Japan? When the U.S. calls for Japanese restraint on exports to the U.S., it should likewise demand that American multinationals give priority to domestic production in the U.S. When these propositions were suggested to a certain U.S. policymaker, he rejected them out of hand, casually reeling off a few simple explanations: "The U.S. government has no authority to regulate corporate behavior. . . . The U.S. has a right to make these demands on Japan because the Japanese government has great influence on Japanese businesses and has obligations to cooperate in eliminating the U.S. trade deficit."

At this critical juncture, Japanese corporations must make a choice: Will they acquiesce in the quantitative restrictions demanded by the U.S. and follow the administrative guidance of the Japanese government? Or will they refuse to abide by these given the fact that the government has no legal authority over the matter and the fact that doing what the government advises will, in this instance, run counter to the interests of shareholders?

How corporate Japan interacts with the government is the critical issue, today and in the future.

PART IV

Japanese Corporations Shedding Old Skin

Chapter 9

What Will Lead to a Solution?

SOLVING TODAY'S PROBLEMS AND MAPPING OUT THE FUTURE

People involved in the management of Japanese corporations are today faced with a number of problems. The solutions to these will not to be found in old ideas. Overinvestment made during the bubble should be cut back. . . . The core of Japanese management is the system of lifetime employment, and that system ought to be maintained. Job security is an indispensable element of Japanese management. Propositions such as these no longer suffice; they provide no answers. Recognizing this is a necessary first step.

We propose to address two areas. The first involves identifying the problems that plague Japanese companies and then devising solutions for those problems. The second involves envisioning how Japanese firms can best be managed in the future and then suggesting the direction we should take to arrive at that future. These are, then, two distinct approaches. One starts with the current agenda and suggests ways to fix any problems it may have. The other leaves aside the current agenda and concentrates instead on formulating the best possible future agenda and mapping out the strategy most likely to achieve it.

Solutions proposed must deal with various levels of management. And responses must not only be solid from an abstract perspective—that is, be true to the fundamentals of management theory—they must be functionally sound as well. After defining abstract goals, we must tailor a functional agenda to achieve them. Such functional measures are essential to solving abstract problems.

Thus, we believe that, when dealing with management agenda, we must determine abstract concepts and functional strategies and that such determination dictates the direction in which to move.

If you want to establish a network-type organization that is more in keeping with the mind-set of young people, it means you are setting a future goal at the organizational structure level that is based on human resources. If a large number of older employees in your firm is pushing up the average wage, and you want to establish a wage system that involves a greater degree of performance evaluation it means you are addressing a current problem at the employee remuneration level. Thus shall we proceed with our discussion, remembering that the solutions proposed or the conclusions drawn will depend on the direction chosen and the degree of abstraction involved.

Varying Forms of Japanese Management

In our common sense approach, when we refer to Japanese management we tend to think of all corporations being distinguished by certain specific characteristics. In reality, of course, there are differences between individual companies in organization and management. And although the differences between industries are often pointed out—with each industry employing organizational activities or management styles that mirror the characteristics of the business it is engaged in—the differences (which are often vast) in the management styles of individual companies within an industry are not given sufficient attention. We must acknowledge that, strictly speaking, the very definition of Japanese management can be ambiguous.

Let us take the case of Fujitsu as an example. Along with NEC and IBM Japan, Fujitsu is engaged in information processing, communications, and multimedia—an industry characterized by fast-moving technical innovations and intense international competition. As the management style of this company is more laissez-faire than anything else, management does not involve everybody from the various business divisions in the process of drafting long-term budgets or exercise undo control over the plans that those divisions formulate. The accounting department does not insist on formal procedures for budget *ringi*; when funds are available, they are provided with the request that they be used effectively; when they are not available, the response is "sorry, no money." That is how the internal control divisions and business divisions interact with one another. Moreover, the *ringi* system of investments and financing has no substantive review standards and no clearly defined procedures. You can classify this company's management as one verging on noninterference.

Because authority is delegated to the mid-level employees of the company, the firm is highly energized and provides an exhilarating workplace for gung-ho employees who want to achieve things using their own initiative.

It is perhaps appropriate here to make mention of the great changes that have taken place in the marketing of computers. Previously, each organizational segment dealt with a distinctive process—salesmen took the orders, systems engineers designed the system, and customer engineers took care of the subsequent maintenance. That is no longer the case today. Now, when a salesman discovers a sales opportunity the systems engineer approaches the customer first and proposes new processes and a new system. That is the only way the firm can hope to get the order. Sometimes, good maintenance performed by customer engineers leads to new orders. In such an environment, it is sometimes necessary to marshal the entire resources of the company to close a deal. To cope with this kind of market—and with the changes in the way customers behave—extensive organizational changes are necessary. The companywide changes in the organization that are now required are far greater in magnitude than those that would, in a traditional environment, be crafted by the corporate planning office, reviewed by top management, and put into force.

In the past, Fujitsu set up an in-house forum whereby the company's directors and general managers got together to discuss the running of the company. General managers spent about 70 hours split into teams and engaged in group studies, discussing and analyzing various business strategies from a variety of different perspectives. The conclusions of those study groups were then passed on to the directors, who are charged with operating the various departments. Some of the teams were only successful in making suggestions, and these were never carried into action. Today, Fujitsu seems to feel it cannot afford the time and money required to conduct such group study efforts, and they have been suspended. But it is interesting to note that Fujitsu—at a time when all firms were under pressure to implement substantial changes in their business structure—tried to involve as many staff as possible in a discussion of management problems with top executives, despite the fact that the company was going through some tough times.

We have heard that similar meetings have also been held during management training sessions at Hitachi. Generally speaking, of course, large companies can ill afford the time required to involve a large number of core employees in a discussion of the company's overall agenda and achieve a consensus from them. Nevertheless, it is worth noting that such efforts have been made, even if it was for only brief periods of time. We note that Hitachi has a corporate climate in which the purpose and methods of business deployment are discussed in the normal course of business, with the traditional entrepreneurial fervor. In a typical large company, however, internal control departments oversee the formulation and implementation of business plans—they exercise the levers of control. Since that is the management structure of the average, large Japanese firm, it shows that Japanese management comes in many different shapes and sizes and that it is difficult to define it with blanket statements.

Chapter 10

The Move toward Change—Case Studies

To what extent are attempts at management innovation to deal with the new age actually being put into practice? Although a number of commentaries and essays have been written that present a future vision for mid-size companies and their business prospects, only a few have focused on large corporations. In this chapter, we want to introduce as many examples as possible of ordinary companies fighting corporate bureaucracy.

GETTING OUT OF FIXED-COST STRUCTURES— REBUILDING DILAPIDATED BUSINESS

While it may seem strange, we would like to take a look at trading companies. A general trading company is an interesting phenomenon. This type of company does not exist anywhere else in the world except in Japan and South Korea. With the help of a trading company, even a manufacturer with no overseas base can export products. When Japan's foreign reserves were limited, trading companies were applauded for the functions they performed at the front lines of international trade. Today, with their functions weakened and their earning power in steady decline the management of trading companies faces a tough test.

But before discussing which trading companies are doing well and which poorly, it should be said that we have reached the point now where the very business of trading companies is going to have to change. Products such as semiconductors, automobiles, computers, and home appliances—the real muscle behind the international competitive strength of Japan's economy—do not

189

depend on trading companies for export. Trading companies principally handle the imports of materials and the exports of processed or fabricated goods and the exports of equipment to make such goods—the kind of products on which trading companies have established commercial rights.

With their main business facing troubled times, trading companies are very concerned about reviving their operations. Many of them are anxious to formulate business strategies or long-term management plans and engage in new business in accordance with the guidelines they establish.

An issue of common concern to all trading companies is reducing fixed costs, which often means reducing personnel costs. But to suggest that a reduction in personnel is the only way to reduce fixed costs is very disheartening to trading companies, as their employees are the only real business resource these firms have. But given the deterioration of functions and the reduction in commission rates, there is no other alternative available.

In addition to contemplating cutbacks in personnel, firms are also looking at ways to overhaul their business plans. As mentioned earlier, very few Japanese companies incorporate in their plans specific programs that are characteristically different from those of other companies in their industry. But trading companies do not follow this pattern. Interestingly, they seem to be the only Japanese companies that formulate business plans that differ from one company to another. Mitsui & Co., for example, is struggling to revitalize itself and is thoroughly reviewing everything—even asking itself what the purpose of a trading company is. It is working to construct a new business structure under the slogan: "A multiple value-added service firm."

Of those business resources that have traditionally supported trading companies—personnel, material goods, and financial resources—Mitsubishi International has chosen to focus on financial resources as it reviews its functions as a trading company, formulating a business plan it calls the K Plan. Itochu International, on the other hand, is trying to segment its various business domains. While still hoping to maintain its traditional product mix, it is focusing investment on electronics and communications and has staked its survival on a realignment of its strategic products. We can assume that Sumitomo Corp. is trying to strengthen management control because it wants to keep investing in projects that can achieve an ROI (return on investment) above a certain level. Clearly, each of these companies is carving out its own distinct strategy and direction.

The need to shed-fixed cost structures is a big issue of concern to all companies that suffer from high overhead costs, high depreciation costs caused by overextended automation, and R&D costs that have become fixed over time. In particular, companies making semiconductors and liquid crystal displays have financial structures characteristic of capital-intensive industries, and their capital spending and R&D costs are equal to about 60 percent of revenue. Their balance sheets already make them fixed-cost-type companies. This leaves them particularly vulnerable to reductions in volume. They can deal with the need to make a variety of different products, but they cannot deal with a drop in throughput. With steep fixed costs, the break-even point is so high that a reduction in volume, even a slight one, means the bottom line takes a big hit. We need to ponder this situation carefully to see if there is anything that can be done about it.

To be sure, the fixed-cost ratio at Japanese corporations has been generally high since the 1980s. There are a number of reasons for this, but principal among them is the fact that the money used to bankroll substantial capital investments during the 1980s was obtained inexpensively through equity finance. And what sort of capital investments were made? The funds were supposed to be used for equipment conducive to a flexible production system— small-quantity production of multiline products. In fact, not a few of the investments were for fixed production facilities designed for specific products only. Some steel companies invested in machinery to produce steel sheets of particular specifications earmarked for specific customers only. Those facilities are not in operation today. From a long-term perspective, the investments made during the latter half of the 1980s may yet turn out to be useful, but for the time being they will remain as high fixed costs because of the high depreciation costs that are associated with these investments, at least for the next few years.

Every company now seems to be stressing the urgent need to reduce fixed costs. But what do they really mean by this? It is clear that what is meant is a reduction in the work force, because in Japan personnel costs are the major component of high fixed costs. With lofty fixed costs, it is not possible to run a flexible operation, reduce throughput, or change products at will. With low fixed costs and high variable costs, you can reduce your operating rate at will without incurring much in the way of additional costs. With high fixed costs, you cannot alter production volume at will. It was easier to reduce labor costs in the past, when personnel could be replaced by machinery. Previously, when the need to cut fixed costs arose many firms could do so by slashing labor, replacing people with machines. Steel companies steadily reduced blue-collar workers in this fashion. Now, for the first time ever, firms are faced with the prospect of having to reduce white-collar workers as well. The white-collars have, of course, always been part of the elite within steel companies. They have never before been subject to retrenchment. The fact that they are now susceptible to dismissal is evidence of just how difficult a time steel companies are having as they try to revitalize themselves.

"Work reform" is a slogan often bandied about in connection with reducing fixed costs. Nowadays, the deployment of information technology to achieve work reform is a topic of endless discussion. Although the specific methods of work reform are yet to be fully developed, there is no doubt that reform will be an important tool in the effort to enhance the productivity of administrative work—the tasks carried out by white-collar employees. In recent years, the notion of re-engineering companies has often been stressed, and its principal component will be none other than work reform that fully exploits information technology.

Ultimately, this will mean downsizing the structure of organizations and the work they do. The objective is to review the whole organization and cut fixed costs. At big Japanese firms, head office overhead represents one of the largest slices of the fixed-costs pie. As the organization is built on the premise that everybody is a manager, communications and coordination take up a great deal of time. Because of this, the costs of coordination involved in obtaining and maintaining consensus are very high. As a result, all of the resources of the company are not available to be mobilized.

Against this backdrop, there is the widespread recognition that we have reached a point in time when cost-efficient work performance has become a vital consideration. To achieve this, many companies are actively trying to introduce network-type computer systems. The aim is to have traditional administrative work performed by the new tools of information technology. Many a company today is teeming with enterprising ideas, with people aggressively pursuing ways to put into practice plans for a computer network that would supplant cross-organizational and hierarchical communication within the firm. It goes without saying that some of the employees who would be displaced by such a computer network will be white-collar workers.

SEEKING THE MANAGEMENT KNOW-HOW OF BIG FIRMS—MOBILIZING THE ENTIRE RESOURCES OF A COMPANY

At big companies like Hitachi and Toshiba there is an ongoing debate as to how they should go about developing their integral power as corporations. Heavy electric machinery and semiconductors, computers and home appliances—these are the types of products that supposedly make such companies what they are. But the parties to the debate find themselves asking questions such as the following: What exactly is Toshiba?

Toshiba is one of Japan's leading companies, with one of the highest sales performance records in the country. But in the area of computers it is outdone by Fujitsu, while in the area of home appliances Matsushita has the upper hand. And in terms of heavy electric machinery, while it may not be bested by them it is certainly rivaled by Hitachi, Mitsubishi Heavy Industry, and Mitsubishi Electric. From whence, then, does its stellar sales performance come? The answer, alas, is not so easy to find, and so the debate continues.

The search goes on for ways to improve operations to reduce high fixed costs and high sales costs, for ways to get more mileage out of the firm's far-flung operations, for ways to make one plus one equal 3.5 or four rather than just two.

In large companies, such as Toshiba, operations usually center on distinct business divisions. And there are walls between the divisions, with each division making its own decisions, so that it becomes very difficult for divisions to coordinate with one another across those walls of separation.

At NEC and Fujitsu—companies that find themselves on the top rung of the computer industry—there is a prevailing fear that their future will be bleak if they continue to ship only hardware. But this is not to say that they are short of systems engineers who can develop software. On the contrary, they have a surplus of such people.

Even large companies like these have serious concerns about corporate management. One principal cause of such concern is size. When a firm is very large, the forces of decentralization and bureaucratization are great, and the time taken up conducting control functions jumps at an accelerated rate. The result is weakened earnings power and a fixed-cost structure with a high break-even point. Such organizations have no opportunity to take advantage of economies of scale.

Large companies seem incapable of defining and focusing on a primary integral power as they carry out their varied business ventures. Their effort to cobble together mammoth multidimensional corporate power results in more personnel at headquarters and more bureaucracy. In light of this, some argue that it would be better to move in the opposite direction, reducing headquarters staff and spinning off subsidiaries. In other words, to give up the goal of a strengthened integral power.

A way to strengthen total corporate power and at the same time improve economies of scale in the area of sales would be to increase exchange between computer divisions and home appliances divisions or, in the case of heavy electric machinery, to sell electric bulbs (home appliance products) as well as elevators. On the technical side, one could argue for the development of common materials, which could be used across the boundaries by different divisions, thereby taking advantage of the benefits of common materials as a catalyst for attaining an integrated corporate power. It seems to us that an increasing number of companies are making efforts to develop a companywide integrating force through improvements in organizational functions such as those described here, particularly in the areas of marketing and technical development. It is often said that a big company tends to try to overcome difficult situations by applying the full scope of its financial and human resources, bringing the weight of its prestige and sheer strength to bear on completing the job. When the divisions of a large company are viewed as individual entities, it becomes clear that they do not necessarily receive large infusions of business resources when compared with mid-level companies. Recognizing this, operating divisions at firms are beginning to explore what the new type of corporation ought to be like and are looking for ways to bring that about. This gives us hope.

GLOBAL MANAGEMENT AND THE CHALLENGE TO IMPROVE EARNINGS

Under the impact of domestic and foreign price differentials and the high value of the yen, many Japanese corporations are under pressure to manage from a global perspective, whether they like it or not. In practice, running a company overseas is no easy task. For one thing, there are various risks attendant with doing business in a foreign country. It seems, for instance, that Japanese companies are aware of the risks they are taking in establishing factories in China, given the current economic friction between the U.S. and China, but they are going ahead nonetheless, feeling they have no choice.

It is generally recognized that it is possible to run a business fairly well in Southeast Asia, but any firm that locates there will be forced to contend with unsatisfactory infrastructure in distribution, communications networks, and highway networks. (Singapore is an exception.) For example, we have heard executives say that whereas in Japan you can run a smooth production operation with about three days worth of parts inventory, in Asia you need about two months worth to ensure a stable operation. The organization of labor unions is also a very delicate matter. In view of a highly mobile work force that moves from company to company, it is still unclear whether a system of enterprise unions such as that found in Japan will take root or whether American-style labor management practices will prevail. This is currently a very touchy issue.

In strategy, the issue of how to strike a balance between globalization and localization is something that goes to the very heart of organizational structure. If you want to make products that closely meet the needs of the locality in which you are situated and enjoy the benefits of economies of global scale you will be hard-pressed to devise a business structure that will allow you to achieve that. On the other hand, if you produce a single uniform product for the global market you may end up making something without character that nobody is interested in buying.

When a large Japanese firm sets out to go global—shifting its manufacturing base overseas and establishing sales outlets there—the move is not often predicated on companywide considerations. Indeed, divisional policies are often given priority. In many cases, a particular business division makes a cost analysis and decides that it must make the move overseas if it hopes to maintain its competitive position, or it decides that, to deal with antidumping suits, for example, it sees no alternative to producing abroad (in this case, in an advanced country). This division—once it is has set up overseas—comes to be dominated by solipsistic considerations, and that makes it very difficult for the company to effect the coordination of its business on a worldwide basis.

It is said that there are three typical forms of global organization. The first is the so-called Ford-type organization, in which each regional headquarters—the European head office, the U.S. head office, and the Asian head office—manages and controls all company business within its region. Although Ford's Asian strategy includes a rather sensitive element vis-à-vis its relationship with Mazda, this type of structure seems to be generally well liked by Japanese giants. There is, however, one problem in connection with this type of organization. It appears that over time the primary concern of the regional headquarters becomes solving problems connected with taxation. So much so that in many cases management is not able to exercise a sufficiently effective integrating function.

The second is the ITT-type organization, in which the company's foreign subsidiaries carry out their business in complete independence, even engaging in their own development work. Although not many Japanese companies adopt this form, some firms will still at times allow an offshore subsidiary a great deal of freedom to make its own business choices, much to the consternation of headquarters in many cases. This type of organization decentralizes operations completely, leaving everything in the hands of the foreign subsidiaries, and coordination is effected through conferences. In a way, this type of organization resembles a grouping of small companies.

The third is the IBM-type organization, in which resources central to the company are consolidated at headquarters and not diffused throughout the organization. Only those functions that are strictly associated with particular local communities, such as marketing functions, are diffused out from headquarters. Today, however, this has changed. Even IBM no longer develops all of its products or concentrates all of its production in the U.S. alone.

Despite the fact that many large Japanese corporations have adopted the Ford-type organization, only a few have actually allowed their regional headquarters to carry out all development, production, and marketing functions, as Ford does. Sony, for example, is organized like Ford. And in the U.S. and Europe, Sony's regional headquarters do execute all functions of marketing, production, and development in an integrated fashion. The company is attempting to establish the same system in Asia, but regional headquarters there is relatively behind in parts production, materials procurement, and the installation of machinery and equipment. Consequently, it is not given the same responsibilities as Sony headquarters in the U.S. and Europe But in general, when Sony shifts its business abroad it shifts all of the functions abroad, and in this sense it is correct to say that Sony is a Ford-type organization.

Yamaha and others also tried to create such a system of regional headquarters. Some companies talk about setting up quadripolar or tripolar structures. If Japanese companies were able to establish foreign subsidiaries that could integrate all management functions—as Ford does in Germany, for example—Japan's global program would be successful. But Japanese firms have been unable to do that.

If a firm tries to concentrate all research and development in its own country, as IBM does, production and marketing functions are diffused to host countries. Although a firm may want to assess the costs of centralized R&D on each foreign subsidiary at a certain rate against the sales of that subsidiary, the constraints imposed by tax laws in the host countries make it difficult to effect. We do not have sufficient experience to completely map out a diffused global organization in which each regional headquarters would undertake its share of the R&D, production, and marketing functions. While we could conceive of a technology-driven headquarters in Japan where all research and development work might be concentrated, devising a method for allocating the costs would be a difficult task and in the end only an exercise in armchair theory. As a global organizational structure can be built only after a full review of a vast array of issues, including accounts settlement policy and international taxation, we must conclude that Japanese corporations lack the experience to create such an organization and have it be stable. If Japanese firms were able to emulate a certain large American concern whose head office charges its regional sales company in Japan 10 percent of its sales as its share of the R&D costs, it would be a different story. But Japanese corporations would be hard-pressed to make a success of a scheme such as that.

Instead of putting everything they've got into their foreign business endeavors, Japanese corporations have been satisfied with half measures. As discussed earlier, Japanese firms built foreign factories after they were hit with dumping suits. A decision to build a factory of a limited size to produce a limited quantity of products that may or may not sell in the local market leaves one wondering if there is such a thing as business strategy in Japan. What is required is the formulation of a more serious global strategic plan and the building of a factory that will have a competitive edge. Unless Japanese companies can identify what constitutes the strengths of European and American multinationals that have been touted for their success, and unless they can emulate those multinationals in terms of integrating functions, strategic functions, and long-term investment connected with overseas expansion, they are likely to discover that all they have really done with their overseas efforts is diffused themselves out to other countries.

As we review actual cases, we are left wondering whether Japanese management is capable of working effectively on the world scene or of dealing with the age of globalization. Are Japanese companies making overseas investments for strategic ends? Nissan Motor, for example, produces cars in the UK. Under a local procurement program it buys parts from a leading German parts maker, Bosch. Because the volume of its purchases is very small compared with those of Volkswagen, it pays much higher unit prices than Volkswagen. The cost of the finished product goes up as a result, and the firm cannot make a profit. Nissan must know what's happening. So why doesn't it do anything about it? As long as it is obligated to purchase parts from Bosch, why doesn't Nissan buy not only the parts it needs for the European market but also all the parts it needs for all of its production worldwide? This would allow the firm to buy parts at unit prices lower than what Volkswagen pays, and it could use those parts it needs for its European production and bring the rest to Japan. Perhaps Nissan didn't really approach its European venture in the right way and therefore didn't know exactly what it was getting into. But if it did know beforehand that it was unlikely to make money with the European operation, then the question is what could those managers who are responsible for profit possibly have been thinking about? We wonder if the managers in question really know their business and can properly assess resources and evaluate a competitive position.

In the same manner as with overseas investments, we see so many cases of firms entering a new business only because they are responding to external circumstances or because their competitors have entered the same business. Why does this happen? We see this as the most serious problem plaguing Japanese management. Maybe it is a by-product of excessive compromise. In making decisions, each functional department is concerned only with the matters in its own area—with production functions under the jurisdiction of the operating division, marketing functions under the jurisdiction of the overseas marketing division, and so on. The head office makes decisions that are nothing more than a response to outside circumstances. What are we supposed to make of all this?

Under this style of decision making you only deal with a problem after it presents itself; you only start a project because your competition has started a similar one; and you only move your operations overseas when you are faced with a dumping suit. And when decision making is simply a reaction to outside developments, or when a company decision is nothing more than the sum of the decisions made by separate functional departments, what you have is bottom-up decision making in the worst sense of that phrase. At the very minimum, firms need to examine what can be done to build a money-making structure and to formulate strategies that encompass the entire structure. Finding solutions to these and many similar problems that mar the performance of companies is a very serious issue.

In fact, there are many possible solutions. A number of measures can be implemented to revitalize or expand the business or operating structure. While we sometimes feel that managers worry too much, we also feel that at other times they are being buffeted about topsy-turvy by forces that are beyond their control. We would even go so far as to say that when global management at a Japanese firm is not running smoothly, it is sometimes not a question of management not working effectively but rather a question of there being no management control of the company whatsoever.

GROPING FOR STABLE GROWTH-TYPE BUSINESS MANAGEMENT

The premise that the market will keep growing is one of the basic environmental factors that have supported Japanese management. But we cannot hope that this premise will continue to be valid in the future. In Japan, all products, including home appliances, automobiles, and computers, have been supplied in quantities sufficient to reach all consumers. Cable TV is available to whoever wants to subscribe. Anyone who chooses to can access an inexhaustible fount of information from around the world. In short, the demand for products has dropped off, and because it has it is only logical to assume that few industries will experience significant growth in the future. In light of this, the pressing management issue of the day is figuring out the most productive way to run a company when the market is not growing.

Heretofore, even firms that established ill-advised overseas operations, ventured into new business areas without properly calculating the risks involved, or made a series of imprudent business decisions would often come out ahead in the end, as the consequences of their imprudent actions were overwhelmed by the prodigious growth of the market. But such luck can no longer be counted on. We already have industries that either have not grown at all or have grown only slightly since the 1970s, prime examples being steel and television sets. Policies and decisions that might have passed muster during the high-growth period just won't work any more. It is clear that business losses will persist and pile up.

As an example of how difficult it is to deal with a period of low growth, let us take the case of Nissan Motor. Because of changes in the market after the bubble collapsed the automobile industry found it was no longer able to sell a lot of luxury cars—expensive products that had until then done very well. Nissan had the added pressure of being second fiddle to Toyota in the industry. In the face of this stagnating market, Nissan maintained full production and ended up with a large inventory of money-losing products. The firm then instituted cost-cutting measures, such as the common use of parts by different models, and changed its cycle for introducing new models. It then raised prices and endeavored to establish a new earnings scheme that would be secured by structuring the industry so that it avoids price-cutting competition.

Several years ago, Nissan's five-year business plan attracted a lot of attention. Its aim was to erect a structure whereby profits would be realized by a strategy that maintained revenue levels and did not increase the number of cars sold. When this plan was announced, Nissan was praised for being true to form in courageously striving to solve an essential problem in the industry. One year later, however, Toyota broke ranks and started lowering prices, plunging the industry into a price war, and the Nissan plan fell apart. What Nissan wanted to achieve was a cooperative industrial structure that avoided price-cutting, shifting from competition over quantity and price to competition over quality.

Honda apparently chose a similar approach. But its stated policy of "avoiding random price competition" became unworkable as Toyota and Nissan engaged in an all-out price war.

As Nissan tried to make clear, it was not the time to engage in competition predicated on company size—competition in price and quantity. Instead, it was a time to focus on quality and to face the challenge of building a business structure with new dimensions. In a mature market, there are but two alternatives—you either engage in quantitative competition and try to put your competitors out of business or you cherish each segmented market and strive to maintain them by continuing to supply differentiated products. We still believe that Nissan's proposal is an option worth considering in a nongrowth market.

It can also be argued, of course, that the Nissan proposal presupposed an oligopolistic structure. We fear that Nissan's proposal was understood to be, in essence, an example of a cartel, under which companies can raise prices and still continue to make money. When such an interpretation became pervasive, the Nissan plan came to be criticized for advocating a management style that is inappropriate in a flat-growth market. The authors now believe Nissan's idea is unworkable, although we remain convinced that what Nissan was suggesting to the other companies was basically this: Let's not fight over market share.

The automobile industries in the U.S. and Europe have striven toward oligopoly and now enjoy the benefits of oligopolistic, or even monopolistic, markets—so much so that the application of antitrust laws is now a real possibility. In a stable growth market, unless Japanese companies are given appropriate stimuli through competition they run the risk of replicating the example of American auto companies some years ago. Their cars were getting poor mileage, but they declined to develop new engines. The cars were selling so they just continued to design new images for their products by designing new bodies for them, seeing that as the best way to maintain the highest possible rate of return on investment. Eventually, they realized that an overwhelming gap in fundamental technology had developed between them and Japanese auto companies. While they maneuvered politically to avoid international competition, they put forth great efforts to catch up with the Japanese, and in four or five years they succeeded in doing so. The automobile industry is not the only example of how monopoly or oligopoly can detract from the vitality of an industry. Philips in Europe ran up against a wall in its diversification program and is now charting its recovery by refocusing efforts on home appliances centered on audiovisual equipment. We believe that the failure of Philips had as its genesis the benefits the company enjoyed because of a monopoly.

Why is it that Japanese corporations are able to conceive of ideas to keep up with the Joneses? Why does each company make similar investments to make similar products and end up with excessive outlays? It is perhaps because there exists in Japan an industrial structure that facilitates the efforts of companies to make investments similar to those of the competition. In the relatively small Japanese market, there are some seven to nine companies making passenger cars. In the United States, automakers have been consolidated over the years into the current three companies. The Japanese market continues to feature cutthroat competition.

Why is this so? We think it is because the industrial structure permits the second, third, fourth, and fifth players to survive. One element that supports this industrial structure is the availability of large subcontractors and parts companies. Even the parts department of a large company looks to reap the benefits of increased production by selling some of its merchandise to other companies. And as long as automakers can obtain parts from these companies, even the fifth or sixth firm can produce cars. The result is we end up with a number of rival companies because of an industrial structure that is crowned by the mentality of keeping up with the Joneses.

The ultimate outcome is excessive competition and the persistence of a very stimulating business environment. That is why it is extremely difficult to steer an industry along a path of cooperation like the one suggested by Nissan. The automobile industry is not the only one characterized by such stiff competition. The electric home appliances industry is the same. In fact, intensive competition is the hallmark of the entire Japanese economy, with the exception of certain government-owned corporations. We believe this aspect of Japan's industrial structure is extremely positive and healthy and something we should be justly proud of.

If Japan's *keiretsu* system is closed down, as sought by the U.S. government, it would likely mean that automobile assemblers, for example, would have to maintain exclusive arrangements with their subcontractors, which would constitute the kind of *keiretsu* structure that was criticized during the second round of the U.S.-Japan Trade Framework Negotiations. Such arrangements would, we suspect, result in inefficient performance. Currently, a Toyota supplier, simultaneous to serving Toyota, seeks to benefit from economies of scale by selling products to Toyota's competitors. Nowadays, this sort of efficient productive activity is being increasingly promoted. We don't think this arrangement fits the definition of *keiretsu*. With respect to each component sold, legitimate market principles operate and arm's-length transactions take place. Such an arrangement is more efficient from the point of view of the industry as a whole. In fact, parts makers these days are detaching themselves from *keiretsu* and moving in the direction just described. Gear parts makers in the bicycle industry are doing the same.

In an environment of stagnant growth, it is necessary for firms to evaluate operations to determine if earnings will support continued investment and to calculate if cash flows balance out. While not many companies or industries have succeeded in doing this, the steel industry was successful for a time. Nippon Steel's market share declined as it helped maintain, at its own expense, a minimum-price cartel characterized by the Trigger Price Mechanism. Steel firms maintained a cooperative relationship while supplying low-priced products. That industry is now plagued by competition from low-priced products from South Korea and China. Whether Nippon Steel will once again practice a policy of self-sacrifice for the sake of cooperation within the industry is a question that has yet to be answered.

Ultimately, the issue is whether business can still run smoothly when growth has stopped. Given a market without growth, how can we create a structure that will allow for well-balanced management; the reinvestment of capital; and the continued, stable operation of companies?

That question has yet to be answered. But if firms are careful not to get hung up on narrow definitions of industry, they might consider deploying outside their usual parameters and maintaining a measure of competitive stimulation in that way. In doing so, it may well be necessary to consider business deployment beyond the realm of manufacturing or distribution.

A good example of this is Kao Soap. The toiletry market is very mature, and Kao, after many years of hard work, is today extremely successful, having set up a sales company, reduced and automated its production process, and realized a distribution revolution by carrying out the bulk of its domestic transportation by sea. It has diversified in such a way that, with the aid of floppy disks and thermal printer ribbons, it is doing very well in an industry beset by tough price competition. (Perhaps the achievement of such success is where the real pleasure lies in running a company in a mature market.) Kao's success does not mean that its competitor, Lion, is not doing well. In fact, Lion is successful in the information industry, running Planet, a VAN company. It also enjoys a considerable share in big supermarkets, such as Daiei, where it deals with the same tough competition as Kao. The toiletry market and the competition that characterizes it are worthy of analysis.

Another significant trend under way is the increased effort on the part of firms to bolster their global competitive position by taking advantage of the power that comes from size—something that was evident in the Mitsubishi Chemicals merger. As Dupont's net income in chemicals is said to be as high as the total sales of this merger, oligopoly is clearly one possible direction for companies to move if they want to maintain their development capabilities.

TRYING TO CHANGE THE TYPE OF BUSINESS YOU DO

There is a company named TRED—Total Restaurant & Eatery Development—and 50 percent of its stock is owned by Ajinomoto and NTT. Tokyo Gas and Nippon Life are also shareholders. The company was established to assist in the restaurant business. It enrolls restaurants as club members (Nippon Shokudo, JR Higashi Nippon Restaurant, and others); it designs buildings or critiques the design of existing buildings; it designs layouts and interiors; it develops and trains cooks; it provides tables, chairs, carpets, utensils, flatware, towels, and other items; and it provides member restaurants with menus and trains cooks in how to prepare the food on those menus. It provides all this at cost. NTT, Tokyo Gas, and Nippon Life either have locations that are appropriate for restaurants or have clients with such locations. TRED finances such clients and provides them with all the know-how necessary to run a restaurant.

Ajinomoto, a food manufacturer, knew little about restaurants. How did it set about gaining know-how it didn't have? It's an interesting story. First, it contacted TRED, and TRED hired first-rate restaurant and food consultants in Milan, Paris, Düsseldorf, London, and New York. These consultants go to different restaurants to sample the fare, and when they find interesting dishes or menus they advise Ajinomoto. Such information is then carried in a special magazine distributed free of charge to specified individuals who are considered to be opinion leaders. If readers show an interest in particular products showcased in the magazine, Ajitsu (Epicurean), a mail-order house, begins to market them. The products are also introduced on Takashima Tadao's *Gochisosama*, a TV program sponsored by Ajinomoto. After screenings, if the products are thought to be in great demand they are brought to TRED's plant and engineered into canned products for distribution, along with menus, to partner restaurants. In this way, the firm has been exploring ways to develop food ingredients comprehensively and to organize a better distribution system.

A classic example of an effective method for providing multiple services to customers is the value-added resellers (VARs) introduced by IBM when it entered the personal computer market. Neither a wholesaler nor a retailer, a VAR is a new kind of intermediate dealer. VARs are, in essence, agencies that handle IBM personal computers as their core products but that also deal in hardware and software made by other companies. In addition, they provide technical service, maintenance, systems education support, equipment leasing—in short, all the peripheral services required to run a computer. (figure 10-1)

For a time, Ajinomoto won acclaim as a company actively involved in its partnerships with foreign manufacturers and in prominent diversification programs. But as far as we are able to observe, the company's diversification projects—whether they involve coffee, mayonnaise, or something else—have had an unexpectedly difficult time increasing market share. The firm is now trying to become a general food producer, but—as was the case with Calpis, which Ajinomoto bought some years ago—it is finding it difficult to break down the barriers whenever it tries to enter a new field, where it invariably encounters specialty stores or other competitors who got there earlier.

Now, suppose Ajinomoto were to decide it wanted to expand its product line. Since it is a technologically advanced company, it would not be impossible for it to produce ham products, for example, and that these would be tastier than those of other com-

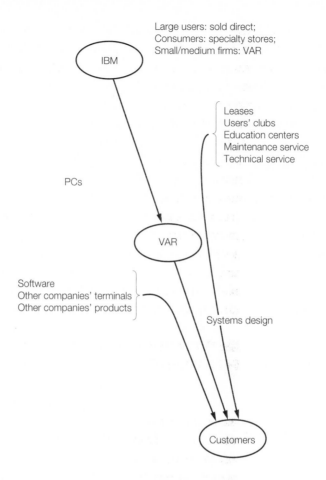

Large users: sold direct;
Consumers: specialty stores;
Small/medium firms: VAR

IBM

Leases
Users' clubs
Education centers
Maintenance service
Technical service

PCs

VAR

Software
Other companies' terminals
Other companies' products

Systems design

Customers

Fig. 10-1. The Concept of Value-Added Resellers

Note: VARs sell comprehensive systems support and products.

panies. It could thus develop these new products, produce them, and send them out through its distribution routes. Even if it did this, however, there is no guarantee that sales would go smoothly. No matter how strong a firm is in technical or product development, it is not easy to pry open distribution barriers and to get into new markets.

A firm looking to break into a certain sector of the food market would want to discuss what it should do with its products that are running second best in their markets. One possible answer would be to not push too hard and to cut back on advertising. The firm might worry that this will cause its market share to drop, but from a profit standpoint this might be a more effective strategy than pressing hard to win the No. 1 position. But that would still leave the question about what to do in the future. The firm should be well aware that the entire food market is changing and that people are eating out more often. It perhaps might be a good idea for the company to aim at supplying its products to a network of eateries. Once the name recognition of the products is established, it might start selling its products as a manufacturer. Unique strategies such as this are often the brainchild of one individual with vision. We know of one young president who successfully ran an entire group of subsidiaries with great success.

The food industry is characterized by stable growth. One of the important concerns within the industry is the way wholesalers service customers. Wholesalers such as Mitsubishi's Bisshoku and Itochu's Matsushita Suzuki are now considering a number of measures. For their part, restaurants are striving to develop new types of venues in order that diners are offered a variety. How should food producers deal with this mature market? The orthodox response would be to develop new products. The response of TRED is to perform the functions of a manufacturer while supporting restaurants, which are the retail sector. And therein lies the uniqueness and brilliance of its approach. It seems to us that instead of carrying on with business as usual, TRED re-thought its entire wholesale and distribution approach and responded in an ostensibly self-denying manner, while continuing to perform the functions of a manufacturer. This is perhaps an indication that new business structures that encompass distribution will become increasingly important in the future.

You can still make it in a mature market if you are able to change the type of business you do. Such a strategy seems to be on the same wavelength as the thinking behind Sony's purchase of Columbia and Matsushita's purchase of MCA. The essence of business management boils down to delving into product concepts and providing consumers with products and services that effectively meet their needs. If you can pursue a new business in a comprehensive way, focusing on the products or functions of the business and not getting hung up on categorizing it as manufacturing or wholesaling or retailing or whatever, we believe the horizon opens up with a plethora of possibilities. The important point to remember here is that there are always ways of dealing with stable growth markets.

ABANDONING THE "KEEPING UP WITH THE JONESES" PRINCIPLE

Until the bubble burst, the market for the most part grew consistently, which made it possible for market players to vie for a share of an ever-expanding pie. Different industries approached this competition in different ways. In most cases, however, the top dog of the industry—IBM in computers, for example, and Kirin in brewing—paved the way and others followed. When IBM introduced its next-generation system, the typical strategy of second and third stringers was to follow along. In beer brewing, almost every brewer who tried to introduce beer that didn't taste like lager, Kirin's principal product, failed.

Mirroring the business concepts of the leading company, the second- and third-rank companies mimicked or tried to rival the leader with similar concepts. But this method of competition is not without its problems. A second fiddle who tries to emulate the industry leader often discovers that the No. 1 company can still excel. To be sure, if this pattern is followed under a stable-growth economy—if all competitors put out to sea together in a convoy—it is not likely to benefit consumers. If keeping up with the Joneses is the only path available to competitors, the industry may well become sapped of its vitality.

But if a firm is willing to consider changing the type of business it does, it may well find plenty of opportunity for improving its position and invigorating the industry. If a second or third stringer can alter its method of selling or its merchandising concept in such a way that the leader cannot easily copy it, or if it can carve out novel, freewheeling methods of business deployment instead of following industry norms it may well be able to expand its market share. To do so, of course, it is necessary to think in terms of making a break with the industry's traditions and accepted practices.

For example, the principal strength of Wacoal, one of the top producers of women's underwear, is its ability to secure sales space in department stores. Indeed, that method of selling underwear was perfected by Wacoal. While a second fiddle may try to emulate this, it would never succeed because Wacoal has an unshakable foothold in department stores. Suppose, however, that a second- or third-ranking competitor were to try a different tack, such as selling by mail order or at home parties. It might well expand its market share by doing so, as there may be some consumers who don't particularly like to shop for underwear at department stores. Initially, results would be limited, but gradually consumers could take to the new firm and its method with gusto. Wacoal, on the other hand, is likely to find it cannot copy the competitor's new method because this would lead to cannibalizing its department store set up. Department stores would surely complain if Wacoal tried to sell its underwear in places other than the stores.

When discount stores made their appearance some years ago, Matsushita Electric, which had been selling its products through its own chain of stores, took an immediate dislike to the discounters. Matsushita found it could not quickly alter its system of a strong, proprietary marketing network. In the meantime, Sharp caught Matsushita flat-footed when it developed new brands with Daiei and introduced these in Daiei stores. Sony expanded its share of the market for electric home appliances by selling at specialty stores in Akihabara. Such changes in the contour of the industry did not come about through product strategies alone. These significant changes can be seen as an indication either of competition between manufacturers and distributors or between manufacturers themselves in response to changes in the environment or changes in the distribution structure.

In the computer industry, when Digital Equipment came out with minicomputers IBM was unable to follow suit. IBM was weak-kneed when it came to personal computers. A similar situation took place in Japan when Fujitsu and Hitachi were late in responding to demand for PCs while NEC moved successfully into the market. During the last few years, in an unexpected twist, Apple Computer has jumped to second place in the Japanese market. And while the performance of Apple's products may have a lot to do with this, it should also be remembered that when the electric home appliance industry had matured and Akihabara's specialty stores had no new merchandise to offer Apple launched its attack on this industry, using outlets that had been selling copying machines, and in one fell swoop it was able to carve out a 20 percent market share.

Generally speaking, even when an industry is mature and a Gulliver-like top dog has established the industry norms, there are still bound to be certain customers who are not happy with the way things are in the market. If second- and third-tier firms can find these customers, they should be able to enjoy respectable business success. And if these new ways of conducting business continue to develop, they could well bring a sea change in the way business is done within some industries, altering their very norms and standards. Engaging in qualitative, rather than quantitative, competition may well be the key to success.

The success of Asahi's dry beer does not seem to derive only from the fact that the company introduced a product that is different from those offered by Kirin, the industry giant. Asahi dispatched a large contingent of its staff to liquor stores to conduct beer-tasting campaigns. The fact that Asahi chose to undertake such marketing gambits rather than simply leave everything to dealers, as it had done in the past, is seen by many as a principal factor in Asahi Dry turning out to be such a success. Recently, taking advantage of the expanded differentials of domestic versus foreign prices caused by the appreciating yen, Daiei began to import Belgian beer, a move that promptly became a topic of hot debate. And the success that the move subsequently achieved was not due simply to the low price of the beer. The reason Daiei, a retailer, was able to offer the Belgian beer at half the price of domestic beer was because it cut trading companies and wholesalers out of the picture and bought the product directly from Belgian producers.

What was broken by this move was the common sense approach of Japanese industry that holds that a manufacturer develops and supplies merchandise, a wholesaler distributes it to retailers, and retailers sells it to consumers. There are other significant changes—many of them tectonic in nature—that are taking place throughout the distribution sphere. The importation of foreign beer is nothing new. In the past, however, Japanese producers had arrangements with foreign producers to sell such foreign products through the domestic distribution channels. The imported goods were treated just like any other merchandise. A new distribution structure was required. And that is why the recent moves are so interesting. It could well be that the principle of keeping up with the Joneses is falling apart.

Chapter 11 | New Industry and the Search for Distinctiveness

In this chapter, we want to look at ways of reviewing corporate management, seeking out the relevant fundamental factors and taking into account the fact that there have been new developments recently in the area of business management.

It is demanded of a corporation that it seek distinctiveness and develop the vigor needed to overcome significant changes in the business environment. Many of the propositions or concepts presented as solutions to prevailing challenges are so abstract in nature and so obscure as to specific measures that people tend to discuss and seek solutions only in terms of personnel concerns, which are the most basic and common to all. To be sure, vitalizing employees, recruiting distinctive personalities, and innovating methods of in-house communication are important items, but these do no more than put in place the necessary conditions for reform. For these to lead to concrete results, functional and specific action must be undertaken and the groundwork prepared to make it possible to open new markets or engage in advantageous competition.

What is essential is a new method of corporate stewardship and the creation of specific management strategies. Otherwise, plans will arouse expectations but produce no results. A good example of such failure is the activities connected with corporate identity that were previously in vogue. Companies talked about corporate philanthropy as an expression of their social concerns, but it was only natural that these activities soon fizzled when firms didn't take them up with enthusiasm. If a firm really wants to change, it must engage in specific actions.

215

INVESTMENT COMPETITION IS RUNNING UP AGAINST A WALL

Japanese companies are running up against a stone wall in a number of respects. In the auto industry, the maturity of the market, the focus on developing luxury cars in complete disregard of consumer affordability, and the yen's appreciation struck a simultaneous blow against Japanese auto companies. In the semiconductor industry, a strategy that put too much emphasis on memory chips allowed American semiconductor producers to run away with the market. Those Japanese semiconductor companies that once proudly proclaimed memory chips to be the technology drivers are now rivaled by South Korean makers. They are faced with competition from American firms if they enter the advanced processor business and from South Korean competitors if they enter the low-rung business. In the past, they had a strategy of maintaining production volume by increasing exports if they ran into difficulties at home. That strategy is just a memory now. They now focus on the management of quality rather than of quantity. And that isn't working either.

It seems to us that the South Korean producers making remarkable progress in the field of semiconductor memory are following in the footsteps of Japanese makers in their management posture and investment attitude. They are making bold investments to seize leadership in the area of dynamic RAMs. But they are on precarious ground. They don't appear to have fully studied which products the chips are to be used in and what consumer needs really are, and they are engaged in an accelerating competition of capital spending, claiming that the investment cycle for semiconductors only runs for three years. It is as if one is looking in a mirror and seeing the typical decision-making process of Japanese corporations.

The approach is precisely the same one that vexed Japanese makers when they tried to bring the production of 4-MB DRAMs up to full capacity. Since only 1 MB was considered sufficient for a laptop computer, it took a long time for the 4-MB DRAM market to get up to speed. While greater integration in semiconductors may be needed for multimedia applications, it seems strange to make the gradual increase in the integration of semiconductors— which are only components—an end in itself without a clear notion of the products in which they are to be used.

The electric home appliance and semiconductor industries have similar concerns. Generally speaking, home appliances have gradually become commodities, and the production of very few of these products is still lucrative. The industry seems to yearn for some new, epoch-making products that will help innovate the industry. But it is not clear how automation at home will develop, and as a result no one can envision new products in any specific form. In other words, we already have, for the most part, the kind of electric or electronic products we need in our daily lives. Moreover, these commodities are now best produced in Asian, specifically ASEAN, countries. What the Japanese appliance makers once did to the U.S. and European appliance makers some years ago is likely going to be done to them in the Japanese market as a result of competition with ASEAN countries and China. Today, China is said to be the largest market for home appliances. The market is huge, and the high-growth period for appliances is about to begin there. The Chinese appliance makers can beat the Japanese makers in this area. At one time, South Korean appliance manufacturers wanted to enter the Japanese market. And although they had a competitive edge in price, they didn't quite make it because they didn't bring with them Japanese-style customer service. But that was only the first phase of the game.

While it is easy to understand the difficulties faced in terms of mature products, it is not easy to judge the maturity of trading companies or their business structures, as their situation is rather opaque. Trading companies now receive less commission from steel companies for handling their products; likewise, because many manufacturers now make detailed technical decisions regarding their plants by conferring directly with the client trading companies are reduced to handling only documentation, and that doesn't yield much commission. Against this backdrop, trading companies are now discussing the need to reduce administrative costs to survive on commissions of between 2 and 3 percent. That is how precarious trading companies' business has become. As a result, not only the reduction of administrative costs but also reductions of personnel are going on in some circles behind the scene.

An industry that finds itself in such an extreme predicament must seek out change. For the short term, firms may be able to see themselves through with personnel reductions, but more will be needed eventually. It is not clear whether trading companies need to be split into separate companies that would then go into the downstream business of distribution or whether such business is beyond the capability of trading company offshoots.

The activities of Japanese trading companies have been the subject of study by Americans and South Koreans. They are the subject of discussion in Japan, regarding whether they should be split into separate companies or become wholesalers. We wonder if it's possible for them to metamorphose their business to the extent that they can use their experience as exporters and importers to gradually move into the domestic markets of the foreign countries they have dealt with or into the upstream or downstream operations they once served. It is questionable whether a company created through a trading company spin-off can prove strong competitively because, depending on the field of business, it is likely to encounter competitor firms already conducting business in accordance with the reality of the field, be they wholesalers or forwarders. There are, on the other hand, trading companies that have succeeded in reforming their business. Otsuka Shokai and Canon Sales, for example, which just recently came into being and which specialize in semiconductors and office automation equipment, are growing rapidly. We think it is quite possible that from now on we will see more of these new types of trading companies, such as semiconductor traders and PC traders and the like, and not only general trading companies.

Banks and department stores also have their problems. Although Japanese banks are criticized for providing excessive services, the earnings of big banks are said to be extremely high, given the fact that the convoy led by big banks ensures that small financial institutions can also continue to do business. In the West, department stores lost out to chain stores in price competition. In

Japan, it is questionable if department stores can survive in the face of criticism against their high margins, lack of confidence in their pricing mechanism, and problems related to the lavish interiors and superfluous personnel at their stores. Thus, it now seems impossible that they can continue with a high-price strategy that is supposedly based on superior quality.

THE END OF THE GROWTH-IS-BEST POLICY AND FUTURE STRATEGY

Which is the toughest to scale of all the walls that Japanese companies have run up against? In the past, Japanese companies needed a growing market to resolve management problems, and business did not run smoothly unless there were waves of growth upon which they could ride. And therein lay their biggest problem. In fact, the protestations of management—"There must be growth; its lack is a problem. . . . The problem is the inability to implement growth strategy. . . . We must find a market that will grow."—could have been management's biggest problem.

It is not correct to say that when a market has matured there is nothing that companies can do. For example, the textile industry, which is cited as the most representative of mature industries, went abroad in the 1970s, principally to Southeast Asia, and started local production. Negotiations with the U.S., which had been its principal export market, bogged down, and MITI Minister Tanaka Kakuei involved himself in negotiations to bring about an agreement. From an international perspective, the textile industry managed to move from a state of excessive competition to a relationship of cooperation. Likewise, the steel industry managed to maintain a stable international relationship under the Trigger Price Mechanism, an arrangement akin to an international cartel. But in 1993, the developing countries refused to accede to the cartel led by advanced countries, which caused a plethora of dumping suits to be filed. Now the cartel has collapsed, and the old competitive conditions have returned.

However, Japan's textile and steel industries have gone into the Asian and American markets, provided capital and technology, acquired companies, and continued to implement different globalization strategies.

At one time, there were discussions among the companies in Japan's shipbuilding industry—which had been forced to take a backseat to South Korea—that they might be able to continue doing business only in auxiliary equipment and control technology. But orders for new ships are now being placed, as Japan has lowered costs through automation and designed double-bottom tankers. Such moves by the textile, steel, and shipbuilding industries, ostensibly mature industries, show that it is not a lost cause trying to improve on products in mature industries. It is a lesson we all ought to learn. These examples of the revival of mature industries through new technology and conformance to changing circumstances seem to give more than adequate answer to those who wonder whether Japanese companies can continue producing such things as automobiles and home appliances in Japan.

Japanese firms producing electric home appliances and cameras, which dominate the world market, have achieved international competitiveness and now have little opportunity to further develop the current market. Many would say they have come as far as they possibly can. Xerox—which once dominated the world with its copying machines—can now best its Japanese rivals only in the area of large machines, as the market now demands smaller and smaller equipment. Thus, in the field of precision machinery, such as cameras and copiers and home electronics equipment, Japanese makers are discovering that there is hardly any room left in the market for expansion. In the auto industry, Japanese makers are being challenged to expand their business abroad as Ford and GM have done and manage it on a global basis.

As the world becomes smaller, it is doubtful that all industries can survive, as an increasing number of examples seems to indicate.

What about computers? Can Japan do business across the breadth of the world's computer market? We doubt it very much. What about communications equipment? This is a field even more competitive than computers, and very little business is won by

Japanese in Europe. What about semiconductors? It doesn't seem possible that Japanese firms can sway the world in any facet of this growing industry. While it looks as though Japanese companies control the world market in peripherals such as printers and storage devices, it is in fact questionable whether they do. To be sure, when it comes to storage devices the Japanese dominate the world market in floppy disk drives (FDDs), but in hard disk drives (HDDs) they face stiff competition from companies like Seagate and Conner and have gained only a small share, despite a strong technological foundation. It goes without saying that the market of the microprocessor—which is the heart of a computer—lies almost beyond the reach of the Japanese.

When we look at these various products from mostly hi-tech fields, we begin to have doubts about the future. We can divide the industries into two groups: those in a gray area and those that have obviously reached their limits and face barriers to growth too formidable to overcome. What on earth is happening to those Japanese industries that are supposed to be technology driven?

Intel and Motorola, which develop processors, and Seagate and Conner, which produce HDDs—are American firms that have maintained their supremacy in the market with a global scheme of collaborating with personal computer makers, their customers, in product design and development, importing components from Japan and assembling products in Asia. In the past, Japanese firms, which lead in FDDs and CD-ROMs, carried out the entire process—from design to production—in Japan. The strong yen forced them to shift the whole system to Asian countries (figure 11-1). One could argue that Japanese firms' management capabilities suffer from a lack of depth and breadth. It leads us to question whether Japanese management is as strong as American management in its ability to approach a market, bring corporate resources together, and devise a winning strategy.

It is clear that a growth-first orientation is not conducive to problem solving. At the same time, it is hardly necessary to shrink a business once it has matured.

Japanese firms do not need to discard their growth-is-best policy. What is troubling is the apparent decline in their ability to

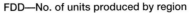

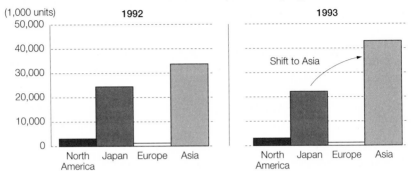

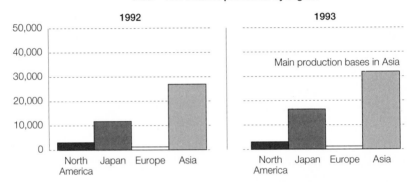

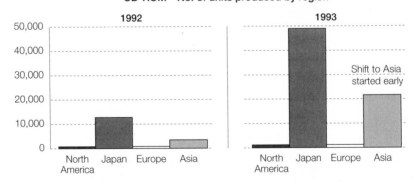

Fig. 11-1. Production Bases of Storage Devices for Computers

Notes: 1. Charts prepared from Dataquest, Japan's *An Analysis of Shift of Production of Electronics Equipment Overseas*, 1994.
2. Total units produced by all manufacturers of the world, including output by Japanese makers.

assess new market needs and to develop products to respond to those needs. That worries us.

COMPANIES AND EMPLOYEES ARE BEGINNING TO ASSERT THEIR DISTINCTIVENESS

What we have observed up to now is competition—in a sense, limited competition—taking place in a favorable environment in which the market keeps growing. Under those circumstances, Japanese firms were certainly competitive in quantity and cost, but perhaps they didn't grasp in a systematic, integrated way just exactly what business management is all about.

Today, the market has matured, and it is no longer easy to expand exports in defiance of international trade friction. What is now strongly demanded is the ability of a company to mobilize its total resources in a well-balanced and well-controlled way. The important challenge for today's managers is whether they can infuse their company with such an ability. In this regard, different companies have started to chart different strategies.

In the camera and copier industries, Canon, Ricoh, and Konica have all changed their business structures. Canon, on the one hand, has identified cameras and copiers as its core products and has made a strong move to deploy internationally through alliances with overseas firms specializing in small copying machines. Ricoh and Konica, on the other hand, have focused their efforts on competing with Fuji Xerox in large copying machines. These companies have developed completely different business structures with sharp differences in performance. We observe that different companies have begun to steer themselves in different directions, asserting their distinctiveness. The fact that companies have begun to show distinctiveness may be evidence that subtle differences in respective companies' strategies, differences in the process of deployment, difficulties experienced in breaking down barriers to competition and market development, and various other factors have now made it impossible to manage business simply by keeping up with the Joneses.

Just as different companies are moving in different directions, the employees who work in those companies are not necessarily of the same mind; they as individuals appear to be going in slightly different directions. Of course, the situation differs from one company to another. For example, at Canon—which boasts broadly deploying worldwide operations with a relatively limited repertoire of products—the company's main ideas permeate each of its business divisions, management has the power to marshal the entire resources of the company, and each employee's discharge of his official responsibilities is more important than his personal dedication to the company business.

Other companies operate differently, either because their main business involves a small market share or because they have gone too far in their diversification efforts. Generally speaking, we find that large corporations usually have some constituent business divisions that have reached their limits and have no prospect of expanding sales. The staff assigned to such divisions are under pressure to go back to the basics and reinstate competitive strategies. When the people in charge of such problematic business segments want to take specific action to improve earnings or expand the size of their operations, they have a number of alternatives. Some may want to maintain the present business and cut back on marketing; others may want to pursue marketing in close collaboration with the production floor. Still others may want to take on new technologies as well as marketing functions. In this fashion, different ideas from the employees of the same company seem to push the company in different directions at the same time.

Among the employees in a business division of a company, there are those who lose interest in the firm's business because of the very nature of that business or for personal reasons. Conversely, there are those who want to continue doing the job in the same old way. Still others want to get involved with the job but to move in different directions. Different people appear to be setting out in different directions. Different views are being put forth as to how work should be performed and how employees should interact with the company as they serve the company. We believe that many individuals are beginning to discover how they should conduct themselves within the company.

It sometimes happens that an employee who believes his company must change its strategic direction decides he will do all he can to help bring about the needed change despite opposition from all sides. But when traditional business structures need to be changed or old strategic concepts supplanted by new ones, it is rare that management will take the lead in planning such structural reform or executing the needed business innovations. In most cases, the more enthusiastic an employee is about bringing about change, the more frustrated he will be when he runs into the impenetrable wall of a corporate organization.

In many companies, we see more and more people who have their own opinions about the direction their companies should take and who keep fighting with their companies, trying in vain to get their opinions adopted as company policy. The companies often deal with these people as if they were crackpots, or at the very least treat them differently than other employees. Often, those managers who avow an interest in distinctive personalities do not have the mettle to set in motion distinctive responses to the efforts suggested by such personalities. There have, of course, been cases where individuals were fortunate enough to have an understanding boss and where, when the suggested change was successful, they have been highly commended for their pluck.

At trading companies in need of reform there are staff who believe there is an urgent need to make greater use of information technology in the distribution business and who advocate a vision of a new trading company built on advanced technology. Some employees at consumer goods manufacturers, fully aware of the competition from imported goods, insist on stronger globalization and downstream strategies. Some working in the information industry assert that the high cost of communications in Japan inhibits business deployment here and that firms should go to the U.S. to start up new businesses there first.

The reality is that very few companies listen to these advocates of new business deployment and allow them the chance of drawing up new business strategies. Most companies have organizational departments that specialize in formulating future strategy, such as a corporate planning office or a new business development office. These units are staffed by men of common sense who are considered brilliant, at least within the company. Some companies will go as far as letting young junior executives draw up future plans as members of a committee. Most of the members of such a committee consist of the so-called elite staffers, most of whom, unfortunately, only trumpet the kind of innocuous plans that will do neither harm nor good.

Sometimes an especially outstanding individual will predict certain changes in the business environment, and when this prediction comes to pass the company is unable to effectively grapple with those changes, and problems mount as a result. At that point, the company may finally act on his recommendation. In such cases, there are always people in the company who will deftly maneuver themselves into a position to claim credit, asserting that they had been in agreement with the prediction all along. It is not the originator of the idea but the people who know how to work the organization that gain credit and come to the fore. That seems to be what happens typically in Japanese companies. There are exceptions, of course. A certain consumer goods manufacturer we know of has made just such a talented individual president of one of its subsidiaries, given him total freedom to implement his ideas, and made him accountable only to the president of the parent company. We are impressed with the insight and mettle of the top management at this company; it is indeed refreshing to observe such a performance.

As history proves, an age of change summons the talent required to effect it. A typical example was the emergence of Kobayashi Koji and Sekimoto Tadahiro at NEC. Previously, NEC had a digital exchange with technical specifications that were different from those of Nippon Telegraph & Telephone Public Corp. (predecessor of today's NTT), which had introduced an electronic analog exchange, and NEC found itself unable to do business in Japan in communications equipment, its major product area. With respect to computers, NEC had a product with specifications different from the technology that was emerging as the industry standard. That product was a machine developed with technology from RCA, with which NEC had an agreement; the machine did not uses bytes, which were then becoming the industry standard. Thus, every NEC product was running into problems. Mr. Kobayashi and Mr. Sekimoto—who were at the time mid-level managers of NEC— were concerned about the future of the company. They came up with an epoch-making business concept of melding computers and communications and staked the future of the company on this concept. They deployed product strategies focused on the development of small yet strong network products. Their move helped create today's NEC. And they accomplished this feat while they were only middle-level managers.

Although their stories are not as well known as NEC's, there are many firms that have been well served by such men of mettle. Thanks to such men, these firms achieved success.

The management of Toray—which has improved its corporate performance despite the burst bubble and the high yen—is attracting particular attention of late. Before the bubble, Toray reviewed its diversification strategy and shifted operations to areas that assured it of competitive strength and an effective performance. That restructuring took place at the same time that the rest of Japan was having fun due to the bubble. Toray persisted in building a solid business foundation. Those efforts laid the foundation for today's Toray.

New business ventures are exciting for engineers, but it is not easy to make them successful. A company may successfully develop new technology or new products, but to build these into a money-making business requires more than the efforts of the company concerned. Distribution and the method of business deployment are also important factors. A firm may have undertaken market research during the development stage, formulated a business plan, and mobilized its operating division and as a result believes it is ready to go. It may then discover that it just missed a particular business opportunity or chose the wrong partner in a joint development effort, and that mistake hobbles its efforts to commercialize its new product. Such cases are not rare. In fact, Toray ran into such problems in the past and suspended the development of a number of technologies. This shows how crucial management decisions can prove to be.

Managers are not the only ones who accomplish good results through distinctive behavior. More intriguing is the behavior of middle-level employees.

It is not widely known that Mitsui & Co.'s general-purpose resin department supplies box lunches to Seven-Eleven convenience stores. People may wonder why the food department of this trading company is not responsible for this. However, the original aim of the resin department was to supply Seven-Eleven stores with styrofoam box lunch containers. The convenience store did not like having different-sized containers because their shelf appearance was not attractive; it wanted a standard size. At each store, a number of local box lunch vendors were vying to supply the box lunches, and size difference was one of their marketing tools. Suppliers, for example, would offer slightly larger box lunches for the same price or a smaller lunch of higher quality for people with a moderate appetite. That was the nature of the competition. For a while, box lunches sold well, but the store's objective of standardized size was still not achieved, and Mitsui's preformed resin containers couldn't solve the problem, as the food suppliers didn't offer a standard size of box lunch. In the end, turned down by all box lunch vendors and left with no alternative, the team that developed the styrofoam containers at Mitsui started supplying Seven-Eleven stores with its own box lunches.

Mitsui set up a separate company, built a computer network, and began an on-time delivery service. In this market, the success of a store's takeout service depends on its performance within a time frame of half an hour or so every morning, noon, and evening. Box lunches won't sell unless they are in the store by 11:30 a.m.; should you deliver them as late as 12:30 p.m., you cannot sell them. If, on the other hand, you deliver them by 10:30 a.m., customers may feel that they have been on the shelf too long and have doubts about the freshness of the food. It's a tough business. That's why Mitsui built an information network to help it plan, change, and adjust delivery routes depending on the degree of street congestion to insure that trucks would follow the optimum routes in making delivery to each client store. It had the good sense to utilize information technology in this regard. The most interesting thing about this venture is that a trading company that originally wanted to supply resin food containers ended up creating a separate company to supply takeout food.

Many companies are fortunate enough to have the kind of nettlesome characters on their payrolls that generate such new business. Generally speaking, these individuals often have certain eccentric traits and are not much interested in getting along with other people in the company. They often have outstanding technical abilities but may be so offbeat that they cannot be team players or sometimes act superciliously. Of course, that doesn't mean that there aren't any well-balanced, superior individuals whose presence is reassuring.

Even some steelmakers, generally reputed to be rather rigid companies, don't lack for captivating personalities. A Mr. A we know of was running a subsidiary in the U.S. His company was developing multimedia, a subject that enthralls the world today. Most steelmakers have only a limited number of directorship slots reserved for men with an engineering background. Just as MITI has only a few high positions available for officials with technical training, there are not many directors in steel companies who are engineers, despite the fact that these firms have a large number of engineers in their organizations. The company that Mr. A worked for has a compulsory retirement age of 55 for all managerial/professional personnel, with the exception of directors. Its American subsidiary had already started developing its multimedia business when Mr. A became president after being forced to retire a few years earlier from the parent under its compulsory retirement system. The company's main business was to collect information concerning hi-tech fields. It just so happened that Mr. A had experience analyzing images of the fluid conditions of material inside a blast furnace and that he also understood computers. In addition, before his retirement he had been assigned to the newly formed electronics and information systems division of the parent company and was put in charge of developing multimedia image chips. After his retirement, he organized the U.S. subsidiary to find a future market for the chips.

In the United States, he interacted with many people in different walks of life, discussing business opportunities and working on systems development. An American communications company thought very highly of the technology he had developed and placed an order with him, creating a budding new business opportunity. How did a steel company succeed in developing a cutting-edge technology in this intensely competitive hi-tech industry? The steelmakers' formidable technical prowess and insightfulness have a lot to do with it, of course, but the fascinating thing to remember here is that it was not Fujitsu or NEC or Matsushita or Sony that made this particular development a success.

There is a mass market for tens of millions of image terminals, but the market for the encoders that input digitized images into computers and prepare image files is said to be no larger than tens of thousands of units. In this multimedia world, where so much technology had been developed and plans for commercialization were being formulated, it was suddenly discovered that nobody had bothered to develop a technology to digitize movies and videos. It is truly fascinating that, amid such intense technological competition, a steel company should have achieved an unrivaled position in the world of multimedia and attracted everyone's attention in the process.

Even when a new development occurs in the area of a key technology, it is not easy to judge whether it should be commercialized. We don't know how a steel company that doesn't have communications equipment or image terminals will go about commercializing its invention. Perhaps it won't. But the interesting point is that it succeeded in developing it at all. The venture is interesting for a number of reasons, not least of which is the fact that Mr. A brought with him the developed elemental technology to the United States and undertook systems development in the U.S. Depending on how you look at it, perhaps Mr. A was a bit too assertive and wasn't exactly the well-balanced personality expected in a company employee. But he was a unique individual who stood out and did not bother himself about matters of commercialization or company affairs.

Chapter 12 | # In Search of a New Management Philosophy

TAKING ADVANTAGE OF THE STRONG YEN TO CHANGE THE INDUSTRIAL STRUCTURE

The basic approach of Japanese corporations in dealing with the appreciating yen has been to rationalize their operations and build a corporate structure to withstand the strong yen, although some have chosen to import components from abroad. Large corporations have given little thought to changing the structure of industry.

Some firms are trying to build a structure to stave off the negative effects of the surging currency. Toyota Motor and Nissan Motor previously had about 20 different steering wheels each. They have now reduced at number. By doing so, they are able to save on molds and engineers, thereby cutting down on the costs associated with domestic production. Thus, as the exchange rate hovers near ¥80 per dollar, they continue to address the problem in the same manner they always have, trying to find yet another group of things to rationalize.

Nippon Steel's Oita operation proudly maintains the world's foremost competitive position, even with the soaring yen. As this operation handles mostly the upstream portion of steelmaking, it uses a lot of raw materials imported from abroad, which makes it possible for it to withstand the effects of the high yen. Its equipment is supermodern, and significant manpower savings have been achieved. Furthermore, the equipment is fully depreciated, having been installed 15 to 20 years ago. Although we recognize the operation's competitive strength, we fear that, in a perverse way, Nippon Steel is putting off the day of reckoning.

In reducing the cost of production, many industries seem to be taking the same measures that they have always adopted to counter the effects of the escalating yen. As shown in figure 12-1, they have lowered prices and continued with their exports, which is risky. The fact that they don't seem ready to change the usual export-driven method of riding out difficult times convinces us that this is really a question of the prevailing mentality of management.

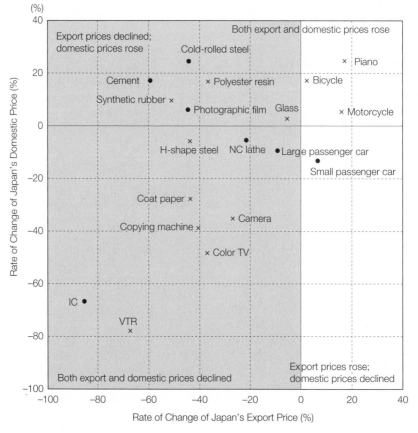

Fig. 12-1. Difference Between Export Price and Domestic Price

Notes: 1. Chart prepared from information quoted from "Pricing and Market" by Julia Lowell, Loren Yager, The Rand Corporation, 1994.
2. The rate of change is from 1980 to 1992
3. "dot" indicates the merchandise subjected to dumping suits, voluntary export restraints, application of section 301 of the U.S. trade law and other trade actions between Japan and the U.S.

Incidentally, the exchange rates have changed such that not only the yen but also the German mark and some of the Asian currencies are all stronger against the dollar. So the situation is really one of a weak dollar not a strong yen. What kind of problems does that present for Asia? The strong yen causes Japanese companies to transfer production abroad, especially to other other Asian countries. This, of course, helps those Asian countries develop their economies and acquire export strength. Because of this, foreign exchange—which in many Asian countries is under government control—will become an important issue and eventually be liberalized. At that point, each Asian currency will rise in value, and those nations will have lost their competitive edge. Such a trend could well continue for a long time. Therefore, the problem should be addressed as one between Asia, including Japan, on the one hand and the U.S. and Europe on the other. We could then look at what Japan should do and what the U.S. should do. It would make for a totally different set of answers and a totally different discussion. When we are able to take a new look at things—with a broad, global perspective—we might perceive a totally different role for Japan.

For example, the Asian market for automobiles has expanded in size, and local consumption has increased tremendously. As a result, there is no transshipment for exports. When a Japanese firm goes elsewhere in Asia and builds a plant, it causes imports of certain components to increase. But the value added remains in the host country. The host country no longer has to buy machinery and everything else, as it did in the past. It need only buy materials, and very soon it will be able to make those as well. The host countries are beginning to develop their economies without having to depend on borrowed money. The earliest to achieve this were Taiwan and Singapore.

In the twenty-first century, Asia, with a population of 2.5 billion, will see massive industrialization. Economic changes on an unpredictably mammoth scale are likely to occur. Staying on its own, Japan's relative international status will only decline. Japan would be well advised to approach business from the perspective of doing all it can do to help elevate the living standards and educational level of the people of Asia.

Incidentally, the yen's upsurge has finally caused Japanese corporations to be less export oriented and more inclined to produce locally. Japanese companies will be producing and selling locally in Asia. They will then export products to developing countries. Next, they will begin producing in those countries, and a chain reaction will set in. This way, Asian countries will further develop and begin to increase their exports to Japan, just as Japan increased its exports to the United States in the 1970s. It is important that Japan's industrial structure should have an impact on Asia's development.

We are talking about an approach different from that of simply going abroad to deal with the sky-high yen and improve the trade balance. We are suggesting that Japan should compete more thoroughly in technology and cost reductions in the international arena not only for its own sake but also for the sake of those countries around it. Japanese companies should reform their structure so that they can manage with a compound eye, putting their faith in the belief that this approach will eventually yield returns.

The very thought of trying to hold down the rising yen is a retrogressive one. Keidanren (the Japan Federation of Economic Organizations) is afraid that the strong yen will cause companies to lose competitiveness and reduce profit levels. MITI is concerned that local industry in outlying regions dependent on exports will no longer be competitive. If one should ask if these export-oriented small and medium-size companies in outlying areas can continue to operate in the same way as they have, the answer is quite obviously no. From the standpoint of consumers and ordinary citizens, the appreciating yen gives us a great opportunity. It is only the producers that are spooked by the rising yen.

We should think in terms of what place Japan should take in the world, not in terms of what Japan's domestic map is going to look like. Then we should consider how we can contribute to the progress of Asia, for example. It is certainly a long-term view. In the shorter term, we must increase imports from within Asia. That would seem to mean that each company will be compelled to adopt a strategy of taking advantage of the surging yen. If firms strive to take advantage of the rising yen instead of trying to overcome it, imports will necessarily increase.

The biggest objective is to enrich the quality of our lives. Our apartments are small, and there is no place to enjoy leisure activities. The pity of Japan is that our life and leisure are so standardized that there is little room for individuality. The Japanese are not yet really affluent and are not confident enough to assert their individuality.

A NEW MANAGEMENT PHILOSOPHY IS NOW BEING SOUGHT

We still don't know with what corporate structure and what corporate systems the new age should be addressed. No new philosophy has been established. Different corporations and different people may use different mechanisms, but one thing is clear—change must occur.

It is organizational structure that makes it difficult for corporations to change. Big corporations in Japan are burdened with ponderous structures and permeated with bureaucracy that values formality. That is why it is difficult to alter long-standing traditions or ways of thinking or to look at an entire company from the outside and reposition it.

It is not bad for a bureaucratized company to lose its competitive edge and be replaced by a younger, more vigorous corporation. Once imbued with bureaucratic ways, where formalities and procedures are held in high regard, an organization resists change to the fullest. Some Japanese companies have become so large that it is more important for them to maintain their organization and procedures, and they have lost their flexibility in the process. If big firms want to survive as vital organizations, we believe they must make a bold decision to break up current operations into flatter, decentralized organizations, and not just in the area of communications.

What is important to management is that officers and employees maintain their vitality. If they stagnate, it's the responsibility of management. How do we make sure that the officers and employees maintain their vitality? One way is to give them the opportunity to apply their entrepreneurship or to enhance their professional skills. A company that can share with everyone not only material benefits but also a kind of excitement will attract many people and prosper as a vigorous concern.

Thus far, Japanese companies have maintained themselves only because they have had hidden assets, such as shares of other companies and real estate. But they are now selling those off. From now on, they will have to manage their business without the benefit of such hidden assets, and they will have to compete strenuously to earn profits.

It is not that all hidden assets will be completely eliminated. Hidden assets in the form of stocks and real estate may be gone, but firms must work hard to accumulate new hidden assets—the abilities of their employees. When a company has the capability to undertake activities that can be expected to earn profits in the future, it is cultivating such hidden assets. It is a question of how many talented employees are being developed and what capabilities they can bring to bear on the fortunes of the firm. We are talking about the kind of ability that might, for example, induce a venture capitalist to invest in a project because a capable, talented individual has been put in charge of the project.

Such hidden assets will become increasingly important in the future. That's why we need the kind of management that will nurture such talent. From now on, when people talk about hidden assets they will be speaking of personal ability. In this respect, the United States—where people are willing to bet a lot of money on creativity—is an extraordinary society. In Japan, there aren't many who will pursue their own projects, even resigning from their companies if necessary, or who will support such entrepreneurship with the necessary capital.

Successful entrepreneurs will tell you that in many cases they fail two or three times before they succeed. They simply refuse to be deterred. They are wonderful people, endowed with an enterprising spirit. There ought to be a system to support such individuals and help them succeed. Venture capital is fine, of course, but in addition to that reliable accountants should be available to help entrepreneurs. Advisors should also be available, but they must be of assistance, they should not be restrictive. These and other incubator functions are greatly needed.

It may be wishful thinking to some extent, but in the future nimble start-up companies will prove to be more advantageous to economic well-being than bureaucratized firms that are possessed of nothing other than the prestige of being large. It seems inevitable that small and medium-size companies overflowing with entrepreneurial spirit will carry relatively greater weight. Instead of confining themselves to quiet positions in their respective communities, local firms should engage in entrepreneurship and actively create new business because success will come from such efforts. Certainly, they may encounter failure. But what is needed today is the hunter-like persistence of entrepreneurs like those in America, who keep on setting up new businesses, success or failure notwithstanding. In the future, we can anticipate a dynamic and flexible industrial structure, one in which individuals determine what they really want to do; take risks; and, if favored by a good opportunity, succeed, instead of seeking comfort and security as members of large organizations.

The days are gone when large organizations can enjoy the benefits of economies of scale. In the United States, all hi-tech companies are small, full of vigor, and create numerous jobs. Large companies in Japan have become so ponderously structured that they are suffocating. More and more people are dissatisfied with their situation and want to leave their companies. While the social environment may not be ready to accept them, people are nonetheless starting new business in a spirit of independence with ever-increasing frequency.

If you look around and identify some of the current needs and address them skillfully, you can begin a new business on a small scale. As you keep at it, you will improve your skills, and demand may increase. You may not strike it rich, but your market will develop nonetheless, as long as the need exists and your abilities continue to increase. From now on, it may be necessary for us to start our businesses on our own in this fashion. As the bubble has collapsed, so has the prospect of Japanese companies living up to the reputed characteristics of Japanese management and securing a place of work for their employees and looking after them for life. With that prospect gone, the conditions for a new start have been put in place.

Excessive diversification is not advisable in terms of management, the utilization of individual capabilities, or competitive conditions. One might propose to organize business divisions and manage them according to return on investment, but to diversify into business areas that top management is not familiar with is to court trouble. The U.S. proved this in the 1960s and 1970s. The age of adulation from simply being big is gone in the U.S. Of course it depends on the industry, but Americans no longer admire bigness simply for itself—size no longer commands the prestige it once did. Nobody refers to GM or USX as representative of American business today. Instead, they name Microsoft and Intel, companies that grew from start-ups financed by venture capital.

Japanese companies have undertaken diversification to maintain employment, but they have failed in that endeavor. It is understandable that they had a strong desire to maintain jobs, but in the process they squashed the latent abilities of employees, which should have been given full scope. In particular, big corporations have monopolized talented employees and wasted them by giving them work of limited scope.

What do people want from a company? It is important for the company to provide an employee not only with pay and position but also with an opportunity to develop his abilities. By working for a company, an employee hopes to be able to enhance his professional skills or to develop capabilities that he can later use to enjoy a second and third career. When the employees of a company fully exercise and develop their capabilities in doing their jobs, that company is cultivating latent capabilities. The employees look forward to enhancing their skills and being adventuresome, and the company benefits from the vitality of such employees. It is possible that from now on people will look upon the security of lifetime employment and the seniority system as something that ought to be eschewed.

What is the possibility of new businesses being created? Already, new companies, though small, are finding it possible to work together with big ones to jointly serve customers or to meet certain needs in a market. We can also envision the possibility of a small company providing general planning services or services limited to a specified area of specialty.

The impact of the appreciation of the yen alone has facilitated structural changes in many industries. New needs have emerged that cannot be met by traditional systems. Only those firms with an enterprising spirit can satisfy them. Of course, they will experience failure as well as success. No matter how hard they try, they may still fail if they aren't blessed with a little luck or fortuitous circumstances. People ought to be more tolerant and less critical about the failures of entrepreneurs. Rather, they should encourage entrepreneurs and approve of their efforts to make yet another attempt.

This is the time when such changes are needed, and we must cultivate a mindset receptive to those changes. What those in management positions must do is give younger people the opportunity to attempt the things they are anxious to accomplish. When business is spun off into a separate company, the parent management should let the new firm's management run the business as they please without meddling in its affairs and thereby incurring the cost of control. The spin-offs should be held responsible for their own operations. As more of them are set up, the parent company should control them as would an investor. In other words, the parent should become a holding company.

Without sitting smugly by and maintaining the present system, managers should go down to the production floor and take a closer look. They will then discover new needs and be able to accumulate new capabilities.

Epilogue

Three years have passed since we decided to write this book at the invitation of Ogawa Mario of Japan Broadcast Publishing Co., Ltd. and started our collaboration. At times during this period, we were led to hope that the adverse effects of the collapse of the bubble might be eradicated. We are sorry to report, however, that Japanese corporations appear to have fallen steadily into a crisis of management under the impact of an extremely strong yen that is widely at variance with the principle of purchasing power parity.

The electronics and automobile industries, which have been recognized for their international competitive edge, have seen earnings grow unbalanced, except for certain special products. Instead of withdrawing from money-losing operations to right the corporate balance, firms have instead generally shifted production elsewhere in Asia and endeavored to maintain business through typical Japanese hard work and perseverance.

Not a few electronics companies have been compelled to reduce prices on computer-related products, such as CD-ROM drives and printers, after price negotiations with computer makers, their customers, and have then found it necessary to shift their production bases from Japan to elsewhere in Asia. We are not speaking here about mature products, but rather about products whose market is growing at a remarkable pace, products in which Japanese companies possess proven competitive strength and have dominated the world market. Indeed, a Japanese firm would have to boast a highly exceptional product, one of exceptional international competitiveness, if it expects to continue its current operations.

The automobile industry is continuing its strenuous efforts to correct surplus investment and redesign high-priced products, but it has not yet succeeded in reversing its declining earnings, as the change in consumer motivations and U.S.-Japan political friction have added to its woes. But we detect no change in the traditional stance of auto companies as they demand of their subcontractors extreme cost reductions at the same time as they revise the selling prices of their cars. During the oil crises and immediately after the weakening of the dollar in 1985, for example, Japanese companies exhibited miraculous adaptability to changed circumstances. But this time, the circumstances are a bit different. As we engaged in discussions in the course of writing this book, we were hopeful that Japanese companies would be true to their inherent nature and come up with effective solutions or initiatives. Unfortunately, our expectations have not been realized.

It is not correct, however, to say that Japanese competitiveness has been eroded in all fields. With respect to liquid crystal displays and semiconductor memory devices, supply has not kept pace with demand, which has ballooned due to rapidly increasing information and multimedia needs. In some cases, the quantity of supply by Japanese semiconductor makers and the selection of consignee companies have become factors in determining the size of the market share of U.S. computer makers. As a result, the price leadership that was once exercised but had waned has been recovered, and price revisions have proceeded successfully, and profitability has improved. We are aware of one company that maintains an overwhelming share of the world market on the strength of its technical prowess. In the electronics equipment industry, there is a communications equipment maker showing overwhelming strength in the U.S. market, riding high on the information technology wave there. Still another firm holds sway in the world market for terminal equipment.

In the automotive industry, it is well known that, despite the surging yen, manufacturers of automatic transmissions and dies are expanding their market share while they revise their prices upward in accordance with changes in the exchange rate. Related to the auto industry, there are small companies that specialize in making prototypes, a service that links design and the mass-production process, and these firms have been inundated with requests from companies around the world in regard to the production and evaluation of prototypes.

Ours is an age in which competitive strength that passes muster anywhere in the world will be directly translated into big earnings. It is indeed encouraging when a small company that was once only quietly appreciated by the other companies in its *keiretsu* group finally sees its capabilities fully recognized by a third party.

If we limit our discussion to the last several years, we must admit that it is difficult to find case histories of big Japanese companies that have grappled significantly with initiatives to reform management, except for some reductions in personnel or a few other restructuring efforts in organization or personnel. Somehow, almost imperceptibly, Japanese companies, especially large ones, have lost their vitality to an almost unimaginable degree. It is distressing for us, as observers of the industrial scene, to see this happen.

When you scrutinize a Japanese company that incorporates the traditional organizational concepts, you may well conclude that it has well-ordered control functions and well-established support functions. In fact, it would be more accurate to say that those functions have become shells of their former selves, with people busying themselves only with the application of rules and formalities. One large company we know of has, through automation, reduced the number of employees in the manufacturing department to such an extent that personnel engaged in control functions, such as those in the manufacturing control department, the quality evaluation department, and the subcontracting department, have come to constitute as much as 80 percent of the firm's total payroll. In the marketing department of the same company, only 20 percent of the total man-hours of the entire department is devoted to substantive marketing activities. Developments such as these are worrisome.

Most people in any given firm believe they are working hard. If a middle-level employee should take a critical view of a certain situation and have the courage to propose a solution, his superior will often quash his recommendation. It is unfortunate that this is the way things are. Management staffers—who are charged with the responsibility of leading the company in the direction it should move—spend most of their time preparing and reviewing ritualized business plans. When their review discovers a divergence between performance and those plans, all they do is drag people from the production floor up on the carpet, without realizing their own responsibility for the situation.

For the last few years, we have observed the decision-making structure and management process of typical Japanese corporations as we have also watched the change in the competitiveness of their products. Such observation leads us to conclude that Japanese corporations, which have experienced repeated ups and downs, are slowly entering a phase of decline. Clearly, Japanese corporations are facing crunch time, and, with their backs pushed firmly against a wall that cannot be scaled by the strategies of the past, they are crying out, "Is there nobody around to help us? . . . Show us how to climb over this wall!"

But one should perhaps not be too pessimistic. Often, problems become so serious that they reach a point of critical mass that allows the organization to realize a massive transformation.

In writing this book, we became acquainted with many middle-level employees and exchanged information with them on an informal basis. We have noted that the following changes have begun to take place in their ranks over the last few years.

Those middle-level executives who are more acutely aware of what is going on than others are already taking action, realizing that there will be no future for them if the situation is left as is. Some are pressuring their bosses; others are carefully conducting *nemawashi*; still others are leaving their companies to set up their own firms. Different people have different approaches, but the important thing is that the number of people who are at least taking proactive steps is slowly but steadily increasing.

It requires a great deal of energy to stir up one's company through innovative action, and a middle-level employee may not be allowed to do what he wants unless the management is favorably inclined to go along with the initiative. But some people, even in the face of opposition, still present their suggestions for change, at the risk of losing their promotion or even their job. As far as we can tell, their actions seem to be motivated by a desire to destroy the bureaucracy governing their particular areas of responsibility or to oppose blustering, sham directors whose objective is to flaunt their positions or challenge any management agenda that is not strictly within the firm's methodology of business deployment. These middle-level managers promote new efforts that reflect as closely as possible their vision of what needs to be done, and they strive to initiate new business within the scope of their own responsibilities. It is noteworthy that their behavior often exceeds the scope of the company's authority and responsibility.

Many may consider such actions as archetypically Japanese, reflective of Japanese firms' valuation of the production floor. An American manager in the same situation would likely quit the company and find a new job with a more vigorous company or set up his own. A Japanese manager's behavior in taking action within his organization may be considered an act consistent with the essential character of Japanese management. Japanese management—which builds consensus through the *ringi* system and the practice of *nemawashi* and maintains a seniority-based organization—essentially leaves undefined the specifics regarding job tasks and the responsibilities entailed. This means that employees who are of a mind to question things are allowed to present their views to the company on matters related to their jobs or to the business that they observe around them.

Some bosses who see such courageous behavior on the part of their subordinates try to thwart these reform movements for fear that other departments or the firm's upper management might see the actions as reflecting poorly on the boss's performance, while others, in their heart of hearts, may say to themselves, "I have not been able to do anything I really wanted to do, circumscribed as I am by company rules and frameworks, and I have endured it as my lot with this company. But these men dare take bold action. How I envy them."

Fewer and fewer managers who work for big companies like those listed on the Tokyo Stock Exchange want their children to work for their companies. This is one of the most remarkable phenomena that we have seen in recent years. The very same parents who previously wanted their children to work for a large company with good pay and fringe benefits and pressured them to study hard so they could get into a good university now feel different than they did—"The last thing I want is for them to work for my company." We consider this to be an expression of their yearning for bygone days, when the company organization permitted free-thinking and freewheeling behavior and employees found their jobs exhilarating.

Will the activities of middle-level managers lead to a breakdown in company discipline or well-balanced management? Not as long as their superiors are well versed in the kind of business that the activists want to promote. What this all means, it seems to us, is that firms don't need those officers who serve only as caretakers of the organization's systems and rules, or those elite executives who only flaunt their power within that system. We believe that valuing the production floor is the very quintessence of Japanese management.

In reality, freedom in business deployment may be restricted by laws and regulations; the extremely strong yen may make it difficult to deploy business within Japan; there may be a shortage of management talent; financial institutions with huge latent losses may not be able to provide ample financing; and many other difficult problems may materialize, each with no easy solution. In the progress of internationalization, Japanese methods of subcontracting and business transactions have become the subject of political friction. Given that situation, is it possible for Japan to participate in this century's greatest phase of economic development, which is now taking place in Asia, introducing Japanese institutions and systems into the effort? Can we successfully implement overseas projects in cooperation with peoples of different cultures, philosophies, and customs? These are indeed very difficult questions.

One thing is unmistakably clear, and that is that one of the most important elements of Japanese management—valuing the production floor—must be conspicuously released from the yoke of bureaucracy. Those managers who are only intent on maintaining a balanced organization and who cannot promote proactive and specific business efforts should retire soon. If they cannot, then they should make every effort to summon the courage to undertake new business. I am hopeful that in a typical Japanese company, it will become more and more likely that revolutions will take place from within. We believe that one way to arrive at a solution would be to break up big companies into smaller units on the basis of the principle of valuing the production floor and to delegate extended authority to each unit.

KONOMI YOSHINOBU
July 1995

The LTCB International Library Foundation
Statement of Purpose

The world is moving steadily toward a borderless economy and deepening international interdependence. Amid this globalization of economic activities, the Japanese economy is developing organic ties with the economies of individual nations throughout the world via trade, direct investment, overseas manufacturing activities, and the international movement of capital.

As a result, interest in Japan's politics, economy, and society and in the concepts and values that lie behind Japan's socioeconomic activities is growing in many countries.

However, the overseas introduction and dissemination of translations of works originally written in Japanese lags behind the growth of interest in Japan. Such works are not well known outside Japan. One main reason for this is that the high costs involved in translating and publishing materials written in Japanese hinder the undertaking of such activities on a commercial basis. It is extremely important to overcome this barrier to deepen and broaden mutual understanding.

The LTCB International Library Foundation has been founded to address this pressing need. Its primary activity is to disseminate information on Japan in foreign countries through the translation of selected Japanese works on Japan's politics, economy, society, and culture into English and other languages and the publication and distribution of these translations. To commemorate the completion of The Long-Term Credit Bank of Japan, Ltd.'s new headquarters and its 40th anniversary, LTCB has provided the LTCB International Library Foundation with an endowment.

We sincerely hope that the LTCB International Library Foundation will successfully fulfill its mission of promoting global understanding and goodwill through enhanced cultural exchange.

March 1, 1994
The founders of the LTCB International Library Foundation